T.H. MEYER was born in Switzerland in 1950. He is the founder and publisher of Perseus Verlag, Basel, and editor of the monthly journals *The Present Age* and *Der Europaer*. He is the author of several books including *Ludwig Polzer-Hoditz, A Biography*; *D.N. Dunlop, A Biography*; *In the Sign of Five*; *Rudolf Steiner's Core Mission*; *The Bodhisattva Question*; *Clairvoyance and Consciousness, Reality, Truth and Evil*, and editor of *Light for the New Millennium*. He has written numerous articles and gives seminars and lectures around the world.

MILESTONES

*in the life of Rudolf Steiner
and in the development of anthroposophy*

T.H. Meyer

TEMPLE LODGE

Temple Lodge Publishing Ltd.
Hillside House, The Square
Forest Row, RH18 5ES

www.templelodge.com

First published in English by Temple Lodge Publishing, 2015

Originally published in German under the title *Wegmarken im Leben Rudolf Steiners und in der Entwicklung der Anthroposophie* by Perseus Verlag, Basel, 2012

Translated from German by Matthew Barton

A CIP catalogue record for this book is available from the British Library

The publishers wish to thank Perseus Foerderverein, Switzerland, for their generous sponsorship of this edition

ISBN 978 1 906999 82 7

Cover by Morgan Creative
Typeset by DP Photosetting, Neath, West Glamorgan
Printed and bound by 4Edge Ltd.

Contents

Preface

The life of a leader of humanity, whose mission is of the highest kind, is an artwork in which angels and human beings work together.

Friedrich Rittelmeyer, *Rudolf Steiner Enters My Life*

This book is not a comprehensive biography of Rudolf Steiner. Excellent accounts of his life and work from an anthroposophical viewpoint already exist. I would mention here publications by Emil Bock, Willem Zeylmans, Herbert Hahn, Rudolf Meyer and the Rowohlt monograph by Johannes Hemleben. All these appeared around the 100th anniversary of Steiner's birth or shortly afterwards (Hemleben). There followed a biography by Christoph Lindenberg and then, a few years back, a mammoth tome by Helmut Zander which presented a huge quantity of information, yet was founded, equally, on huge prejudices and a striking lack of reflection. The same author released a biography to mark Steiner's 150th anniversary, and similarly partisan monographs by Heiner Ullrich and Miriam Gebhardt also appeared around this time.

Painstaking and sometimes minutely detailed chronological accounts of Steiner's life—Christoph Lindenberg's above all— simultaneously reveal and conceal their subject. They offer a wealth of information which all those interested in Steiner's life and development will immerse themselves in gratefully. But precisely because their content is so copious they may also cover up certain key aspects: everything presented seems equally important, and accent or emphasis can be lacking.

Symptomatic milestones

This present volume does not seek to be *the* complete biography by adding further biographical details to those already available, or by offering a full evaluation of Steiner's work. Instead, I wish to focus on key events or facts in Rudolf Steiner's life which, despite often being known, have so far received little attention. I see these as milestones, indicators of Steiner's thinking and actions over many decades. The approach here is not cumulative but symptomatological: from a wealth of largely known facts I have chosen those which shed an especially illuminating light on Steiner's primary spiritual impulses and on his far-reaching quest for knowledge. It is a method I previously employed in my book *Rudolf Steiner's Core Mission, The Birth and Development of Spiritual-Scientific Karma Research*. This present book however surveys a much broader field of events and facts.

It is impossible to practise this kind of historical symptomatology without *selecting* from a wealth of details, yet this is something from which modern biographers and historians recoil in alarm, thinking that they will succumb to subjectivity. They prefer therefore to adhere to 'objective' facts without value judgements. But this is a twofold illusion. Firstly, no one has access to the full scope of facts — for which he would have to wait until the end of Vulcan evolution! Everyone therefore, inevitably offers a selection. And secondly, and more importantly, not all objective facts have the same weight or emphasis. In the unfinished series of events that compose world history, the very greatest significance of all must be accorded to the Mystery of Golgotha. Deeper insight into why this is so can awaken understanding for a symptomatological view of history. Without finding the *courage to highlight things of key importance,* we will fail to understand either the Mystery of Golgotha or the nature of a symptomatological approach; and the significance of temporal rhythms such as that of 33 years 4 months, as embodied in the historical life of Jesus Christ, will likewise remain a closed book to us.

What this book does not contain

Let me say without prevarication what you will not find in this book: there is no account of Steiner's work on Goethe, a rough knowledge of which is assumed, nor any explicit mention of *The Philosophy of Freedom*, Steiner's major work, or any other of his basic works. I have not included any account, either, of the complex events which led to Steiner's expulsion from the Theosophical Society and the founding of the Anthroposophical Society at the end of 1912. Studies on this theme have already been published.[1] As regards the forming of the Anthroposophical Society and the role which Mathilde Scholl played in this, I would like to refer to the excellent monograph by Ekkehard Meffert.[2] There is no need to reiterate what this author has already presented.

Nor have I given any special emphasis to the founding of institutions upon which Steiner pinned some hopes that were not in the end realized. I am thinking here, for instance, of the School of Spiritual Science. No one else proved able to enlarge on this Michael School's primary spiritual content of 19 lessons,[3] given by Steiner in 1924.

Thematic emphases

The contents page will show, by contrast, the primary focus of this book to be different in kind from previous works: it includes Steiner's encounter with an unknown person in 1879, his experiences with modern projective geometry, the importance of his recognition of the dual stream of time, and of the universal laws of involution and evolution as constituents of *all* development.

A long chapter emerged from a study of Friedrich Nietzsche's importance in Steiner's development. Steiner saw an instance, in Nietzsche, of how humankind was once more approaching states of 'Inspiration', with all its attendant dangers if this happens in an unbalanced way, as was the case with Nietzsche.

I placed particular emphasis on Steiner's relationship to the true spirit of German culture, which has continually been misunderstood even within the anthroposophical movement itself.[4]

The Holocaust not only failed to diminish the importance of this spirit but it can now emerge still more clearly by comparison to the pseudo-German culture of the last century, in which it played absolutely no part. It was this latter spirit, deeply bound up with the nature of anthroposophy and the deeper zeitgeist, which Steiner sought to further.

In connection with these efforts it was important to highlight Steiner's relationship with Helmuth von Moltke, whom Ludwig Polzer-Hoditz said was the 'last whole man' left in Germany at the outbreak of war. Moltke suffered defamation and mis-understanding on a scale second only to that inflicted on Steiner himself, as is amply demonstrated by the biased publications of Annika Mombauer or others. The chapters related to this theme were written with a view to the anniversary year 2014, when new attacks are likely to be made both on Moltke and Steiner.[5] It is my hope that leading anthroposophists will not succumb so easily to these attacks as they did to the racism attacks in the 90s of the last century.

Some chapters of the book do not keep to chronological order and sometimes also extend into the present day, thence returning to their starting point and leading on to the next milestone.

Reflections on a seemingly unimportant quirk of Steiner's childhood, raised but not elaborated on in the first chapter, conclude the main part of the book.

The volume ends with a survey of the development of anthroposophy, the anthroposophical movement and the Anthroposophical Society after Rudolf Steiner's death. This is an extended study with numerous subsections, and ends with the prospect of a second great energetic cycle of anthroposophical activities in the future. In writing this chapter I was guided by perspectives that I would like to briefly outline here.

Involution and evolution as governing principles

Every developmental process has two fundamental, opposite aspects, that of evolution and involution.[6]

The first of these means that, emerging from a spiritual realm, spirit enters into the sensory realm of matter, while the second indicates that substance passes over into spirit again. These two phases alternate in the seasons. From midwinter to midsummer, nature is evolving; and then, in the second half of the year, the reverse process occurs. If we survey the globe as a whole we see that both processes—which we can also call upbuilding and declining—occur simultaneously, and interact harmoniously with each other.

These phases can be distinguished in humankind's history too. The era that led from Augustine to Meister Eckhart was primarily marked by involution processes, or in other words of spiritual internalization. There followed a phase of largely evolutionary processes with outward voyages of discovery, world conquest, technological development and so forth. Rosicrucianism tries to harmonize both poles of development, as does anthroposophy. The anthroposophical movement should develop through harmonious interplay of these two principles.

But this interplay can only be harmonious if the two poles themselves are healthy. Something that usually does not figure in natural evolution can indeed occur in *human* development: involution processes can grow unhealthy, leading to mysticism, superstition, sectarianism and so forth; and this will lead in turn to equally unhealthy evolution processes, in which we lose ourselves in the external world.

The history of the Anthroposophical Society, especially following Rudolf Steiner's death, despite all partial success that it can demonstrate, is one of continually distorted, one-sided or 'false' involution processes, followed or even accompanied by equally distorted and one-sided processes of evolution. Let me give just one of many possible instances: on the one hand a narrow emphasis on the significance of the Christmas Foundation Meeting of 1923/24 and Steiner's supposed 'indissoluble' connection with the Anthroposophical Society; and on the other an urgent, undiscerning impulse to enter the public domain and meet with increasing 'recognition' from more and more people but only by increasingly concealing anthroposophy itself. These are false, or in other words unhealthy involution and evolution processes which seem to exclude each other but which in fact are mutually determining and supporting.

Disharmony between these two poles, increasingly apparent

for decades now, and at odds with the core impulse of anthroposophical development, could only be harmonized or 'healed' again through unwavering recognition of reality. Such recognition has a healthy involutionary character and can therefore lead to healthy evolutionary steps, or in other words to new upbuilding actions. It is fully informed by freedom and does not arise by necessity or compulsion from past realities — which is why it has largely not figured in the previous history of the anthroposophical movement — but instead emerges as something entirely new. It is therefore, in Steiner's phrase, 'creation out of nothing'.

The present anthroposophical movement appears to need insights founded on this kind of creation out of nothing in order to cure and rebalance involution and evolution processes that have grown one-sided or even aberrant. Naturally no single individual can accomplish this alone, and this book seeks only to offer a small contribution to the healing process. Those who consider some things in the final chapter to be stated in an excessively stringent or even unrelenting way may like to reflect that a sickness cannot be cured without an absolutely truthful diagnosis.

Overall, this book tries to evaluate the world-historical grandeur of the life work of Rudolf Steiner and the healing powers of anthroposophy with its capacity to reconcile all opposites. Anthroposophy continues to work on in an involutionary way in many souls who have crossed the threshold of death after endeavouring to attain spiritual knowledge on earth. Helmuth von Moltke was one such soul. While alive he belonged neither to the Theosophical nor the Anthroposophical Society; and yet the meditative Foundation Stone which Steiner gave at Christmas 1923 lives on in him, as it can in all those who strive for truth and knowledge. From such internalized foundation stones the mystery centres of the future will be built, initiating a new phase of anthroposophy's evolution in and for the world.

Thomas Meyer
Basel, 7 March 2012

1. 'For One Use Only'

In December 1923 Rudolf Steiner started to write his *Autobiography*, which initially appeared in regular instalments in the journal *Das Goetheanum*. He died on 30 March 1925 and a week later, in the issue of 5 April 1925, the 70th instalment was published as the last of the unfinished series.

In the second instalment, published in the issue of 16 December 1923, Steiner described a 'curious peculiarity' of his as a very young child:

> From the moment I was able to eat unaided, people had to watch over me carefully since I had formed the view that a soup bowl or a drinking cup was only to be used once. Each time, therefore, that I had finished eating or drinking I would, if not watched, throw the bowl or cup down on the floor so that it broke into pieces. When my mother came up to me I would shout out to her: 'Mother, I've finished now.'

Rudolf Steiner commented on this as follows: 'This cannot have been rage or destructiveness on my part since I treated my toys with painstaking care and kept them safely for ages.' He said no more about it, yet what he describes makes this 'curious peculiarity' still more remarkable—not just a seemingly inexplicable little trait but something that might need deeper attention and explanation. Steiner does not interpret it further, simply defining in negative terms what this characteristic was *not*. It was not an expression of rage. He leaves it to the reader to ponder and, perhaps, discover the real explanation.

Most readers will probably simply read on without attributing much importance to the matter, seeing it as odd or amusing but nothing more. But one wonders whether the founder of spiritual science, undertaking a serious review of his whole life, would have considered this worth reporting if it really had no further importance. Is it possible, rather, that this peculiarity conceals something of deeper significance which we might fathom through deeper reflection?

In the preface to his book *Theosophy*, published in 1904, Steiner had written: 'This book cannot be read in the way people generally read things in our times. In certain respects, the reader will need to work hard to take possession of every page, and even many sentences.' Steiner's *Autobiography* is not of course *Theosophy*; but it is true nevertheless that he had no intention of writing the kind of autobiography generally written today. It emerged from the same mind as *Theosophy*, after all, and it is perfectly reasonable to assume, when reading it, that it contains pages or sentences that will not easily disclose their meaning to a reader who merely rushes through it, let alone urge itself upon him suggestively.

The little anecdote quoted above is an easily overlooked matter. What lies hidden within it will only be discussed further at the end of this book. Its profound and encompassing character can probably only be understood after we have first surveyed the nature and development of the impulse of spiritual science which Steiner introduced into the world.

2. The Experience in Pottschach

When Steiner was seven, something very incisive occurred in the waiting room of the little railway station in Pottschach (Lower Austria), and was to be of great significance in the later emergence of spiritual science. He gave an account of this incident — which Marie Steiner first published in *Das Goetheanum* in 1946[7] — on 4 February 1913 at the first general assembly of the newly founded Anthroposophical Society.

Here Steiner countered the lies spread about his life by Annie Besant merely by offering a description of his *actual* development. He adopted a third-person, distanced stance to the narrative, since he was only disclosing it because of the lies. In this account of his life, whose printing Steiner immediately authorized (though for various reasons it was not published at the time), the following passage occurs:

One day he was sitting in that waiting room on a bench, quite alone. The stove was in one corner, and a door stood in the wall opposite the stove. The boy, still very, very young, sat in the corner where one had a good view both of the door and the stove. And as he sat there the door opened. It was no surprise to him that a person, a lady, entered whom he had never seen before but who bore an extraordinary resemblance to a member of his family. The lady came through the doorway, reached the middle of the room and proceeded to make gestures and to speak words to the boy, too, which could roughly be reproduced as follows: 'Try to do as much as you can for me both now and later!' She remained a little longer, making gestures that can never fade from memory if one has ever seen them, then went to the stove and disappeared into it.

This incident made a very powerful impression upon the boy, but there was no one in the family he could have spoken to about it; and this was because he knew he would be told off in the severest fashion for his 'stupid superstitions' if he had told anyone.

After this had happened, the following occurred soon afterwards. The boy's father, otherwise a very cheerful man, grew very sad; and the boy could see that his father was keeping something to himself. After a few days had passed, and another member of the family had been let in to the secret, what had happened was revealed. A long way from that railway station — at least as distance was viewed at the time by the people concerned — a close family member had killed herself at the same moment that the figure had appeared to the boy in the waiting room. The boy had never met her nor had he ever heard much about her because he was in some respects — and this should be emphasized — rather unavailable for stories told in his vicinity: they went in one ear and out the other. He heard few of the things that were discussed around him, and he therefore knew little about the person who had killed herself.

This occurrence made a strong impression on him, for there can be no doubt whatsoever that he had been visited by the spirit of the person who had killed herself, and that she had come to entrust him with the task of doing something for her in the period following her death. In addition, this spiritual event coincided with events on the physical plane, as became very apparent in the following days.

If someone experiences something like this in early childhood, and seeks to understand it as well as his inner disposition allows, he will, if this experience is conscious, be aware henceforth of how one experiences things in worlds of spirit.

This is how Steiner described the full dimensions of the experience he had around the age of seven, which opened supersensible portals to him in the midst of the physical world. From then on he knew that one enters the world of spirit in *three* ways: firstly through a supersensible experience that is pictorial in nature, secondly through supersensible hearing, and thirdly by penetrating to the essential core of what has been revealed in the first or the second way.

This experience at a young age later developed into Steiner's systematic account of the three forms of supersensible experience of *Imagination, Inspiration* and *Intuition*, which are also of course the foundation for spiritual-scientific research and enquiry. He first described these stages of higher knowledge systematically in writing in the chapter of *Occult Science* entitled 'Knowledge of the Higher Worlds'. The book was completed in 1909.

It is clear from this experience he had as a boy how decisive is Intuition, the third stage of knowledge. We should try to imagine what would have happened if the incident had been revealed to him only up to the second stage, ending with the plea to him from the lady appearing to his occult vision. The boy would have remained in almost unendurable ignorance about the *essential nature* of what he had experienced. But he was able to relate it to what occurred in the following days at home: it became utterly clear to him who the being was who had appeared to him in Imagination and Inspiration, and only because of this could he understand the whole thing.

It is significant here that he could reconcile an esoteric experience with the realities of physical existence, giving rise to a sense of conclusion and completeness which Steiner's spiritual research in future would require of all spiritual experiences: they must be embedded in a healthy way in the whole context of one's life.

It is also characteristic that the incident did not occur in a sleeping or dreaming state but in full, waking awareness. It unfolded within the boy's very ordinary object perception (of the physical reality of the waiting room) which is the lowest of the four stages of knowledge, and one that we all possess quite naturally. All four stages of knowledge and perception were therefore involved in this event, and thus we can call it a *total* experience.

In the same way that Rudolf Steiner's first total esoteric experience occurred in the midst of his waking perception, his later spiritual research took its point of departure from the waking perception and thinking of ordinary object awareness, and developed from this all higher stages of knowledge. This contrasts strongly with somnambulistic or trancelike forms of awareness that lie below the level of waking perception.

Finally, we can accord special significance to the fact that this first total esoteric experience approached him from the *objective* world to which the soul and spirit aspects of all being belong, and that it was associated with a plea to help. In this respect too this formative experience appears archetypal in nature. In a sense, the boy was approached by the soul of a humanity at risk of drowning in materialism, sinking into despair and desperation through lack of spiritual sustenance and, oblivious of the higher nature within it, murdering itself yet at the same time begging for help.

In this incisive and seminal occurrence we can discern how esoteric capacities awaken in order to serve humankind and the world. The whole of the spiritual science later elaborated by Steiner represents nothing other than a reply to the—mostly unconscious—cry for help from the human soul deprived of spirit and impelled towards destruction and self-destruction.

There is one further 'side effect' of this total experience that I would like to highlight, which Rudolf Steiner expressed as follows in the 1913 lecture:

> Since I intend to speak of the influx of spiritual worlds only to the degree directly necessary in this context, I will indicate merely that from that event onwards a life within the soul commenced for the boy, revealing to him worlds through which not only outward trees or mountains speak to the human soul but also underlying realities. From that moment on the boy lived in communion with the spirits of nature that especially inhabit a region such as this; he lived with the creative presences behind all things, in the same way as he experienced the influences upon him of the external world.

The experience in the waiting room thus also opened portals to the spirits of nature. The soul in the first period after death lives within this world of nature or elemental spirits—of which there are basically four kinds. During this period we gradually divest ourselves of attachment to the physical, sensory world, passing through regions of burning desire, the flux of stimulus, of wishes, and of like and dislike, as these are described in *Theosophy*. Altogether these four regions, which correspond to the elements of earth, water, air and fire, constitute what is called kamaloka. This 'locus of desires' is the moon sphere in cosmological terms. No wonder, therefore, that the 'visitation' of the dead person's spirit, just entering kamaloka, also started to open to Steiner the realm of nature or elemental spirits.

The fairy tale of the miraculous spring in Steiner's second Mystery Play, *The Soul's Probation*, has some resonance with his spiritual experience of nature that began with this event. The boy who figures in this tale perceives nature beings in the form of female figures whom, with his youthful clairvoyance, he sees thronging in 'moonlight's silver shimmer and moonlight glimmer' around the spring he loves, which he visits on an evening walk. This is not to say that the female figures described in this tale do not also bear a higher aspect than is granted to mere nature beings.

3. Joy in Geometry

Rudolf Steiner's first experience of joy was entirely spiritual in nature. It did not approach him through any outward means — in the form of a wonderful gift, say, or friendly word, or warm, loving glance. Instead the young Steiner made a discovery in the room of Henrich Gangl, an assistant teacher at the village school in Neudorfl, where the family had moved soon after the incident described in the last chapter. He saw a geometry textbook and was allowed to take it home with him. In his *Autobiography* Steiner describes the enthusiasm with which he pored over it: 'For weeks my soul was filled with congruence and the affinity between triangles, rectangles, polygons; I racked my brains to work out where parallels actually meet, and Pythagoras' Theorem entranced me.'

This enthusiasm for geometry gave the young Steiner his first experience of inner joy:

> I was deeply contented to find that the soul could live inwardly in the elaboration of forms perceived purely inwardly, without the need of any outward sense impressions. This consoled me for the mood that had arisen in me in consequence of unanswered questions. To comprehend something in spirit alone brought me inward joy. *I know that it was geometry that first gave me an experience of happiness.*[8]

Clear, cool thinking capable of kindling warm feeling was the primary experience that arose here: personal feeling which is not, as ordinarily, kindled in response to outward things or emotional matters, but instead is born from an active engagement with an objective mental or spiritual domain. In *Theosophy* Steiner speaks of the 'new' kind of feeling arising from active cognition, saying: 'No feeling and no enthusiasm can match the warmth, beauty and exaltation kindled by pure, crystal-clear thoughts relating to higher worlds.' The young Steiner had already experienced this as he formed pure geometrical thoughts.

Here too we can find the primary experience that later leads Steiner, in chapter 6 of *The Philosophy of Freedom*, to define the nature of an 'authentic individual', as one who 'elevates his feelings to the greatest degree into the ideal realm'.

A true individual is not distinguished by unfeeling thinking or unthinking feeling but by feeling engagement with the activities of pure thinking. Steiner puts this as follows:

> There are people in whom the most ordinary ideas still bear the distinctive hue that reveals their connection with the mind who thinks them. Others, by contrast, have concepts that reach us with no trace of any individual nuance, as if they do not come from a human being of flesh and blood at all.

Kant is an example of the latter, Schiller of the former; or also the young Steiner himself who, as a boy already, embodied authentic individuality in the manner described above because he was able to feel transports of happiness through the activity of his thinking.

4. 'I Have Shown You Who You Are'

Steiner's initiation in the autumn of 1879

In November 1890, when he was living in Weimar, Steiner wrote as follows to Friedrich Eckstein, an important contemporary and friend of his youth: 'There are two events in my life which figure so importantly in it that I feel I would have been a quite different person if they had not happened. Of one I must remain silent; the other is the fact that I met *you*.' The event which Steiner says he must remain silent about is his encounter with one of the two persons involved in his initiation.[9] He said still less about the second.

Although this was a moment of the profoundest importance in his biography, we have nothing to go on but the brief account Steiner himself later gave in the autobiographical lecture of 1913. As far as the date of the encounter is concerned, it is apparent from the aforementioned Berlin lecture that it occurred in the first year of Steiner's university studies, in October 1879 in Vienna, and predated his first reading of Part II of Goethe's *Faust*, 'which he studied as an 18- or 19-year-old youth'. In the autumn of 1879 Steiner was still 18 and he could only have begun reading *Faust* after he commenced his studies in October, encouraged by his teacher Karl Julius Schroer. In the *Autobiography* he relates that he visited Schroer at home after only a few of the latter's lectures, and that among other things they discussed the second part of *Faust*. Thus he must have begun reading Part II in November or December 1879, *after* his encounter with the unnamed person. Let us try to examine these important weeks of Steiner's life in closer detail, since together they represent one of the most important milestones in his whole life.

From the beginning of August of that year, the Steiner family had moved to Oberlaa near Inzersdorf, south of Vienna, to be close to Rudolf Steiner's place of study. On his very first visit to

Vienna Steiner had procured a 'large number of philosophical works' which he was able to exchange for the school books he no longer needed at a second-hand bookseller's. He read Kant, Hegel, Schelling and Darwin, in particular undertaking a detailed study of Fichte's *The Science of Knowing* during these summer months. Steiner composed a text which 'rewrote' Fichte's ideas, in which there seemed to be no place for his spirit vision. As a consequence of his early total esoteric experience, there lived in the young Steiner a capacity to perceive the spiritual individuality of every human being, 'which was merely manifest in physical corporeality and in outward actions in the physical world, and united with the physical germ originating from a person's parents' (*Autobiography*).

The two streams of time

During this summer period between the end of his schooling and the start of his university studies, Steiner made a very significant discovery which, unlike the rest of his studies and self-enquiries, and the characteristic mode in which he engaged in these, was directed — in his words — 'entirely from the realm of occult life' and 'was not related to these other studies'. This is how Steiner himself put it in an autobiographical sketch which he wrote for Edouard Schuré in 1907.[10]

Schuré was well prepared to understand this occult influx into Rudolf Steiner's biography, and was receptive to it, since he himself had been preoccupied with the great initiates of humanity's history. Steiner communicated these things to Schuré in the summer of 1907, during a visit that he and Marie von Sivers made to Barr. This three-part account, written in his own hand, has become known as the 'Documents of Barr'. Much of what he told Schuré, over and above the written text, found its way into the long introduction which Schuré wrote for his French translation of Steiner's book *Christianity as Mystical Fact*, published in 1908.

The knowledge 'directed entirely from the realm of occult life' was something Steiner counted among the 'external occult influences' in his development. It related to 'complete clarity about ideas of time': the insight that 'the forward progression of evolution is at the same time informed by a reversed, astral-occult developmental direction, and that spiritual vision is dependent upon this knowledge'. Elsewhere Steiner described these two opposite streams of time in the words 'evolution' and 'involution', and associated a great deal more with them than may at first be apparent. I would like to illustrate this with an example of current relevance.

Brief digression on modern economics

It is of critical importance in our time to ask how many people really grasp the fact that, alongside the laws of growth and evolution, everything in the world is also governed by involution, or in other words that besides synthesis—the up-building powers at work in nature and in ourselves—break-down and decline also operate, as we can see clearly in the cycle of the seasons. In the world of economics, for instance, we must count on both factors, seeing that, like the commodities which money should represent only as an accounting symbol, without itself becoming a commodity, money is also subject to the laws of decline. On 13 December 1918 (GA 186), Steiner spoke of this as follows: 'Emergent and upbuilding powers are looked upon with favour. People always want endless growth and development. But besides evolution or upbuilding forces in the world, involution or decline is also at work.' We may not acknowledge this, but it is a reality nevertheless. In relation to our current financial and economic crises, we are being forced to recognize this reality, which teaches us greater wisdom through major downturns and inflationary processes. Steiner showed how, in economics, such 'unwilled' devaluation processes could be replaced by rationally integrated involution processes, for instance by setting a date when a money note would lose its value, just like the commodity which it represents; and how, in the same way that food must be consumed before it goes bad, so a note ought to be brought into circulation *before* this expiry date as purchase, gift or loan money. The mere hoarding of money never leads to higher value, but instead ultimately to its complete loss of worth.

The 'agent' of the master

Steiner's fundamental insight into the interplay of evolution and involution was soon followed by his acquaintance with a man who turned out to be the precursor of another, whom we must regard as the young Steiner's initiator. The latter acted as his inspiration while remaining entirely in the background and anonymous.

To attend university, from October of that year onwards Steiner made regular train journeys to one of Vienna's railway stations (Suedbahnhof), during which he made the acquaintance of the herbalist and occultist Felix Koguzki. Steiner relates this encounter in his *Autobiography*, in the autobiographical sketch, and memorialized it also in his first Mystery Play *The Portal of Initiation*. Koguzki, an unusual figure and someone whom others found hard to understand, travelled once a week to Vienna to sell his herbs to pharmacies. On his way to the Technical University, Steiner accompanied him along the narrow Alleegasse (today called Argentinerstrasse) in the direction of Karlsplatz, and witnessed the smiles of 'some who occasionally joined them' as they walked along.

This important figure was in fact 'the precursor of another individual', as Steiner stated in his Berlin lecture of 4 February 1913. 'Like Felix, this outstanding man pursued a nondescript outward profession,' but in contrast to the former, we know nothing about his name, origins or 'nondescript profession'.

Rudolf Steiner thus encountered him some time between October and December 1879. Did this encounter happen on the route he and Felix took from the railway station through Argentinerstrasse? Did the unknown figure join them one day, not smiling but knowing? Was the young Steiner introduced to him *en passant* by Felix, and did he walk further with him? We do not know.

From Fichte to *Occult Science*

Whatever the truth of it, this individual used a 'particular means to kindle in the young man's soul, which already stood within the world of spirit, things of an ongoing, systematic nature with which one must be familiar in this world'. The 'occult schooling' which the unknown figure now undertook with the 'youth' started from the very works of Fichte which Steiner had been studying intensively in the previous months:

> This person [...] used the works of Fichte, linking them to certain reflections which formed the germinal foundations of the book *Occult Science*, later written by the youth when he became an adult. Much of what subsequently emerged as *Occult Science* was discussed at that time in relation to Fichte's ideas.

Fichte's works are based on perception of the spirituality of the I. But how could the world and its origins be reconciled with the origins of this spiritual I? Clearly this was an unanswered and painful question for the young Steiner at the time.

But his eyes were opened: it was a matter of showing how the spirituality of the I had emerged from the spirituality of the whole world. *Occult Science*, published at the beginning of 1910, was the reply to this tormenting question in relation to Fichte, and it was the unknown figure who pointed him in this direction.

Deepening insight into time

The unknown person also helped in another respect, enabling Steiner to broaden and deepen those insights of his into the nature of time which had been 'directed from the occult realm'. To do this he used an unnamed and so far unidentified book 'as a kind of reference point for something that is little known in the external world [...] by means of which one can be guided upon very specific spiritual paths'. What did Steiner learn in this way? 'Vividly before the youth's soul appeared those distinctive streams that pass through the occult world, and which one can perceive only through awareness of a dual stream that both rises and falls.' Thus Steiner in his autobiographical lecture in 1913. This dual stream is that of *time*, encompassing all growth and decline. In addition to the flow of time we perceive in ordinary awareness, which is future- or forward-oriented, there is a second, corresponding to astral consciousness, which flows in reverse. One is the stream of evolution, the other that of involution. The living move primarily in the first, the dead chiefly in the second, in a reverse experience of their past life. At the age of eight already, the young Steiner had encountered both these streams, and also became aware of them in his occult perception of nature. In the life of the earth as a whole, these two streams exist simultaneously too, and act in opposite reciprocity to one another: when spring arrives in the northern hemisphere (growth), nature is entering autumn (decline) in the southern hemisphere, and vice versa.

What the unknown figure taught Steiner enabled him to integrate much of what he himself had already experienced in a more 'systematic' schema.

Concluding what he has to say about this important encounter with the unknown person, Steiner says:

> The youth was introduced to these esoteric realities before he had as yet read *Faust*, Part II. There is no need to speak further about this aspect of the occult schooling of the youth into whom the younger boy had grown. All these things remained in the young man's soul; he experienced them within him as he continued to pursue his outward path.

From then on, having undergone a systematic training, he was able to move more self-assuredly through both the sensory and supersensible world simultaneously.

Words for the further journey

In the biographical sketch, approved by Steiner, which Schuré wrote as introduction to the French edition of *Christianity as Mystical Fact*, we can read the farewell words which the 'master' gave to his pupil to accompany him on his further path:

If you wish to fight the adversary, you must first understand him. You can only conquer the dragon if you slip into his skin. You must take the bull by the horns. You will find your weapons and battle comrades in the most adverse fortune. I have shown you who you are—now go, and remain yourself![11]

These words contain the quintessence of the whole schooling Steiner had received from the unknown man, and they culminate in a prospect of all the future deeds required in consequence. As Steiner wrote to Friedrich Eckstein, he became someone 'quite different' through this encounter.

*

Here we stand before a milestone of the very greatest significance or, we might say, at a nodal point of Rudolf Steiner's whole development, which cohered from the most diverse threads: his exoteric studies embodied primarily in the great figure of his teacher Schroer, complemented and augmented—through the mediation of Felix Koguzki—by esoteric schooling from the unknown person. During September 1879 Steiner himself was passing through his first moon node. In November 1879 the Time Spirit Michael assumed the period of his regency, which is to last 350 years. Simultaneously the doors opened for the young man both to what mainstream science could attain at the time, and to the heavenly realms. Between these stood the great figure of the unknown teacher, as mediator between the two spheres in which he himself, clearly, had long since learned to live.

5. 'As if a Great Weight Had Fallen from My Shoulders'

A few years later, Steiner's early experience of joy in geometry is picked up again and led a good deal further. As a boy he had among other things 'racked his brains' to work out where parallels meet. Clearly this remained an unsolved problem in his joyous embrace of geometry at the time. Yet the boy seems to have been certain that parallels, like any other two straight lines, must inevitably intersect somewhere. But where?

The answer to this dawned on him during his studies at the Technical University in Vienna. In the *Autobiography* we read that 'a decisive experience was granted me in my studies of mathematics at the time'. He had been struggling with the riddle of space, and had not felt it possible to reconcile himself with the idea of space as a 'void extending on all sides into infinity as was posited by scientific theories prevailing then'.

In lectures he attended, and private study of synthetic geometry, a new field at the time, he developed the view 'that a line extended infinitely towards the right will return from the left again to its starting point. The point infinitely far to the right is the same as that lying infinitely far to the left'. Thus he had come a step closer to answering the question of his boyhood as to where parallels intersect. The name for this 'locus' is infinity.

In his *Autobiography*, Steiner writes: 'It seemed to me that ideas of this kind in modern geometry would enable one to conceive of space other than as a rigid void. The straight line returning to itself as if in a circle struck me like a revelation.' And then he describes a moment that seems to be of great significance in his development: 'I left the lecture during which this first occurred to me as if a great weight had fallen from my shoulders.' In other words, precisely in this field of enquiry, Steiner had learned to *suffer* the pain of incomplete or immature ideas! One such was of space as a rigid void; and all the greater, then, was his pleasure at the discovery of the solution: 'I was overcome by a sense of liberation. Again, as in my boyhood, geometry granted me an experience of happiness.' Around the same time Steiner, who had embarked on a very intensive study of Kant when only 16, was also making a thorough study of Hegel's philosophy. And Hegel states at one place in his *Science of Logic* that the concept of infinity is the 'underlying concept of all philosophy'.[12] In a Whitsun lecture of 1910, Steiner himself emphasized that the 'infinity of the spirit is its most significant attribute' (GA 118). The seeds of this insight lay in the moment a 'great weight' fell from him on leaving the lecture.

The logic of Aristotle and likewise Euclidean geometry did not recognize the infinite. Humanity had to be led into the finite realm with its seemingly insuperable contradictions. Two thousand years later it had once more to discover a connection with the infinite. Both Hegel's treatise on logic and the new geometry offered something of an impetus for this: contradictions in the finite realm could be resolved by ideas about the infinite. In infinity, such contradictions find a higher unity, as is apparent in geometry in relation to the question of where parallel lines meet. In finite terms, they never do and never can; but from the perspective of infinity they meet everywhere and all the time. Great minds actually *suffered* from the direct repercussions of the problem of infinity. We can see an example of this in the Hungarian mathematician Bolyai, who warned his son against worrying over the problem of parallel lines. His misfortune arose from the fact that he himself was unable to resist this temptation (see GA 174).

Just as, in the time of Scholasticism, the question about the reality of concepts was one of pervasive existential dimensions, so this was true also of the question of infinity in the nineteenth century, which at the same time represented the quest for the 'most significant attribute of the spirit'.

As well as calling Hegel the greatest philosopher of all time, Steiner also pointed in his lectures to the truly innovative importance of synthetic or projective geometry. On one occasion 'an older author who has written much about spiritual matters' asked him, at a first meeting,

> 'How did you first become aware of this difference between per-ception of the sensory world and of the supersensible?' I replied, because I prefer to be outspokenly honest about such things: 'At the moment I learned the inner meaning of what is called the new or synthetic geometry.' (GA 82)

Steiner stresses in this context that the question made a 'powerful impression' upon him, and also reveals that, as he answered, the other gave him 'a curious look'.

This 'older gentleman' was none other than a figure we have already referred to several times, the French writer and theo-sophist Edouard Schuré.

*

But as in his first experience of happiness, which still left him with the unresolved question of parallel lines, a question remained for him and led to further creative endeavours. This related to the *riddle of time* which could not be solved in the same way as that of space, although Steiner initially wondered if it might be. 'Might it be possible,' he asked after solving the riddle of space, 'to conceive time progressing into an 'infinitely remote' future in a way that also contained its return from the past?' But it soon became clear to him that this could not be: 'All my endeavours led me to acknowledge that I must guard very carefully against introducing tangible concepts of space into views of time.' And then came a sentence that shows, again, how profoundly Steiner's search for insight was rooted in his whole soul: 'All the disappointments which a quest for knowledge can bring surfaced in relation to the riddle of time.' (*Autobiography*)

The liberating experience after the lecture with all that it triggered for him occurred *after* his encounter with the unknown man. This can give us pause for thought. Surely he had already gained 'full clarity about concepts of time' before he met this person; and during his esoteric instruction he had, after all, as he stated, come to know the dual, rising and falling stream. Why therefore was he suffering the 'riddle of time' once more?

Things are not that simple. Steiner's insights into time, 'directed from the occult realm', were not as yet sufficient. Through his *own unaided activity* he still needed to reconcile this with the concept of time that existed in exoteric science and philosophy.[13] Initially this appeared to be impossible. Although the new geometry had revealed a new concept of space, no similarly satisfactory scientific concept of time existed. The young Steiner suffered from this fact, even after his instruction and initiation by the great unknown figure.

6. The Night When Steiner's I Was Born

We now arrive at a key moment in Steiner's development, and, from a certain perspective, *the* key moment: a milestone exceeding all others in importance. Once again we can give the precise date this occurred: during the night between 10 and 11 January 1881. This was the night when the I of Rudolf Steiner was 'born'.

This phrase—the birth of the I—may annoy some readers. Surely we all have a sense of I or self, starting from our earliest memory? And surely this self-awareness and the little word 'I' itself accompanies all the phases of our development from that early moment onwards? Why therefore do I speak of the 'birth of the I' in a 20-year-old who, like others, has long since possessed self-awareness?

As Rudolf Steiner describes in many lectures, there are in fact four 'births' in the stages of human development: of the physical body firstly, then of the etheric body, the astral body and finally the birth of the true I. If our development proceeded as the Spirits of Form envisaged, who endowed the human being with the spark of individuality, of the I, in Lemurian times, these separate births would have succeeded one another at seven-year intervals. The birth of the physical body would be followed seven years later by that of the etheric body, after 14 by that of the astral body and after 21 years by that of the true I. But due to the luciferic and later the ahrimanic influence, these births were temporally transposed into each other and in a way modified. Thus an infant nowadays appears to possess an ether body, astral body and I. Yet more careful observation will show that up to the seventh year the child is wrapped in the mother's ether body until his own is born; then the mother's astral body forms the astral envelope for the child until the age of 14, when his own astral body is born. And only by 21 do we awaken to our own I power, if we ever really do.

The pedagogy established by Steiner pays heed to these eso-teric births of ether body, astral body and I which still underlie more apparent phases of development. Often however the for-mer are drowned out and go largely unnoticed because of materialistic influences in a child's surroundings and education, and this is truest of all of the birth of the I. Today, in their childhood and youth, many people appear secure in their seemingly fully-formed 'I', and, along with most adults, would ridicule the idea that this is only truly born at the age of 21. Yet what kind of 'I' is it that awakens here prematurely? It is one kindled by Lucifer in relation to and in engagement with the sensory world. And of what does it consist? Of memories of experiences undergone in body and soul since the age of 2 or 3. This ordinary, early-woken 'I awareness' does not encompass either a memory of pre-birth experiences or a sense of the eternal nature of the core I. But it is precisely this individuality, in its eternal essence, that dwells in each one of us and must be awoken by ourselves, that the Spirits of Form introduced into the sheaths of physical body, ether body and astral body during Lemurian times. This eternal being within us usually remains deeply concealed in the unconscious because of our prematurely awoken sense of I. Around the age of 21 this divine spark can awaken, at the hour of its birth appointed by the Spirits of Form. But rare are those in whom this occurs in a way fully and clearly distinct from the youthfully awoken sense of self, so that they become aware of the eternal nature of their core I.

Rudolf Steiner was one of these few. Let us read the account he wrote of it two days later to his friend Josef Koeck:

My dear, loyal friend

I did not sleep a wink in the night between 10 and 11 January. Until half past midnight I had been studying certain philosophical prob-lems and at last threw myself upon the bed. Last year my efforts were focused on ascertaining the truth of what Schelling says: that in all of us there dwells 'a secret, wondrous capacity, to withdraw into the inmost self from transitory things, from all that has come to us from without and, dwelling in our naked self, to look there upon unchanging eternity'. I believed and still believe I have clearly discovered that inmost capacity within me — having long intimated that it existed — and now the whole of philosophical idealism stands before me in a greatly altered form. What is one sleepless night compared to such a discovery?! (*Briefe* I, 13)

The 'discovery' was nothing other that that of Rudolf Steiner's higher I. It is clear from Schelling's words *which* I is here referred to: not the mundane self, awareness of which awakens in childhood, 'that comes to us from without' (from the sense world, in other words). He is speaking of the inmost self, unveiled of all externalities. Steiner discovered — and activated — the capacity to 'look upon unchanging eternity' in himself.

As the letter continues we sense the huge psychological momentum that this discovery gave rise to:

And the morning dawned — an icy, cold one ... I was up and ready for the journey — and found a letter awaiting me, soon seeing from the address that it came from you. I read it on the train, by pitiable light — it is already quite impossible for me to describe the feelings I had during those moments; I was outside myself — hugely moved, not knowing what to do to calm myself — clearly there was nothing!

A stammering account of an event that not only brings an awareness of the eternal I but at the same time also conveys an experience of the continual alteration undergone by the finite (or in other words, soul-physical sheaths) of our being. He continues: 'The whole day long I was a different person from the day before — naturally in a material sense, not in form.' The intense changes in all physical and soul *substance* are suddenly vividly apparent to the eye of spirit, which has at the same time become aware of the immutability of its *form*.

It is noteworthy that Steiner uses Aristotelian opposites of matter and form to describe his revelatory experience. Anyone with the least knowledge of these concepts will be aware that 'matter' here not only designates physical, sensory reality but also non-sensory aspects of life or soul, in fact all that is governed by the laws of spirit, by 'form'. Thus, through his experience of the immutably eternal (form), the young Steiner became aware in tumultuous fashion also of the temporal mutability of everything not eternal (matter) in himself. This belongs to the dual character of the experience: in so far as the I is clothed in matter, it bears qualities of time and mutability; and in so far as it can become pure form unclothed of all matter, it can become aware of the immutably eternal within it. The former invariably plays into prematurely awoken self-awareness while the latter only dawns at the moment the true I is born.

Steiner had already recognized the dual stream of time in 1879. Now, one-and-a-half to two years later, this is complemented by awareness of something lying above and beyond all temporal things, which Schelling called 'the eternal'. The eternal 'I form' dawned upon him. The gift of the Spirits of Form, to which Steiner as spiritual scientist will later refer, has awoken in him like a flash of lightning, one might say, yet following long reflections and preparations which include his encounter with the unknown teacher.

What we can truly call the 'birthday letter' to Koeck is the earliest extant letter by Steiner! In his *Autobiography* he recalls this friend of his youth,[14] who had a somewhat dreamy, introvert and quixotic nature. He cultivated the friendship with Steiner with great loyalty, but after the latter moved to Weimar it gradually ebbed away.

As the rest of the letter shows, Steiner felt he needed to support his friend with good counsel, reminding him of the high ideal of selflessness also in matters of the heart. He advises Koeck to stop reading Heine even though this has a clarifying effect on himself, and instead recommends Rueckert or Uhland, also pointing him in the direction of Goethe's *Faust*. His patron and friend Schroer had just reissued the latter work around this time. Steiner also tells Koeck of his deep esteem for Schroer; and towards the end of the letter (whose conclusion has not survived) he tries again to cure him of his predilection for Heine, saying vehemently: 'You have also studied Plato after all! And no doubt also his *Republic*! Do study him again; you may form other views if you do.'

It seems remarkable, given the karmic connection between Schroer and Plato as Steiner described it near the end of his life, that these two figures are both named in his very first surviving letter! And it is still more remarkable that the night when Steiner's I was born fell on Schroer's birthday. Karl Julius Schroer was born in Pressburg on 11 January 1825.

Thus Steiner's revered teacher, whom he describes so warmly in the letter, stands as a silent witness behind this deeply incisive moment of the birth of Steiner's I.

We will later encounter the figure of Schroer again, as 'mid-wife' of Steiner's development, at the moment when the latter takes up his 'core mission'.

*

The specific character of Steiner's I experience is embodied in a meditation that he offered his audience in London in September 1923. These words, he says, 'can be inscribed, as a kind of meditation for possession of the I, in the soul of every person today'. It runs:

> I look into the dark:
> In it light arises,
> Living light.
> Who is this light in the darkness?
> I am it myself in my reality.
> This reality of the I
> Does not enter my earthly existence.
> I am but an image of it.
> Yet I will find it when,
> With good will for the spirit,
> I enter through death's door again.

(2 September, GA 228)

What had dawned on Steiner at the threshold of his 21st year is the eternal entelechy which does not incarnate and therefore is not reincarnated either. This is the unborn, immortal aspect which we all bear within us although it usually is in deepest slumber. Only the *image* of the I referred to in the words of the meditation incarnates and reincarnates. Not until seven years later was Steiner to begin studying the developmental journey of this image through time, at the birth moment of his real karma research. But the birth of his I, as described here, was the moment when this later research was first anchored in the eternal realm.

From the birth of the I to *Occult Science*

I would like to refer to another context here too. In his lectures on the Gospel of St Mark, Steiner showed the importance in human biography not only of the seven-year rhythm but also of certain multiples of seven. He speaks of a small-scale rhythm of 28 days in relation to minor impulses, and of 28 years in relation to much greater ones, saying that this rhythm can be observed, for instance, in the work of great artists: 'In Goethe, for example, we see something surfacing in his soul but only maturing after four times seven years, appearing then in a form different from the one in which we first observed it.'[15]

Steiner too can be regarded as a great artist: a master of the art of thinking, in fact, from the very outset. All other artistic work in which he engaged emerged from his thinking artistry; and the law he refers to above can also be seen to relate to him. Twenty-eight years after the transformative moment when his I was born, he gives the world the book *Occult Science*, which describes the evolution of the world and the human being from a spiritual-scientific perspective.

In relation to his encounter with the unknown master, Steiner spoke of how the instruction he received from him, with its starting point in Fichte, and the spiritual awakening this initiated, laid the seeds for what would later become *Occult Science*. Exactly 28 years later, when Steiner visited Edouard Schuré in Barr in September 1907 (see chapter 4), he gave a first, unique account to Schuré of his awakening by the unknown teacher.

His spiritual awakening by the master was followed during the night of 10–11 January 1881 by the moment of *self-awakening* through his own I, an I experience which, after four times seven years, became manifest as a *spiritual experience of the universe*.

In the *Occult Science* of 1909 therefore, we can discover the profound fruit of the birth of Steiner's I in 1881. This arc of development in him corresponds to many intermediate phases passing from the Spirits of Form, who embedded the spark of the I in human sheaths, to the *complete cosmos* of the hierarchies from which not only the human I but also the whole of Creation emerged.

7. The Origins of Karma Research

In my book *Rudolf Steiner's Core Mission* I examined from various angles the central moment of 9 November 1888 when Rudolf Steiner first became vividly aware of his previous incarnation. After the lecture Steiner gave on 9 November 1888 at Vienna's Goethe Association, Father Neumann uttered the name 'Thomas Aquinas' and at this moment Steiner perceived his last incarnation. He later confirmed this in a personal conversation with Friedrich Rittelmeyer.

Seven years after the birth of his super-temporal I, in a way that relates to the meditation quoted in the previous chapter, Steiner made a sudden breakthrough in perceiving pictures of the I as it passes through incarnation and reincarnation: he became aware of the previous I image of his own eternal individuality. Only the *image* passes on from one embodiment to the next, always only as a more or less perfect reflection of the eternal individuality.

This moment when Steiner, in a flash, became aware of his past as Aquinas, is a complex one. It was triggered not by *just anyone* but by someone very particular, a man with whom Steiner had been on close and intimate terms for years, who was highly knowledgeable about Aquinas's philosophy and outlook. There lived in Neumann an unconscious memory of his former life with Steiner as Aquinas, and what he said at this moment came from a kind of inspiration. This event showed Steiner that knowledge of reincarnation slumbers in the depths of modern souls, but only emerges with difficulty into clear awareness. Neumann himself was an instance of such difficulty since his ecclesiastically trained mind was not in full accord with the inspired depths of his soul. On 9 November 1888, Steiner must have had a vivid experience — though he never expressed this in so many words — that reincarnation knowledge seeks entry into humanity, and lives in the depths of human souls, and yet human heads have the kinds of thought that offer this knowledge no purchase and even dismiss it.

And so the very person who first kindles awareness in Steiner of his last incarnation shows him at the same time the dilemma of the modern soul: it lives in a split between what exists in its depths and what it bears in a thinking schooled in materialism. How can this split be healed?

Once again, as in his experience as a boy in Pottschach, this becomes an impulse in him to alleviate or remedy an inner plight.

Just as Karl Julius Schroer was in a sense unconsciously present at the moment when Steiner's I was born — which coincided with Schroer's birthday — he was also implicated in the event of 9 November 1888, since it was he who had urged Steiner to give the lecture in the first place.

The meeting with Fercher von Steinwand

There was an important prelude and sequel to this incisive moment of 9 November 1888. The prelude was Steiner's encounter with Fercher von Steinwand. For the first time, through this meeting initiated by his friend Fritz Lemmermayer, his impressions of the past incarnations of a human being assumed tangible shape. This was in the summer of 1888, and thus at a time when Steiner, as he records in his *Autobiography*, 'came to certain perceptions of human reincarnation. I had been close to them before, but they had not as yet come into clearer, sharper focus.' This changed when he met Fercher:

> In this countenance and its expressions, in every gesture of Fercher's, I witnessed a soul being that could only have developed around the time Christianity began, when Greek culture of a pagan kind still played into its development.

The anthroposophical biographer of Fercher, Friedrich Zauner, points to the only historical individual he thinks could possibly fit the bill here: Dionysus the Areopagite, a well-known pupil of the apostle Paul. Texts in which the Pauline doctrine of the hierarchies survived through the Middle Ages can be traced back to impulses living in this individual, although they were only written down several centuries after him. Study of Dionysus, alongside Aristotle, was a central, deeply devoted preoccupation of Albertus Magnus and his pupil Thomas Aquinas. In the *Autobiography* Steiner writes: 'I regarded the fact that I made Fercher von Steinwand's acquaintance as one of the most important experiences of my youth.' Of the very numerous important figures whom Steiner met, and who are described in the *Autobiography*, Fercher von Steinwand is the only one upon whom Steiner brings karmic insights to bear. This alone demonstrates the importance of this man in the development of Rudolf Steiner's karmic research.

The birth of systematic karmic research

The sequel to the Aquinas experience occurred at the beginning of the following year, 1889. On 30 January 1888, news of the death by suicide of the Austrian Crown Prince Rudolf had shaken the whole kingdom. His action seemed to come out of the blue or at least was incomprehensible by ordinary standards. Shortly after the tragedy, Steiner went to visit his teacher Schroer in Vienna at 5 Salesianergasse, where he lived. Steiner had not intended to speak to him about the suicide, but Schroer immediately 'uttered the word "Nero", as if this surfaced from obscure depths of spirit'.

In his karma lecture on 27 April 1923 (GA 236) Rudolf Steiner states that he fell 'by chance' into karmic research as a result of this sudden utterance. 'It was really seemingly by chance that the fate of Nero dawned upon me,' he says in relation to this visit to Schroer, but then states more precisely: 'And yet it was only *seemingly* by chance that this Nero destiny suddenly appeared to me so vividly.'

Schroer's soul stood in the background of the birth of Steiner's I; the physical birth of the former coincided with the spiritual birth of the latter. And it was Schroer who had urged Steiner to give the lecture on 9 November which elicited the profoundly important utterance, 'Thomas Aquinas', from Neumann. Now, yet again, he uttered a name that was to initiate Rudolf Steiner's first systematic karma research. Steiner asked himself, as he had done when Neumann referred to Aquinas, why Schroer had uttered this specific name. And Steiner had a thorough knowledge of *Schroer's* soul too: he knew of the latter's profound spirituality, which was of a kind that might well convey special significance through *seemingly* unimportant comments, and also of his reluctance to embody this spirituality fully in an intellectual form. This led him to study more closely a rationally incomprehensible name spoken by his mentor and friend. And what was the result of this study? 'That something had been uttered from the Akashic Records through the medium, only, of a human voice.' At this key moment Schroer acted as the bringer of a higher task to Rudolf Steiner. If karma research was to be born and develop, the name 'Nero' had to be taken up by Steiner at this moment; and thus it was anything other than 'chance' that the name was uttered when karma research was born.

That this birth was not easy or straightforward is also intrinsic to the nature of such research. It has to penetrate through all illusions, even reaching beyond the most accurate and correct inspirations to purely intuitive insight into the occult connection between different incarnations of a human individual.

It was not enough to ascertain that Schroer had voiced a 'correct' inspiration about the connection between the individualities of Nero and Crown Prince Rudolf. This was only the starting point for a form of research that has to discover the eternal and never incarnated individuality overarching and joining the threads of these different 'images'. This can only be done with the aid of the *fourth* mode of cognition, Intuition, in its strict and rigorously methodological sense. As far as potential illusions are concerned, Steiner had plenty of opportunity to meet them precisely in this very first process of systematic enquiry. He encountered a whole number of reincarnated 'Neros' as he delved into the matter so that it 'naturally proved necessary to counter and combat the subjective power issuing from these reincarnated 'Neros' before he could make any headway.

In describing the destiny of Nero in April 1924, Steiner stressed that this destiny must inevitably appear senseless without knowledge of matters relating to karma and reincarnation. Very few lives indeed, he said, were better suited than those of Nero or of Crown Prince Rudolf — whose life in a sense reflected Nero's destiny — for showing that such apparent senselessness could be overcome through karmic enquiries. And in this same lecture he emphasized the need, in our time, to 'school the capacity for karmic vision', and the fact that the forms of the First Goetheanum aimed to support and awaken this capacity.

Something of the power of these forms to waken such vision was perceived in the sphere of certain dead souls. In an after-death communication from Helmuth von Moltke, transcribed by Rudolf Steiner, we read the following for the date 8 February 1918 (a year and a half after Moltke's death in June 1916): 'In the "forms" in Dornach which I now feel, I perceive lines that prepare something by means of which in future one soul will be able to understand another more inwardly.'

This is all the more astonishing a statement if we know that Moltke had never set foot in the Goetheanum while he was alive, and knew it at most from photographs.

As I have described at length in my book *Rudolf Steiner's Core Mission*, the mission referred to concerned research into matters of karma and reincarnation. Unknowingly, Schroer gave the impetus for the 28-year-old Steiner to take up this mission when the latter visited him after the suicide of the Crown Prince. Distinct from this impetus was the fact that Schroer also instigated Steiner's efforts to establish the epistemological foundations of such research. These foundations should have been created by Schroer himself, yet he was unable to do so because of the strange 'spiritual blockage' that arose in him due to his intellectual cast of mind. Only after making this 'detour' to accomplish another's task did Steiner take up the full scope of his own intrinsic mission in the last year of his life and work. In the lecture on Nero he discloses to his audience the 'chance' impulse that began his systematic karma research. But since, as we have seen, this impulse was so closely connected with Schroer's being and personality, it was only natural that Steiner concluded or, as he put it himself, 'rounded off' the karma lectures with communications, until then entirely unknown, about the background of Schroer's own destiny. On 23 September 1924 (GA 238) he revealed — thus coming full circle to the starting point of his 'core mission' — that Schroer had been incarnated as Plato in ancient Greece, and as Roswitha of Gandersheim in the medieval period.

Although Karl Julius Schroer failed to develop anthroposophy itself, it is to him that we owe the first impulse to elaborate spiritual-scientific karma research.

In even clearer terms than elicited in Steiner by the karma inspiration living in Wilhelm Neumann, a few months later the following became inwardly apparent to him in relation to Nero's destiny:

> Without schooling the capacity for karma vision, humanity will end in a kind of spiritual suicide. All human life will appear pointless; and we can only counter this meaninglessness by developing a science of reincarnation and karma.

At a moment of incisive destiny with Schroer, the true sphere of the Time Spirit resounded in Rudolf Steiner's soul. He hearkened to this call and followed where it led.

8. Friedrich Nietzsche and the New Capacity for Inspiration

The prelude to the next milestone begins in the same year, 1889, that Crown Prince Rudolf killed himself. Turning our gaze to northern Italy, we see Friedrich Nietzsche embracing a flogged horse with great compassion in the middle of the street.[16]

Here he wrote letters and postcards which he signed 'Dionysus' or 'The Crucified One'. On Christmas day 1888 he even signed one letter 'The antichrist'. This mental breakdown followed, with inevitability, from a long phase of psychological turmoil.

The same year, at the start of his time in Weimar, Rudolf Steiner first began to read Nietzsche's works.

At the beginning of the nineties the decisive meeting occurred between the two in Naumburg, where Nietzsche was being cared for by his mother while his sister, Elisabeth Foerster-Nietzsche established a Nietzsche archive there. She asked Rudolf Steiner to help her with this task. As he records in the *Autobiography*, Elisabeth led him into Nietzsche's room on his very first visit to Naumburg. This would have been no later than May 1894 and may have been a little earlier. It was the first and only time that Steiner saw Nietzsche. The encounter inspired his book *Friedrich Nietzsche, Fighter for Freedom*,[17] first published in the spring of 1895.

This encounter, too, belongs to the key moments of Steiner's life. Two written records of it exist, one in the form of a diary entry[18] composed immediately after his visit, and the other, based on the latter, in the *Autobiography*.

Steiner also discusses it in the karma lecture on Nietzsche of 15 March 1924 (GA 235). At the time they met, Steiner's *Philosophy of Freedom* had already been published (December 1893).

In a letter to his first wife, Anna Eunike, which he wrote during a stay of several days (January 1896) at the Nietzsche archive in Naumburg, Steiner described Nietzsche's works as 'those of the greatest mind of our time' (*Letters II*, 278). In the *Autobiography* he writes:

> I found the free-floating release from gravity in his ideas compelling. This hovering element, it seemed to me, had shown him thoughts that had likewise formed in me although by means that were quite different.

Steiner saw in Nietzsche a 'free spirit', and this is what he most loved in him:

> But I was particularly attracted to a trait in Nietzsche's work which struck me as a disinclination to try to make the reader share or accept his views. You could feel quite free in your devoted enjoyment of his insights; you felt that his words themselves would have started to laugh if you were to feel beholden and assent to them, as Haeckel or Spencer expect you to.

Steiner also admired Nietzsche's keen perspicacity, for instance when, in reflections on the will for truth, he calls out: 'Yes, it is assumed we want truth; but why not rather untruth?'[19]

Nietzsche's idea of the 'eternal return of the same' ('eternal recurrence') and his longing for the 'superman' or 'overman' seemed to Steiner to be distorted pictures of the idea of reincarnation and the higher human self.

Is it possible that, in his encounter with Nietzsche, Steiner again took on a vital task that the latter was no longer able to accomplish? If so, what was it?

Meeting face to face

How did Rudolf Steiner experience his direct encounter with Nietzsche? Let us first look at Steiner's own account, published on 6 September 1924 in *Das Goetheanum* magazine:

> There he lay on a chaise longue, the benighted one, with his wonderfully beautiful forehead, that of an artist and thinker equally. It was early afternoon. These eyes, still appearing soulful though their

light was extinguished, absorbed nothing but an image of their surroundings which found no way through to the psyche. There I stood, and Nietzsche knew nothing of it. And yet one might have imagined from his spiritualized countenance that this was the expression of a soul who had been formulating thoughts all morning, and now wished to rest a little. In my own inner tumult it seemed almost as if I might be transported into understanding of and communion with the genius whose gaze was now turned upon me but did not meet mine. The passivity of this long, long gaze elicited the understanding of my own gaze which could give free rein to its powers of soul without them being reciprocated.

In a subsequent visit to Naumburg following this remarkable afternoon, Steiner was able to peruse still unpublished texts by Nietzsche. Besides this, Elizabeth Foerster-Nietzsche read to him and other visitors, including the writer Gabriele Reuter, passages from the manuscript of *Antichrist*, written in 1888. On 23 December 1894 Steiner writes to his friend Pauline Specht in Vienna: 'This is one of the most important books to have been written for centuries!' (*Letters II*, 238). And in a letter of 20 August 1895 to the author Rosa Mayreder, also a friend, he refers to Nietzsche's autobiography *Ecce Homo*, likewise written in 1888, as 'Nietzsche's greatest unpublished work' (*Letters II*, 256).

The mind of Nietzsche

There are three distinctive and characteristic aspects of Nietzsche's mind: the deep connection in him between his artistic sense and his power of thinking, his vivid inner connection to those who have died and, associated with this, his inclination towards inspired experiences and insights. In the lecture 'Friedrich Nietzsche in the Light of Spiritual Science', in June 1908, Steiner describes the impression made on him when he saw Nietzsche.[20]

He then gives a specific example of how Nietzsche's soul, in a manner very different from ordinary academia, always sought to penetrate to the spiritual core of another human being:

We can see this best in an example. Let us consider Thales of Miletus. An ordinary academic will study his teachings, but will regard them as being really of only historical significance. In the figure of Thales he studies the nature of those times. But for Nietzsche this philosopher's thoughts are only a means to reach the soul of Thales himself: Thales incarnate stands before him in tangible form. He becomes his friend, can interact with him in a completely personal relationship of friendship. For Nietzsche every figure becomes real, forms a real connection with him.

Inspiration from Schopenhauer

But this immediacy of relationship was not one that Nietzsche formed only with figures from ancient times; it was the same with contemporaries who had passed away. The best instance of this is his connection with Arthur Schopenhauer who had died in September 1860. We need only read the description that Nietzsche himself gives of his encounter with the work and mind of this recently deceased philosopher. In October 1865 Nietzsche moved into a flat in a house belonging to an antiquarian bookseller, on the very day of his 21st birthday — when the 'I' is born. He had just lived through a painful period in Bonn, where he had studied theology and classical philology for two years, taking sudden flight from there like a refugee. He was suffering from inner turbulence and volatility and was, in his own words, 'hanging helpless in the air, without principles, hopes or any sustaining memories'. In this outer and inner turmoil he discovers Schopenhauer's chief work, *The World as Will and Idea*. He writes:

> Now one should consider what effect reading Schopenhauer's major work must exert on oneself in a state such as this. One day I found in Old Rohn's bookshop a copy of this book, picked it up as something of little interest and leafed through it. *I do not know what demon whispered in my ear: 'Take this book home with you.'* I did so, anyway, against my usual custom of taking my time to reflect carefully before purchasing books.[21]

We should take such sentences by Nietzsche far more literally than modern Nietzsche scholars ever dream of doing, since they describe the birth moment of a very tangible spiritual influence in Nietzsche's soul. The following sentences show still more clearly the mood of inspirational receptivity to Schopenhauer's work that Nietzsche conceived:

> Back at home I threw myself upon the sofa with the treasure I had just procured and began to let that energetic, gloomy genius work upon me. Every line of it cried out with renunciation, negation and resignation; it was a mirror in which I caught sight of the terrible grandeur of the world, life and my own sensibility. In it the full, disinterested solar eye of art looked upon me, and here I saw reflected sickness and healing, banishment and refuge, hell and heaven. My need for self-knowledge or indeed for relentless self-analysis took powerful hold of me. Restless, melancholy diary entries bear witness to this period of radical change in my life, with its useless self-accusations and desperate *lifting of my gaze to the sanctification and transformation of the whole human core.*

It could scarcely be put more clearly: at the time when Nietzsche's I was born, in a quest for the 'sanctification and transformation of the whole human core', the empty vessel of his soul, now open to Inspiration, begins unreservedly and most intensely to fill with the spiritual content of an individuality (Schopenhauer) already dwelling in the supersensible realm. This initiating act of inspiration lasted for two weeks, during which he read Schopenhauer into the early hours of the morning.

Rudolf Steiner later studied the 'other side of this coin': in other words, what it meant for the soul of Schopenhauer to find a soul so devoted and open to him. In November 1917 Steiner presents the findings of this research:

> What does Schopenhauer want? What he wants [...] is not so much to see his writings themselves living on but his thoughts working on [...] In Nietzsche's soul he develops the impulse to perpetuate his ideas [...] We can say that Schopenhauer's fundamental nature consisted of a transcendent egotism. As a soul he stands in the world of spirit, and inspires Nietzsche in order that his ideas may be perpetuated. This is a transcendent egotism that continues in life after death. You see, egotism does not always have to be wrong or bad.[22]

In the sphere of Ahriman

The real inspiration instigated in Nietzsche by Schopenhauer's soul occurred at a time of conflict in the world of spirit between the spirits of darkness and Michael and his hosts, ending only in November 1879 with the fall of the spirits of darkness. In as much as Nietzsche himself was receiving inspiration *from the realm of this spiritual battle*, he also came into contact with these spirits of darkness. 'He is exposed to the danger,' says Steiner in 1917, 'that the spirits of darkness will lead him down very grave paths.' That he was not too strongly affected by them is something he owes to his meeting and growing friendship with Richard Wagner. After 1879, the fallen ahrimanic spirits of darkness no longer worked in the world of spirit but in human hearts and human minds, where they inspired anti-Michaelic intellectuality. This intellectual spirituality, with which Nietzsche's inspired soul had previously made acquaintance, now found entry into his *earthly thinking*, exerting an influence upon his soul that became ever stronger after the death of Richard Wagner on 13 February 1883.

Nietzsche's last books, *The Antichrist* and *Ecce Homo,* can only be understood in terms of this ahrimanic inspiration. Steiner later states that these brilliant and remarkable works were in fact not written by Nietzsche at all but only *through* him by Ahriman.[23]

Thus in these works Ahriman appears as an author for the first time in the world's history: they were the first of a whole host of literary products that draw on the same source of inspiration. Given this, it is only natural that Steiner also studied the question of Nietzsche's past karma, and communicated the results of this research in a lecture on 15 March 1924 (GA 235).

The after-death influence of Richard Wagner

From the world of spirit, Richard Wagner's great individuality perceived the growing danger for Nietzsche that he might succumb entirely to the spirits of darkness now working upon earth. And hence he began to exert an after-death influence upon his former friend, who had eventually become his opponent, of a kind quite different from that which had come from Schopenhauer: Steiner writes:

> When Wagner rises into the world of spirit, the spirits of darkness are already below on earth. In a sense he rises into a quite different atmosphere. One has to express things that seem paradoxical and yet are true: from the world of spirit he governs Nietzsche without egotism.

Wagner, after death, did not try to see his own work perpetuated on earth through Nietzsche, as Schopenhauer had done. Instead of 'perpetuating his ideas' he does something quite different:

> He lets Nietzsche play in a channel that is fully appropriate for him through the benevolent deed of shrouding his mind in darkness at the right moment; he prevents him *consciously* entering dangerous regions.

The mental breakdown of Nietzsche as benevolent deed? Steiner realized of course that this is not the easiest thing to understand! He continues:

> Naturally this seems very paradoxical, but it arises from the unegotistic way in which Richard Wagner's soul works upon Nietzsche from purer regions of spirit than Schopenhauer's soul initially worked. Schopenhauer was still in the throes of the battle of the spirits of darkness against the spirits of light in the world of spirit. What Wagner seeks to do for Nietzsche is, as far as possible, to protect him in his karma from the influence of the spirits of darkness now descending to earth.[24]

What exactly was the nature of this great 'benevolent deed'? In his benighted state. Nietzsche was protected, after *Antichrist* and *Ecce Homo,* from 'writing' further works, whose actual author would have been Ahriman. That might perhaps have continued for many years, but would have trapped Nietzsche in a net of the most intense ahrimanic influences. His karma would have been entirely ahrimanized; and to some extent this was prevented by the benevolent deed of Wagner from the world of spirit.

Steiner furthers Wagner's good deed

But only to some extent. While Nietzsche's *consciousness* was protected from ahrimanic spirituality by being shrouded in darkness, the effects of his increasingly ahrimanic inspirations continued after his death in the world of spirit. In a hitherto unpublished esoteric lesson which Steiner gave on Whit Monday 1914, he says that a certain figure of the nineteenth century was not able to grasp the spiritual realm during his lifetime. He continues: 'This person was now in danger of losing his intellect to Ahriman in the world of spirit after death. And for years I wrestled with Ahriman to give this person's intellect back to him.' Steiner does not give the name of this person, or at least there is none to be found in the relatively brief transcript. But it seems most likely that he is speaking here of the 'greatest mind of his time' whose destiny he had witnessed in such vivid fashion. This communication offers us a glimpse of a silent, very significant spiritual battle of which the world remained in complete ignorance, but which Steiner fought not with Nietzsche but with Ahriman, who had begun to employ this intellect and wished to appropriate it entirely after his death.

In the same esoteric lesson Steiner reveals something else, again without mentioning a name:

> Let us assume that this individual wrote a book on the physical plane, and that it now becomes necessary for someone lovingly and faithfully to think through and reflect on what he put into this book, so as to help prevent Ahriman appropriating his intellect after his death.

If we apply this to Nietzsche and assume that Steiner is referring here either to *The Antichrist*, or *Ecce Homo* which was published shortly after, then it is clear that Steiner himself was the person who undertook this loving, faithful work. He did, after all, read with great dedication and love everything Nietzsche wrote, in particular his last, terribly brilliant writings. And he did so with great 'faithfulness' to the eternal individuality whose great gifts he recognized and whose tragedy he witnessed when these great abilities succumbed to the misuse of dark spiritual beings. And is there any record of this loving deed of human understanding? Indeed there is: in Steiner's book on Nietzsche! There he hints obliquely at this, as follows: 'It is strangely moving when people on the physical plane repeatedly ask why one has written a certain book. This may have been done in order to help someone by lovingly rethinking or thinking through his ideas.'

Thus, in the same esoteric lesson of 1 June 1914—twice seven years after Nietzsche's death—we learn why Steiner wrote his book on Nietzsche.

Basel was a key place in Nietzsche's life and work. It was from here that he set out in 1869 on his first of many trips to Tribschen near Lucerne, where he met Wagner. It was surely not by chance, therefore, that Steiner's profound love of Nietzsche—for his work was far more than just academic research—was something he revealed in Basel, nor just chance that he shed such illumination on the spiritual destiny of the greatest mind of his age on a Whit Monday.

Nietzsche's concept of inspiration

Nietzsche sought inspiration in his work, achieving this in the profoundest way as we have seen (through Schopenhauer among others) and ultimately, fatally, through Ahriman. Let us here examine what Nietzsche himself understood by the word inspiration. Nietzsche offers his best account of it in a chapter of his autobiography *Ecce Homo*, written shortly before he was plunged into mental darkness. (As already mentioned, Steiner knew this book before it was published since Nietzsche's sister had allowed him to peruse it during a visit.)

He says here in relation to his book *Zarathustra*:

At the end of the nineteenth century does anyone have any clear idea of what poets of more vital eras called *inspiration*? In case not, let me describe it. If people had even the least inner residue of superstition they would scarcely be able to dispel the idea of becoming a mere incarnation, mere mouthpiece, mere medium of mighty powers. The term revelation simply describes a reality in the sense of Something suddenly becoming visible and audible, perceived with unspeakable certainty and subtlety: something that shakes, shocks and convulses you to the roots. You do not listen or search but receive without asking who it is who gives. Like lightning a thought flashes out with utter necessity, unhesitatingly, unquestioningly. There is no choice in the matter. It is a rapture whose huge charge can trigger a stream of tears, which involuntarily quickens your step to great rapidity and then slows it again; it is being utterly outside yourself with the most vivid awareness, accompanied by numberless fine shivers and tingles right down to the toes; a profound joy with which the greatest pain and gloom are not at odds but instead are felt to be the necessary accompaniment, a vital colour within such overflowing life; it is an intimation of rhythmic relationships encompassing far-flung realms of forms — and this wide scope, the need for an expansive, encompassing rhythm, is almost the measure of the power of inspiration, a way to compensate for its pressure and charge ... All this occurs involuntarily, with the greatest degree of inevitability, but it feels like a storm of freedom, of release from determination, like power and divinity [...]

This is *my* experience of inspiration; and I have no doubt that one would have to look back through millennia to find someone who could say: 'Yes, and it is also mine.'

Nietzsche does indeed give us here an exact account of an *ancient* form of inspiration — one that was quite normal at a time when a sense of freedom was as yet only germinally present and not yet fully developed. One finds an echo of this in Homer, and also Plato. The latter gives a wonderful description of this ancient form of inspiration in his work *Ion*. It is a condition of being lifted away from the sphere of reason, of possession by the power of the Muse and suchlike.

But precisely because there is no place for freedom in this form of inspiration, it becomes an alien abnormality if transposed into our era. It overpowers a person's soul and spirit and negates his sense of freedom. What does this awareness of freedom consist in? The ability to question. Nietzsche says 'you receive without asking who it is who gives'; and this shows us that this form of inspiration is an outmoded and limited one.

Nowadays we have to ask 'who is giving' if we are to avoid falling into the worst spiritual dependency, which regards inspiration as the supreme authority to which we must submit.

As early as the age of eight, Steiner was *asking* about the source of his perceptions, and only thus was he able to discover their true value.

Nietzsche as an 'open secret' in humanity's evolution

Around Michaelmas 1920, the first anthroposophical schooling course was launched with an initial celebratory event in the as yet unfinished Goetheanum. The course was entitled 'The Boundaries of Natural Science' (GA 322), and what Steiner says about Nietzsche there is of special importance for our theme, and draws again on his impressions of the benighted Nietzsche in the early nineties of the nineteenth century. In the lecture of 1 October 1920, Steiner says:

The phenomenon of Nietzsche stood shockingly before me when, a few years after Nietzsche fell ill, I entered his small room in Naumburg and saw him on the chaise longue where he lay prone after eating. He recognized no one in his surroundings, and gazed at you like an idiot and yet still with a light in his eye irradiated with his former brilliance. As one stood before this ruined Nietzsche, this wreck of physical life, reflecting at the same time on everything one can experience in his world-view, his inner world of pictures, seeing this image of him in one's soul rather than regarding him clinically, as a 'psychiatric case', then it became vividly apparent that this human being had sought to see into the world to which Inspiration grants access [...] The whole tragedy of our modern culture, its quest for the world of spirit, its devotion to what can flow from Inspiration, was something that could be learned from such a sight. For me — and I will not hold back here from speaking personally — this moment could be numbered among those called 'Goethean'. Goethe says that nature has no intrinsic secret that she does not somewhere reveal; the *whole* of nature contains no secret that is not made apparent and palpable in some way. Our current stage of human evolution bears in it the secret that a striving is unfolding from humanity, a tendency and impulse that rumbles in the social convulsions of civilization.

This impulse and striving is to try to see into the spiritual world of Inspiration. And *the human being Nietzsche was one locus where nature reveals its open secret, disclosing to us the striving that is at work in all humanity today*; showing too what we must aspire to if all people today embracing education and modern science—as all civilized humanity will gradually do, since such knowledge must become widespread—are not to lose their I and plunge civilization into barbarism.[25]

Nowhere more clearly than in these words do we find evidence of the world-historical importance of Rudolf Steiner's encounter with Friedrich Nietzsche, his work and his destiny.

Lack of Intuition knowledge

Concluding his discourse on Nietzsche in the Whit Monday esoteric lesson of 1914, Steiner said the following: 'Humanity will be in danger of losing its intellect to Ahriman if it does not make proper use of thinking.' To use this intellect 'properly' means not only developing the right concepts of the natural world and its creatures but equally also of the world of spirit and the beings who populate it. Spiritual science came into the world in order to develop this proper employment of thinking. It did not yet exist in Nietzsche's time; and yet a first germ of it was already present in the form of Steiner's *Philosophy of Freedom*. It was a matter of profound regret for Steiner that Nietzsche was unable to read it. 'I count Nietzsche's illness,' he wrote to Pauline Specht on 23 December 1894,

> among the worst evils that modern science and philosophy have had to suffer [...]. For myself, Nietzsche's illness is particularly painful. You see, it is my firm conviction that he would not have remained insensible to my *Philosophy of Freedom*. He would have seen that I had carried further a wealth of questions which he left unresolved, and would doubtless have acknowledged that his views of morality, his philosophy of immorality, find their culmination in my freedom philosophy, and that, rightly sublimated and traced to their source, his 'moral instincts' arrive at what I characterize as 'moral imagination'. This aspect of 'moral imagina-

tion' in my 'freedom philosophy' is the very thing lacking in Nietzsche's *Genealogy of Morality*, although everything in it points in that direction. And his *Antichrist* is merely a particular enactment of this view of mine.[26]

If Nietzsche had read Steiner's fundamental work, he would not only have found there an ethics entirely in accord with his own individualism and nature as an artist but could also have embarked on the first steps in developing an *intuitive* mode of thinking. It was the power of Intuition that was lacking in Nietzsche's Inspiration-oriented disposition. Intuition unfolds in pure, sense-free thinking and is the only faculty capable of giving the right orientation to the Inspiration increasingly entering humanity. Its lack led to the volatility and ultimately the fatal misuse of capacities of Inspiration which Ahriman was thus able to appropriate.

In a sense *The Philosophy of Freedom* leads us directly to the schooling of Intuition: to knowledge of beings with whom we must be familiar if we wish to be clear, in very specific terms, what our source of Inspiration is. If we recall Steiner's Pottschach experience, described in chapter 2, we can see that there might well have been dire consequences if the boy had not gone *beyond* Imagination and Inspiration. Intuition was necessary for him to understand what being had appeared to him in the waiting room, and he could then 'deal' with the experience. It is precisely because humanity is at present progressing towards new capacities of Inspiration that it needs a systematic schooling of Intuition if the former is not to lead us astray or even plunge us into madness, as was Nietzsche's fate.

Thus, through the world-historical 'evolutionary moment' of Nietzsche, Steiner realized that humanity is striving for Inspiration once more. He also recognized no less clearly that humanity will thrive if this develops alongside a spiritual knowledge founded on Intuition and appealing to pure thinking, but if not, that Ahriman will usurp our capacity for Inspiration along with our unspiritualized intellect.

Ahrimanic inspiration — from Nietzsche to the present day

There is no doubt that the new capacity of Inspiration we can discern in the 'evolutionary moment' of Nietzsche has become ever more pronounced since his day, but that the spiritualization of the intellect has not kept pace with it. This has led to a growing number of experiences of Inspiration in people who fail to question who has 'given' them, their source — which, to an unprejudiced observer schooled in spiritual science clearly displays an ahrimanic (and sometimes also luciferic) character.

The whole history of the twentieth century is an arsenal of evidence for a capacity of Inspiration sliding into the ahrimanic realm. Elsewhere I have written, for instance, of Theodor Herzl's Whitsun experience in Paris, which led to his political programme for a Jewish state.[27]

Or one can reflect on the far more dire effects of the young Adolf Hitler's inspiration experience in November 1906, as described by his friend August Kubizek. This occurred after listening to Wagner's opera *Rienzi* in Linz. On the waves of Wagner's music, Hitler's soul was lifted from his body and possessed by some unknown power. During a night-time walk the young Hitler revealed his dreams for Germany to his friend, seeing himself as a liberator of the Fatherland, a new Rienzi. This was the moment when his demented mission for the German people was born. Kubizek observed that

> *It seemed a different I was speaking out of him,* one that he himself was as much transported by as I was. It was an ecstatic state of complete rapture in which he transposed his experience of *Rienzi* [...] into a grandiose vision relating to another plane [...] He now spoke of a mission which he would receive from the people to lead it upwards out of its subservience to the heights of freedom.[28]

Neither the young Hitler himself nor his friend asked who was 'giving' the inspiration for this 'mission'. Their intellect remained entirely untouched by ideas of spiritual reality ...

One can think here also of the individuals in key positions at the outbreak of the First World War. Rudolf Steiner stated on several occasions that they were in a 'dulled' state of awareness — that is, their thinking was not awake or alert — in the hours when critical decisions were made, even though conscious in their sensory perceptions. This condition is one that offers a gateway for ahrimanic demons to gain entry.[29]

We can think too of numerous books written in the twentieth century whose real authorship has to be questioned. They range from *Mein Kampf* through to Samuel Huntington's political polemic *The Clash of Civilizations*. The same question arises in relation to the *Memorandum* published by the Anthroposophical Society in 1935, which stirred up fanatical responses and led to the tragic exclusions of many members. The later work of Valentin Tomberg might also be examined from this perspective, not to mention very recent publications of 'anthroposophical' secondary literature.

Then there is LSD, which in recent years has become popular again for 'research' purposes. The Basel chemist Albert Hofmann, and many thousands if not millions of others, believed they had found in it a miraculous means to spiritualize consciousness. But where are we led by a 'spiritualization' that leaves our intellect entirely untransformed instead of furnishing it with spiritual *concepts*? Or rather, where does the impulse for *this kind* of spiritualization originate? When Hofmann studied the consciousness-altering effects of the substance at first hand in April 1943, he wrote in his research report: 'A demon entered me, and took possession of my body, my senses and my soul. I leaped up to free myself from it, but then collapsed powerless again on the sofa.'[30] If Hofmann had been aware of spiritual concepts, he might have traced the real sources of this experience. For him, 'demon' remained only a metaphorical expression for the huge intensity of the 'trip'.

Then we can consider the mass phenomenon of young people unconsciously driven by an urge towards inspired heights, who numb themselves with earphones day and night rather than learning to take this urge into productive activity.

Yet where will they find teachers who might guide them to do so?

Common to all these phenomena is the fact that sources of inspiration are here at work that remain hidden and disregarded, thus opening the door to spiritual beings of an anti-Michaelic character. These are the spirits of darkness referred to earlier, who seek to insinuate themselves into human heads and hearts after their fall from the spiritual sphere in 1879.

An archetype of this type of modern inspiration can be found in scene 12 of Rudolf Steiner's fourth Mystery Play, *The Soul's Awakening*. Here we see how a human soul—in the play the character Ferdinand Reinecke—is unconsciously inspired without him having the least inkling that this is happening or where it comes from. And Ahriman himself discloses very precisely what the best conditions are for his own success in inspiring someone: the relinquishment of earthly understanding. If this earthly thinking were to imbue itself with spiritual concepts, it would indeed be able to acknowledge that such beings as Ahriman exist, and in consequence refrain from succumbing to them unconsciously. This secret of the potential of earthly understanding is one Ahriman knows very well—unlike the numerous people who find it more comfortable to fail to make 'proper use of their thinking' and thus lose their intellect to Ahriman.

One hundred and twenty years after Nietzsche was ahrimanically inspired, the world is full of inspired Reineckes. They write books, work as MPs, rule whole countries, and above all they have leverage in the deceitful money-creation mechanisms of large international banks. Our current social and economic conditions are merely the expression of an epidemic of intellectual narrow-mindedness in millions of people who refuse to take up spiritual concepts.

Gazing upon the 'common populace' in its spiritual sleep, Mephistopheles tells Faust that 'Little folk can never tell / The devil has them in his spell / Even when he has them by the throat.' Steiner often quoted this passage in relation to the need to have knowledge of Ahriman. His eyes were opened in this regard when he encountered Nietzsche's destiny. On one occasion, when showing a visitor to his studio in Dornach the head of Ahriman that he had modelled, he pointed to an armchair and said

> ... that he had kept Ahriman fixed in that chair until he had completed his work. Then *he*, Rudolf Steiner, had ended the sitting but Ahriman had taken his angry vengeance, destroying the great purple window of the West front of the Goetheanum, which suddenly had a great crack in it from top to bottom.[31]

Steiner was also already very familiar as a youth with the other spiritual power, later called Lucifer. He does not refer to this directly in his *Autobiography*, but there is a comment he made from which we can easily infer this. In connection with the Goethe work he took over from Schroer, Steiner makes a profound remark that we ought not to ignore: 'I would have been swept more quickly into the world of spirit, but then I would have found no reason to engage in the struggle of diving down into my own interiority.'

Reflections on the incisive encounter between Steiner and Nietzsche can give us a key to understanding spiritual conflicts waged both then and in our own time, and this is why I have given so much space here to this milestone in Steiner's development.

9. Spiritual Storms and Knowledge of Christ

Kali Yuga, an epoch of spiritual darkness lasting five thousand years, ended on 19 February 1899. This period had served to brighten human sensory awareness, as such fulfilling its necessary and beneficial task in human evolution. The task had now been accomplished. Sensory consciousness and the science born from it had taken a hold on all human life, accompanied by a materialistic outlook. Twenty years after the beginning of the Michael epoch humanity was ripe for a new phase of spiritual consciousness. A host of spirits of darkness opposed this vehemently, seeking to confuse and mislead human consciousness and keep it in the dark. Rudolf Steiner speaks of 'spiritual storms' that also raged in his own soul. In fact, the scientific mode of thinking, founded on exact observation, offers the best support for developing a science of the spirit that the modern world needs. Science, Goetheanism and spiritual science: these three aspects stood clearly before Steiner as a developmental path; but this was and is countered fiercely by the fallen spirits of darkness who seek to keep Goethe as a poet alone and the 'spirit' as something fit only for mystical musings and established religions.

The problem here was not the scientific mode of thinking but the tendency to see it as the only valid form of thinking, to constrain it within narrow bounds rather than seeing it as a developmental point of departure. Underlying this one-sided tendency, Steiner experienced the activity of specific spiritual beings, saying in the *Autobiography*:

> One-sided knowledge is not merely the cause of abstract confusion but this confusion actually means spiritual engagement with living *beings*. I later spoke of *ahrimanic* beings when I sought to refer to this. For these beings it is an absolute truth that the world must be a machine. They live in a world that directly adjoins the sensory realm.[32]

In relation to the destiny of Nietzsche, Steiner had seen deep into this world of living beings, in which, after all, was rooted the later source of inspiration of this 'greatest mind of his time'. Steiner *learned* this in direct perception of Nietzsche himself, which also protected him from this danger:

> My own ideas never succumbed for a moment to this world, even unconsciously. I was very careful to ensure that my knowledge and insight unfolded in *reflecting awareness.* All the more conscious also, therefore, was my inner battle with demonic powers that emerge not from a knowledge of nature drawn from spirit vision but from a mechanistic and materialistic mode of thinking.

There was no doubt for Steiner of the tangible reality of his spiritual experience of these ahrimanic beings:

> Anyone who seeks spiritual knowledge has to *experience* these worlds rather than think about them in a theoretical way only. At this time I had to safeguard my spirit vision in inner storms that raged behind my outward experience.

The first-hand experiences Steiner had of these storms became an image for him of the situation facing all humanity:

> At the time it dawned on me that the turn of the century must bring new spiritual light to humanity. It seemed to me that the sundering of human thinking and will from the spirit had reached a point of culmination, and that human evolution now needed a radical new direction.

At this time of a new influx of spiritual light, Steiner sought direct access to Christianity unmediated by historical documents. Like Nietzsche, he had been unable to find what he sought in traditional religious confessions. This is why he thought so highly of Nietzsche's *Antichrist,* which was such a stumbling block for many others. Steiner hugely admired the keenness with which Nietzsche dismissed the mendacity, hypocrisy and emptiness of a 'Christianity' composed largely of mere phrases. In the *Autobiography* he writes:

After a period of trials had exposed me to severe inner battles, I had to immerse myself deeply in Christianity itself, specifically within the realm where the *spirit* speaks of it. [...] At a period when I made comments about Christianity that were in such stark contrast to the words I was to utter later, its true content had begun to unfold germinally within me as an inner manifestation of knowledge. Around the turn of the century, this germ increasingly unfolded. The inner trials I underwent occurred before the new century dawned.

And now there follows a single sentence which points to Steiner's inner perception of Christ. This key moment in his life, which may have lasted weeks or even months, is of central importance for his whole development. He says:

My inner development was founded upon the fact that I had stood before the Mystery of Golgotha in an inmost festival of insight of the most profound and earnest kind.

Furnished with all his soul capacities of thinking, feeling and will, the I of Rudolf Steiner stood here in the keenest spiritual manner before the central reality of humanity's whole evolution, the Mystery of Golgotha. If we form an inner picture of this sentence, another may come to join it, that of someone who, in a festival of insight of the most profound and earnest kind, had once stood *physically* under the cross, before the Mystery of Golgotha: Lazarus-John, the first of those initiated by Christ, and none other than the unknown person whom Steiner was permitted to meet at the age of 19. The way in which Steiner speaks of 'having stood' before the Mystery of Golgotha can invoke this other picture. It is one of the sentences in his work that are far more resonant with meaning than may be apparent on first reading.

10. 'The Question Was Put to Me'

17 November 1901

Responding to a newspaper announcement, in the autumn of 1900, Marie von Sivers, who was 32 at the time, paid a visit to the leaders of the Theosophical Society (TS) in Berlin, the Count and Countess Brockdorff.

Edouard Schuré, whose work *The Great Initiates* she was translating, had told her of the existence of this society. Thus it was that she attended the first lecture given by Steiner for the TS in the winter of 1900, although she was not a member. In the following year, 1901–02, Steiner's lectures there on the Greek and Egyptian mysteries became of profound and growing interest to her. Edouard Schuré had alerted her to certain shadowy aspects of theosophy, with its Anglo-Indian emphasis. During a social evening organized by a theosophist called Nina Gernet, Marie von Sivers and Rudolf Steiner had a conversation whose importance for Steiner's activity within the TS and later in the Anthroposophical Society (AS) can hardly be overestimated. Gernet, a fanatical adherent of the Theosophical Society, had organized the gathering to be held on the anniversary of the founding of the society by Henry Steel Olcott and Helena Petrovna Blavatsky on 17 November 1875 in New York. The room was decorated with many chrysanthemums, which later led to the whole occasion being called the 'chrysanthemum tea party'. During this gathering it seems that Gernet tried in vain to get Steiner to collaborate more closely with the TS. Of much greater importance however was the brief conversation that took place there between him and Marie von Sivers. Steiner gave an account of this on 11 October 1915 (GA 254) as part of a review of the development of theosophy and anthroposophy:

I would like now to mention a conversation that took place in the autumn of 1901 between myself and Frau Dr Steiner as she now is, during that 'chrysanthemum tea party'. She asked me whether it might not be necessary to create a spiritual movement in Europe. During this conversation I spoke clear words to this effect: 'Certainly it is necessary to launch a spiritual-scientific movement, but I myself would only be part of it if it were founded on western occultism alone, and developed from this foundation.' In this regard I said that one must start from Plato, Goethe and such figures. I indicated the whole programme of development that has now in fact been realized.

According to Johanna Muecke, a Berlin colleague of many years standing, Steiner said during a conversation about the beginnings of theosophical work, in Marie Steiner's presence,

> that Frau Dr Steiner had asked him at the time whether it might not be possible to impart these wisdoms in a way more in keeping with European cultural life, and with consideration of the Christ impulse. Herr Dr Steiner then added words that I will never forget: 'This gave me the opportunity to work there in the manner I had envisaged. I had been asked the question, and in accordance with spiritual laws, I was then able to reply to such a question.'

*

Towards the end of his time in Weimar, Steiner had been wondering whether he must remain silent about his inner spiritual visions, for which there was no openness in the academic and scientific circles of his day. He answered this question initially by taking on editorship of the *Magazin für Litteratur* in 1897. In this journal he tried, as Schuré reported in 1907, to bring 'a spiritual stream to the awareness of a public interested in the arts and literature'.[33]

On the 150th anniversary of Goethe's birth, 28 August 1899, Steiner published in this journal his essay on 'Goethe's Secret Revelation' as expressed in the fairy-tale *The Green Snake and the Beautiful Lily*.

This attempt to spiritualize cultural life in the public domain likewise failed since leading cultural figures, whom Steiner hoped to address, 'soon fell either into inanity or naturalism'.

The next group to whom Steiner sought to introduce his spirit visions, and thus not remain silent, was the workers' educational college in Berlin. Although the workers loved his lessons, he was soon dismissed by its directors, whose leanings were decidedly Marxist.

All these failed attempts can give us a greater sense of the importance of Marie von Sivers's question on 17 November 1901. In the truest sense she gave Rudolf Steiner a voice.

In the sacred service of spirit evolution

In 1902 Steiner was asked to become the general secretary of the German section of the Theosophical Society; he only accepted on the condition that Marie von Sivers would be his colleague in this role. But her assent alone would not have been sufficient either. More than this was needed. On 9 January 1905 he wrote to her as follows about various problems of substance and personality within the TS:

> If the master had not been able to persuade me that, despite everything, theosophy is necessary in our time, I would have gone on writing only philosophical works after 1901, and expressed myself in literary and philosophical terms. (GA 262)

In other words, Steiner's activities in the TS were founded on esoteric counsel, a 'voluntary task' which furthered the initial task which he had received as 19-year-old from the unknown figure.[34]

And Marie von Sivers was the one who knew of this esoteric background and grasped the super-personal, spiritual nature of her connection with Rudolf Steiner. In 1904 he wrote to her:

> For me you are the priestess present in the gaze you directed at me as I recognized your individuality. I esteem the purity of your soul, and only for that reason may I be devoted to you. We live with one another because we belong inwardly to each other; and we will always have the right to be for each other what we are if we are clear that our personal relationship is immersed in the sacred service of spirit evolution.[35]

And so the liberating questioner became a comrade-in-arms in the service of humanity's spiritual evolution. Therein lies Marie von Sivers's decisive contribution to the development of Rudolf Steiner's anthroposophy.

Marie von Sivers recognizes Rudolf Steiner's karmic past

Marie von Sivers's acknowledgement of the essence of Steiner and his work was infinitely deepened when, entirely through her own resources, she recognized his karmic antecedents. This happened already 'during the first year of our shared work', as she wrote to Schuré in 1907. Thus it must have been in 1902 or 1903.

While reading the book *Esoteric Christianity* by Annie Besant, she realized Besant's basic shortcomings in relation to a deeper understanding of Christianity. She was aware of Besant's previous incarnation as Giordano Bruno and that Besant herself knew this—probably through Rudolf Steiner who prefaced the first edition of his book *Theosophy*, published in 1904, with a dedication to 'the spirit of Giordano Bruno'. As she read Besant's book,

> I realized, as in a revelation, with a certainty and a light that excluded all doubt, and without my having sought it [...] that the greatest teacher in Christian scholarship is amongst us; it is Herr Steiner, and he is Saint Thomas Aquinas whose universal knowledge was enhanced and enriched by study of reincarnation which, though previously known, had been veiled and hidden for a certain period due to the particular mission of Christianity.[36]

Rudolf Steiner was clearly surprised when his colleague revealed her insight to him. He confirmed that her vision was true. 'The intimate experience I had was confirmed both by Herr Steiner, who was greatly taken aback, and also through a thousand small details.' We will return a little later to the significance for Edouard Schuré of this karma communication by Marie von Sivers.

11. Decisions at the Whitsun Congress in Munich

The friendship between Schuré, Marie von Sivers and Rudolf Steiner was to bear important fruit. In the spring of 1906 Marie von Sivers arranged a first meeting between Schuré and Steiner in Paris. As soon as the late summer of the same year, the couple stayed as Schuré's guests in Barr, at the foot of Mont Odile.

This was the first of a total of five visits in the following summers. Rudolf Steiner and Marie von Sivers did not pay such regular and lengthy visits to anyone else.

Marie von Sivers had translated Schuré's work *The Great Initiates*. But the Frenchman had also written plays relating to the ancient mysteries, especially in Greece. He was seeking a new unity of art, science and religion, as Steiner also urged and gradually, consistently realized.

Together with Rudolf Steiner, Marie von Sivers translated a play by Schuré set in the fourth century, entitled *The Children of Lucifer*. This was followed by *The Sacred Drama of Eleusis*, which centres on the mysteries surrounding Persephone, and was performed in Munich in the summer of 1907. All this was the prelude to performances of Steiner's own plays. In this context, dramatic art took its point of departure from ancient mystery culture.

With the performance of Schuré's Eleusis play on 19 May 1907, Steiner introduced an entirely new aspect into the theosophical movement in Germany. This occurred as part of the Whitsun Congress of the Federation of European Sections of the Theosophical Society. The concert hall rented for the conference was decorated in an appropriately artistic manner and included seven seal designs, relating to the seals of the Apocalypse, which Steiner had commissioned especially for the gathering. Busts of Schelling, Fichte and Hegel were also erected as a visible sign of

Steiner's aim of relating the theosophical esotericism—which *he* represented—to central European spirituality. This accorded fully with the 'programme' envisaged at the time of the chrysanthemum tea party.

After the four-day congress, Rudolf Steiner gave the lecture cycle entitled *Rosicrucian Wisdom* (GA 99). Following these events a divergence became apparent in relation to the manner of esoteric schooling within the TS. While Annie Besant, who had travelled to Munich from India, retained the Indian orientation initiated by H.P. Blavatsky, from then on Rudolf Steiner taught quite independently of her in the Esoteric School established for members of the German section. At this period therefore Rudolf Steiner's pupils had to decide which kind of esoteric schooling they wished to pursue in future.

The 'renewal of primordial karma'—Ita Wegman's decision

Ita Wegman (1876–1943) was one of those who had to make this decision. At the time she was studying medicine in Zurich, having first met Steiner in Berlin in the late autumn of 1902. First encountering theosophy in Indonesia, she was initially closer, through her Dutch friends there, to the Indian orientation cultivated by Besant. The moment of decision arrived, and she described this as follows:

> Rudolf Steiner welcomed me with gravity and a questioning look. Not much was said, we understood each other very well. Since my feeling was that he understood how things stood, I simply said, 'I will stay with you.' His gaze became radiant, he took my hands in his, gave me the Michael sign and said important things to me that I may not repeat. A primordial karma existing between us was renewed. But I only became aware of the full scope of this meeting many years later.[37]

Steiner had had to wait five years for Wegman to weigh in the balance the different theosophical outlooks of Besant and himself, and take the decision to follow his lead. This moment marked a new phase for Steiner, literally in the sign of Michael. It is not known that he had previously given the Michael symbol to anyone else. But there existed a primordial karma between himself and Wegman, uniting them in two previous Michael eras, first at the time of Gilgamesh and Eabani, and secondly in that of Alexander and Aristotle. This moment of the passing to Wegman of the Michael symbol, which occurred 28 years after the start of the Michael age, placed their connection immediately in the context of a Michael karma of world-historical dimensions, and was a further distinctive milestone.

Yet many years were to pass before this moment bore its full fruit in Wegman's soul, during the night of the Goetheanum fire, when the decision was born to place her life 'in the sacred service of spiritual evolution' as Marie von Sivers had long since done.

Seventeen years after the Munich congress, Rudolf Steiner at last spoke of this significant moment in Munich in answer to a lost letter from Wegman. On 11 June 1924—the day on which Alexander the Great had died[38]—he wrote to her: 'You walk beside me when I lecture. And in our case this [...] is the right preparation for walking together in the world of spirit.' And then, looking back to his separation from Alexander in the previous Michael era, he wrote:

I had grown old when you departed from me in those past times; and this elderly feeling overcame me so strongly just at the time of the Munich congress which you refer to. No one noticed this outwardly. I appeared lively, perhaps even industrious to many. I kept giving myself up to the world of spirit, and this prevented my weariness from becoming outwardly apparent. Yet it was nevertheless a weariness towards everything except the spiritual stream of anthroposophy. This weariness was the karmic reflection of my ageing after you had parted from me. And now [in Munich in 1907] you were there in the auditorium. But the dividing line between Asia and Europe was still there between us in the karmic reflection [choice between Besant and Steiner]. Now all that is past; and I can also speak to people in a different way from before. The spiritual powers that come to expression in anthroposophy look benevolently, lovingly now as I rely upon the love I nurture for your soul, which I hold in such high esteem. And this is my strongest support.[39]

In these later words of Steiner we can discern the profound importance of the meeting in Munich, and Wegman's decision 'for Europe'. The dividing line had fallen, and this was the birth moment of Steiner's *second* close collaboration with a human soul on behalf of the mission of anthroposophy — at the very time when his work with Marie von Sivers and Schuré was showing its first fruits.[40]

Esoteric revelations in Barr

In the late summer of this decisive year, Rudolf Steiner was once again staying in Barr with Marie von Sivers. This was to be the most important of their five visits there. Hitherto the part played by Marie von Sivers in arranging this visit, and especially in supporting the intimate and confidential course it took, has scarcely been acknowledged. This consisted in a letter which she wrote in two consecutive parts from Rome, and which must have cost her great inner efforts. The letter was only rediscovered, and published, in 2002. In it Marie von Sivers replies to a question which Schuré had once asked her during a walk, about Rudolf Steiner's karmic past. In a few sentences written in French, dated 18 August, she tells Schuré of her realization and Steiner's confirmation of it (see chapter 10). Thus she initiated Schuré into Rudolf Steiner's past as Thomas Aquinas. Those who are familiar with her character will know that this was an act of trust of a kind not equalled in this way at any other point in her life, except towards Steiner himself.

Schuré was therefore prepared for much deeper communications from Steiner than during the latter's first visit there in 1906. He was working on the French edition of Steiner's book *Christianity as Mystical Fact*, and needed biographical details for his introduction to it. Steiner responded in both written and verbal form: the written testament, as previously mentioned, became known as the 'documents of Barr' (in GA 262). There Steiner revealed parts of his esoteric development connected with the figure of the 'unknown person'. He referred for the first time to his 'master', and to his fundamental insight into the dual stream of time as a 'condition of spiritual vision'.[41]

As we saw, he also spoke of this on a later occasion to members of the newly founded Anthroposophical Society. Steiner likewise gave Schuré a condensed outline of the karma of H.P. Blavatsky, later drawing on key aspects of this material in lectures to his pupils. But he never again discussed essential things which he told Schuré about Christian Rosenkreutz, his 'master'.

This also relates to what he told him about a specific aspect of western 'Christian-mystic initiation':

> Within this whole stream the initiation of Manes, who in 1459 also initiated Christian Rosenkreutz, is regarded as a 'higher degree'. This initiation consists in true knowledge of the function of evil, and with its deeper context it must still remain entirely concealed from the population at large for a long time to come. You see, whenever even the smallest ray of light has fallen from it, finding its way into written texts, it has had disastrous effects, for instance through the noble Guyau whose later pupil was Friedrich Nietzsche. (GA 262)

It is only here that we learn that Manes was the one who initiated Christian Rosenkreutz. In August 1909 Steiner deepened this picture of Manes. On 31 August 1909, in the Munich lecture cycle *The Orient in the Light of the Occident* (GA 113), he described how Manes summoned a supersensible council in the fourth century which was to oversee the spiritual future of western development. A 'plan for the future cultural evolution of the earth' was resolved upon, and this was 'carried over into the mysteries of the Rose Cross'.

In saying these things to Schuré, Steiner was revealing something of key importance about the initiator of his own esoteric teacher. This occurred, almost to the month, *28 years* after he had first met his unknown teacher in Vienna.

In 1907, therefore, Steiner's creative activity stood under a twofold star: the meeting with the unknown figure, and that of Michael in whose emergent period this meeting had taken place.

The first of these is apparent in the Rosicrucian impulse underlying the Munich congress and in Steiner's confidential utterances to Schuré, the second in his encounter with Ita Wegman, who was very likely the first person to receive the Michael sign from him.

Another striking indication of the efficacy of the 28-year rhythm lies in the fact that Steiner did not speak of the beginning of the Michael age in November 1879 until 18 October 1907, in an esoteric lesson in Berlin. On 23 October and 5 December he made further comments in this regard in Berlin and Munich. All three of these presentations were given 28 years to the month after the Michael age began.[42]

If we seek evidence of the influence of four times seven years in the work of Rudolf Steiner, we must study this connection between the impulses of 1879 and those of 1907; and then we will discover that the seed sown spiritually in 1879 flowers in 1907 in the form of diverse Whitsun blossoms.

The impulse for the Goetheanum building

From blossoms, fruits develop. The most important was born from the desire of a great many members to erect a building dedicated to the plays first performed between 1907 and 1913. Initially the intention was to do this in Munich, and the Johannes building association formed with this in view, a name chosen because of the figure of Johannes Thomasius in Rudolf Steiner's Mystery Plays. But the association was denied a building permit, no doubt for reasons that went beyond merely technical considerations. Richard Wagner had previously tried to build an opera house in Munich, and had met similar difficulties before he moved to Bayreuth instead. Thus a 'vacuum' arose in Munich: the central location of the theosophical-anthroposophical movement became the centre too of the anti-anthroposophic movement (Karl Heyer). Instead of a building serving spiritual purposes, the 'Brown House' was built.[43]

In 1912 a plot of land in Dornach was offered. Travelling to Dornach in the late summer of 1913 to lay the foundation of the new building there, Steiner told a few members who had gathered at Munich railway station to see him off: 'Now we are going into exile.'

12. Laying the Foundation Stone in 1913

The rain was pouring down at seven in the evening when the foundation stone celebration began, to which only members of the Johannes building association were invited. These had arrived in advance but were only told the exact time of the event one hour beforehand. The word had gone round very quickly, though, and a total of 70 people were present for the laying of the foundation stone.

The clay soil had been softened by a whole day of rain. The members of the Johannes building association who gathered to witness the event frequently sank to their ankles in mud. The foundation stone was a double dodecahedron made of sheet copper. The larger measured 63 cm in circumference, and the smaller 54 cm.

Steiner inscribed the foundation stone document on a large ox-skin: two pentagon dodecahedrons with the Rose Cross initials, as symbol of the human being, encompassed by the lines of influence of all the hierarchies. Below this were the signatures of the building association executive committee.[*]

Rudolf Steiner rolled up this document and placed it inside the casing of the double dodecahedron, which was then soldered shut.

Here it is worth noting a specific relationship between the foundation stone and the actual building. Two iron pyrites, procured by Steiner himself, had to be inserted into the foundation stone: a larger one for the smaller dodecahedron and a smaller one for the larger. And they had to be suspended freely within these outer casings. Ehrenfried Pfeiffer comments further on this largely overlooked and rather mysterious detail. He was

---

[*] As reported by Max Benzinger, who had taken on technical preparations for the foundation stone. See *Erinnerungen an Rudolf Steiner*, p. 148ff.

not present at the event, and only came to know the building in its later phases. Since the two cupolas had nothing supporting the area of their intersection, the young scientist always worried that the large cupola might crush the smaller one in a heavy wind or storm conditions. When he told Steiner of his concerns, the latter told him about a 'crystal' that had been inserted into the foundation stone in order to stabilize the two cupolas. For Pfeiffer this was one of the few acts of 'magic' that Rudolf Steiner ever used in his work.[45] The destruction of the First Goetheanum in an arson attack ten years later was of course not in any way due to a 'construction error' in the two cupolas ...

Five people placed the foundation stone into a previously prepared concrete hole, upon a concrete plinth. The large rear part of it was carried by Felix Peipers, who had played the part of Zeus in Schuré's Eleusis play, and Benedictus in the four plays by Steiner. This larger part faced eastwards, the smaller westwards; in other words in a precise inversion of the position of the cupolas in the finished building. Steiner then gave a half-hour address. Fortunately, someone who could take shorthand made notes of what he said, leaning a notebook on the back of the person in front, so that we know more or less what was said on this occasion (in GA 245). As short as it is, the content of this address is of incisive importance.

The mission of spiritual science as part of the mission of humanity

Standing in the trench under canvas, Steiner began to speak as follows:

> Let us rightly understand what we are doing on this festive evening. This action in a sense represents an inner pledge. Our endeavours hitherto have brought us to this point: of standing here in this place — from where we can look out in the four primary directions of the compass, the dome of the heavens — and of erecting here this true symbol of modern spiritual life. Let us realize that by connecting inwardly with what we have symbolically placed into the earth here, we are dedicating ourselves to the spiritual stream of humanity's

evolution that we have recognized to be right. My dear brothers and sisters, let us try to pledge ourselves inwardly in this way. At this moment, let us try to look beyond everything of minor and mundane importance that inevitably binds us to daily life. At this moment let us try to awaken in ourselves the thought that the human soul is connected with the dawning of a new age and the endeavours connected with this. Let us try to think for a moment that in doing this deed that we perform here this evening, we must bear within us an awareness of gazing outwards into far, broad realms of time, and perceiving how the mission whose symbol this building is to be, will be incorporated into the great mission of humanity upon this planet earth.

Steiner then directed his listeners' attention to the 'eternal Gospel of divine, spiritual life' to which souls were once receptive, even still at the time of 'great Plato'; and he highlighted the 'luciferic and ahrimanic influences' that had since come to the fore, so that humanity had lost all connection with 'divine universal existence', leaving nothing more than a 'vague, inadequate yearning and hoping for the spirit'. He urged his listeners to

> feel hearingly, in laying the foundation stone of our true emblem, how a cry becomes audible in this vague yearning and hoping of humanity for the spirit, a cry for an answer: for the one that can be given where spiritual science can hold sway with its Gospel of the spirit and the message of the spirit.

Furthermore, he stated, 'that today humanity stands at a point where souls would inevitably grow arid and empty if this cry of longing for the spirit is not heard'. And then he speaks of the spiritual battle against ahrimanic powers that work to impede the fulfilment of this longing for the spirit. And the Gospel of the new age, he says, resounding in fourfold manner from the East, must encounter a fifth from the West, in which is reflected the spirit forgetfulness caused by ahrimanic powers. Steiner then uttered as it were the foundation stone of this Fifth Gospel, the 'Gospel of Knowledge'.

This foundation stone verse is the primal form of the Lord's

Prayer and describes humanity's lapse from the spirit from a macrocosmic perspective. It runs as follows:

AUM, Amen
Evils hold sway,
Witness to sundering I-hood,
Selfhood's debt incurred through debt of others
Experienced in daily bread
Wherein the will of heaven does not rule
Because man sundered himself from your realm
And forgot your names
You Fathers in the heavens.

This cosmic Lord's Prayer teaches us from a cosmic perspective of the spirit-forgetfulness which has led to the plight of modern existence; thus we learn of the powers which led us from original heights of the spirit into our narrower, lower selves, and to forgetfulness of our connection with the spirit. These powers are Lucifer and Ahriman and their hosts. Someone who passes through the gateway of this macrocosmic Lord's Prayer prepares himself to receive the tangible revelations of the Fifth Gospel as these have entered the world as spiritual science.

Speaking of this prayer, Steiner says:

If we learn to understand the meaning of these words, we will seek to receive the seeds that must flower if earthly evolution is not to become arid but to thrive and bear further fruit, so that, through human will, the earth may attain the goal that was envisaged for it from primal beginnings. So let us feel this evening that wisdom, and the impulse of new knowledge, new love and new vigorous strength, must come alive in human souls.

And he ends the address thus:

The sense that remains with us from this evening is one that should kindle in us the striving for knowledge of a new revelation given to humanity, for which the human soul is thirsting, and from which it will drink—but only when it wins through fearlessly to faith and trust in what the science of the spirit can proclaim, once again reuniting what had to be sundered for a while through the process of human evolution, that is, religion, art and science. My sisters and brothers, let us take this thought with us on our further way as remembrance of this moment we have spent together in shared celebration, and wish never again to forget.

In this festive moment, Rudolf Steiner thus invested humanity's further evolution with the great mission of spiritual science.

'... one of the most beautiful starry nights ...'

To conclude this chapter I will cite three subtly different yet concordant testimonies by people who took part in this great event of the laying of the foundation stone.

Marie Steiner wrote as follows in her preface to Steiner's address:

No doubt the powers adversarial to the ascending direction of human evolution were aware that this moment had placed a mighty impediment in their way. It was as if they summoned natural forces to their aid to prevent the event taking place. The elements raged, the rain streamed down, and there were furious winds. Many boots got stuck in the softened clay of the terrain. But no one among us would have thought for a moment of postponing the laying of the foundation stone for such reasons. Destiny had decreed that it should happen then.

Dr Steiner's spirit-filled voice won through over the raging elements and penetrated every heart. The friends stood around in a close throng, and one of them managed, albeit with a few gaps, to record Dr Steiner's words so that this day, 20 September 1913, can be remembered by posterity too.[46]

Ludwig Polzer-Hoditz reported the celebration as follows:

Before the event began a pile of wood was lit. The rain was pouring down. Some of us held burning torches. We stood in a close circle around the pit as Rudolf Steiner approached it. First he invoked all the spiritual hierarchies one after another; and then, in the address which followed, he gave us a brief survey of evolution from a spiritual-scientific perspective, right up to the present moment of 20 September, 1880 years since the Mystery of Golgotha and 1913 years since Christ's birth. At this moment Mercury was visible as evening star in the constellation of Scales. Twelve red roses and one white were placed on the foundation stone, and it was lowered by a cross of straps. I remember holding the torch in my hand with some anxiety, partly because I was so moved by the occasion but also because drops of fire were falling from it and we stood so closely together, some with open umbrellas. The image of this event, lit by the burning bonfire and the torch flames, inscribed itself deeply in my soul. I knew that I was participating in a rite that would be of decisive significance for centuries to come.

As the anthroposophic movement emerged in this way into the public realm in the form of the building later called the Goetheanum, grave opposition and attack began upon Rudolf Steiner and the movement.[47]

Max Benzinger, who was responsible for all the practical and technical preparations, recorded the following memory:

Then followed an address lasting half an hour. I was profoundly moved, and so vitally connected with it all that I did not look up to the sky; but then I did, and saw the clearest and most beautiful starry heavens: the stars were shining as if they were far closer than usual. Venus [Arcturus? TM] and Jupiter stood close together in the south-west, and twinkled down, and it was one of the most beautiful starry nights that I have ever witnessed ...[48]

We can say therefore that this ritual act of the laying of the foundation stone was, quite literally, one of the great 'star moments' in the unfolding of anthroposophy upon earth.

13. The Birth of the Threefold Movement

If we take the year when the Michael age began, 1879, as the nodal or mirroring point, then 1841—when the battle of the spirits of darkness began, which ended in the victory of Michael in November 1879—is mirrored in the year 1917. Thus 1917 is also connected with this spiritual battle.

In March that year the Tsar abdicated, and in April the USA entered the Great War. Wilson and Lenin began literally to squeeze the centre of Europe in their pincers. At this time of seeming obduracy from both West and East, the voice of the centre was raised. Three individuals were destined to hear it first: Count Otto von Lerchenfeld, Ludwig Polzer-Hoditz and Walter Johannes Stein.

Lerchenfeld was Imperial Councillor and had connections with the Bavarian royal family. In July 1917 he asked Steiner what might be done at the centre of Europe to work for a peace befitting human dignity—a decisive question asked of the anthroposophical movement, comparable to Marie von Sivers's question in November 1901 about a *western* form of esotericism (see chapter 10). At the time Rudolf Steiner was developing ideas about social reform which could have offered a way forward. Lerchenfeld had urged various ambassadors and people of public standing—including Prince Lichnovsky (the German ambassador in London) and Walther Rathenau—to attend a discussion with Steiner. They all thought they had more important matters to attend to, and declined the request. Count Lerchenfeld also arranged a discussion between Rudolf Steiner and the German Foreign Minister Richard von Kuehlmann, but nothing came of it. Likewise fruitless was a meeting, in Lerchenfeld's presence, which Steiner had with Count Bernstorff, the former German ambassador in Washington.

Michael's call to the House of Hapsburg

Steiner sent a telegram to Ludwig Polzer-Hoditz asking him to come to a meeting in Berlin. Despite the difficulties of travel in wartime, he arrived in Berlin on 13 July, the same day that the German Chancellor Bethmann-Hollweg announced his resignation.

Polzer knew immediately that this meeting would be of the greatest importance. It took place in the summerhouse of Steiner's apartment at 17 Motzstrasse. Over three days Steiner explained to Polzer the basic aspects of 'social threefolding', and gave him a first memorandum on the subject. A few days later he gave him a second memorandum which specifically related to circumstances in Austro-Hungary, and was intended for Polzer's brother Arthur, who, since May 1917, was Lord of the Cabinet for Kaiser Karl, with whom he had been friends since his youth.

Steiner saw an opportunity here. He suggested that Arthur Polzer should try to secure the post of Foreign Minister, and hoped the Kaiser would show some interest in the ideas contained in the memorandum. He told Polzer that the West

> would never hearken to canon power, but only to the power of thought, and that Rome's dominion, which still overshadows Europe, would vanish like mist in the sun. Also that Bismarck's words—'when Austria's Kaiser gets up on his horse, all nations will follow him'—would be fulfilled.[49]

For Steiner this was at the same time a test of 'whether Michael's call can reach the Hapsburgs'.

Polzer felt the burden of responsibility on his shoulders and said, 'You are placing a great deal in my hands, and I will make honest efforts. I will place in the scales of destiny the fraternal love that has united us.'

As his teacher perceived the trepidation in Polzer's soul, he said: 'Be tranquil. We must also be prepared to stand by and watch as nations go under.' But then he added: 'If this attempt fails, catastrophes will follow, catastrophes.'

'Put it on top of everything else in your suitcase'

At this moment of destiny appeared the third figure who was to be directly involved in the social threefolding impulse. This was W.J. Stein. He had come to Berlin for a quite different purpose, wishing to discuss his doctoral thesis with Rudolf Steiner, who had commissioned him to write a theory of spiritual knowledge. In his memoirs he writes:

> Count Polzer was just hurrying away as I arrived at Rudolf Steiner's door. I had known him a long time and we were close friends. At this moment he was deathly pale, and I asked him what was wrong. 'I have to carry an important document over the border,' he replied, 'a letter to Kaiser Karl of Austria.' 'Give it to me,' I said. 'No, no; or at least I must first ask the Doctor.'

The two friends went in to Steiner together and Stein declared his willingness to act as mediator, at which Steiner read the whole memorandum to Stein. When asked how the document should be got across the border, Steiner said: 'Place it on top of everything else in your suitcase.' At the border customs Stein had to open his suitcase. The customs officer took out the document and rummaged through the rest of the contents of the suitcase; then placed the document carefully on top again, closed the suitcase and stamped it as 'passed'.[50] In Vienna it must have reached Polzer again, for he gave it to his brother there on 24 July.

Arthur Polzer did not dare pass on the document, for he had succumbed to the cross-fire of various political intrigues which, against the Kaiser's will, led to his enforced resignation in November 1917. Only after this did he hand it to his old friend, who was clearly interested, and later referred to it expressly. Polzer even had to prepare an itemized summary of it for him.

When Steiner spoke to Polzer again in November, he told him that it was time to bring these ideas into the public domain. Thus began the second phase of the threefolding movement, although this could only be initiated in November 1918, after Germany capitulated.

Systematic silence

Arthur Polzer-Hoditz first published the memorandum he had received in the appendix of his monograph on Emperor Karl, which appeared in 1928. He also noted in his book diverse discussions with his brother Ludwig about this truly central European social impulse of Steiner's. When the American and English edition was published two years later, the memorandum no longer figured in the appendix, and all references to Rudolf Steiner and Ludwig Polzer-Hoditz had been excised from the text. The world was to be given a picture of the last Austrian Kaiser, but all reference to the only really new social idea in central Europe was to be expunged from it in a way indiscernible to anyone unaware of these things.[51] This was symptomatic of the underhand spiritual battle waged ever more fiercely against anthroposophy and its social impulses since the foundation stone had been laid in September 1913.

Thus ebbed the last attempt to awaken understanding of a social organism constituted in three relatively autonomous spheres: the free life of spirit, a fraternal economic life and a rights life founded on human equality.

*

After this failure of the first threefolding initiative ('threefolding from above') Rudolf Steiner himself initially turned to further work on his book *Riddles of the Soul* (GA 21) in which he first gave a systematic account of the human being's threefold physiology and soul faculties.

14. Basic Lessons in Vienna

Steiner gave something like private esoteric tuition to all three pupils referred to in the last chapter. On one occasion he said to Lerchenfeld: 'Never work for the sake of success!' This may not seem very esoteric, but it contains a secret of truly fruitful and creative endeavour. In the fourth of Steiner's Mystery Plays, Romanus says, 'Success comes only to those who do not fear failure.'

In his many private conversations with Steiner, Polzer received inestimable intimations that led to deep insights on his part, especially in relation to the occult background of world politics. Polzer's father had led him to Steiner, and in 1908 he attended the first lecture by him in Vienna. After his father's death the relationship was reversed: Steiner now led Polzer to his father in the world of spirit; and this was accomplished through small remarks such as one he made following a lecture: 'Your father was present again today.' Or: 'Your father is of great help in the world of spirit.'

Accompanying readers through all their future lives

Stein, too, whose persistent questioning and daring gave Steiner great pleasure, received private instruction on various occasions. One such moment occurred in Vienna. The date is uncertain and could have either preceded or followed the gathering in Berlin; but it is one of those incisive, eternal moments with pupils that they carried with them throughout the rest of their lives.

Stein's older brother Friedrich, a classmate of Eugen Kolisko, had blown himself up with his redoubt during the war, on 22 March 1915, after first leading his company back to safety. Becoming a Russian prisoner of war was not something he wished to contemplate. Although he was W.J. Stein's only brother, the latter once referred to him in a letter to Steiner as 'his favourite brother'!

In his memoirs, Stein describes passing through the centre of Vienna with his teacher one day. As they were passing the square of Michaelerplatz, Steiner suddenly pointed with his umbrella towards a silverware shop there, and said: 'It was here that it happened, here where this shop window is. It was here that I sat and wrote the book that your brother is now studying, in thoughts that are as crystal clear as mathematics — the book about Goethe's theory of knowledge.' His astonished pupil did not at first understand.

'This is the site of Café Griensteidl,' explained Steiner. And then Stein began to see what he meant:

> Steiner was experiencing how my brother, in his after-death existence, was working through the book he (Steiner) had written here many years previously; working through it point by point and thought by thought. I was deeply moved, for I had never before encountered in such tangible reality how the dead live on, nor how a living person can perceive what they are doing.

Stein had given this book to his brother as a last gift before the war broke out, having finally succeeded in locating a copy of this out-of-print volume. As his letters testify, Friedrich Stein had studied it carefully at the time, along with other works by Steiner. And now he was working through it again in the reverse passage through his life!

In the quiet of the nearby Church of St Augustine, undisturbed by the noise of trams, Steiner explained to his awestruck pupil: 'I must accompany through all future lives anyone who has read even one line of *Knowledge of the Higher Worlds*, to help and support him further. This is the law by which I must abide.'[52]

Here we see the occultist as the helper and server of others' development. As an eight-year-old already, Steiner had been urged to *help* the female relative he perceived after her death; and this vivid moment with his young pupil shows how much he had since taken such a task to heart and made it his inner practice.

Stein commented as follows on this fundamental lesson Steiner gave him at Michaelerplatz:

> Rudolf Steiner taught his pupils to live with the dead, showing us that when we live in sympathy with them, we come to know what work they are engaged in; and thus the two worlds were no longer sundered. As I was writing my dissertation I often spoke to people who had been close to my brother while he was alive; and a small portion of this otherwise hidden world was revealed to me. The content of my thesis can in part be attributed to this fact.

For his dissertation Steiner had set Stein the task of developing the theory of spiritual knowledge contained in his (Steiner's) epistemology, and it was therefore more than a merely academic treatise. At moments such as the one described, Stein's teacher had awoken his pupil's capacity for spiritual experience and cognition.

With ongoing help and advice from Steiner, therefore, W.J. Stein wrote the first thesis on anthroposophy, submitted under the title 'Historical and Critical Thoughts on Modern Philosophy' for which he was awarded a doctorate on 4 December 1918.[53]

The college of professors of Vienna's Faculty of Philosophy acknowledged, despite certain criticisms, that overall 'this thesis testifies to a power of thinking substantially exceeding the level of dissertations on philosophical themes of a good standard'.

15. A Whitsun in Germany

With the Kaiser's abdication on 9 November 1918, and the outbreak of revolution in Germany, the old empire along with its centralized state crumbled into ruins.

On the evening of 9 November, Steiner arranged a recitation in Dornach of the poem 'Chorus of Primordial Dreams' by Fercher von Steinwand. This was its first ever performance. Fercher had prefaced the poem with the motto in both Greek and German, 'The true nature of being'.

Thus at a moment of social collapse was invoked a figure whose poetic endeavours had been a full expression of the true nature of Germany. Fercher von Steinwand had played a key role in the development of Steiner's karma vision, as we saw in chapter 7, and this moment was therefore incisive and symptomatic. Fercher will again shine into Steiner's biography like a good star at a dark moment of his life in 1922.

In the lecture of 9 November 1918 following this performance, Steiner, without beating about the bush, asked a question that would be decisive for the coming fate of the German people—that of so-called 'war guilt'. Emil Molt, an industrialist from Stuttgart, was in the audience. Few questions have been so shrouded in illusions as this one right up to our own day, even amongst students of Steiner. Steiner had already laid the basis for these reflections in his text 'Thoughts during a time of war, for Germans and those who believe they should hate them'. There he had pointed to the war preparations focused on central Europe that had been underway for decades both in the West and the Russian East. In 1916, also, he had drawn attention to the prize-winning book by Swiss author Jacob Ruchti, entitled *Zur Geschichte des Kriegausbruches* ('On the History of the Outbreak of the War').[54] Ruchti had studied official government documents with a discerning eye, and felt called upon to expose the mendacious role of British foreign policy at the time the war began. But the victorious powers insisted that the central Axis powers should bear the blame. Their only argument was, and remains, the *apparent* course of events, which does indeed suggest Germany was to blame. The German government felt it had to *initiate* the series of declarations of war[55] since its efforts — undertaken up to the very last moment — to reverse apparently unmotivated Russian mobilization, and prevail upon England to assume a neutral stance, bore no fruit.

To this day, this fact is taken by all to show that Germany was at fault. Largely concealed behind this apparent German guilt, however, and therefore unmentioned, is the question of why Russia wished to intervene at all in a conflict that had nothing to do with it initially — the dispute between Austria and Serbia — and why it mobilized for war; and likewise why England could not have remained or did not wish to remain neutral in a conflict between Germany and France.

In view of the European alliances of the time — Russia was committed to standing beside France in the case of war — a war on two fronts was inevitable following Russian mobilization. The so-called Schlieffen Plan had been devised with this eventuality in view. To speak of a 'German desire for war' in this situation and, for decades, to conceal the real desire for war on the part of its adversaries, is completely at odds with the truth. The life and sufferings of a man at the centre of these tragic events — Helmuth von Moltke — can show us the nature of this supposed German 'desire for war'.

Helmuth von Moltke's record of the outbreak of war

The General Staff of the German army played a key role in Steiner's efforts to give real substance to the question of guilt.

After he was ousted in September 1914, Moltke wrote a record of the outbreak of war and the events in Berlin immediately before it, which remain one of the most important documents about the start of the First World War. This record was intended only for his wife, Eliza von Moltke, to read; and for this reason alone Moltke had no reason for presenting a cosmetic account of the facts and of what he had experienced. His report is an unvarnished testimony.

Moltke died on 18 June 1916 in Berlin, in the middle of the war. Rudolf Steiner, who 'by chance' had been delayed in Berlin at the time, gave the memorial address, and also remained connected with Moltke's soul after death. His wife had been an esoteric pupil of Steiner's since 1904 and supported him meditatively in these efforts. Moltke's soul underwent an after-death development that figures among the most significant of those uncovered by Steiner's spiritual-scientific research. Over an eight-year period, uniquely, Steiner recorded Moltke's posthumous experiences.

In January 1919 the preliminary negotiations for a so-called 'peace' began in Versailles, in the same mirrored ballroom where the German Empire had been founded in 1871. The victorious powers were as certain as anything that the central Axis powers were to blame, especially Germany. At the beginning of May, in his observations of Moltke's occult development, Steiner noted a change of intent regarding the record which the former had left behind. He now wished them to be published, and to act as a reality factor to counter illusory or mendacious formulations about Germany's role in the outbreak of war. Eliza von Moltke sent Steiner the document, and he wrote a foreword to it. This foreword shows the nullity of all political action in Germany at the time, and that *for this reason* everything had become weighted towards a purely military decision. In view of the growing encirclement this decision—and ultimately, if necessary, war— required corresponding preparations. These were not the actions of an aggressor but sought to safeguard Germany's survival. Steiner's foreword is a vehement condemnation of the utter dilettantism of German policies, which, after the demonic interlude of the Third Reich, we can see is scarcely different today.

Moltke's document itself confirms Steiner's diagnosis in a frighteningly vivid way. If one reads what happened in Berlin the day before war was declared, and pictures the confusion and vapidity of the Kaiser and his ministers, one will inevitably cease talking of any intentional desire for war on the part of the German government. While Moltke's record is a terrible indictment of German politics, it must be regarded as the very opposite of a proof that Germany systematically pursued a policy of warfare either before or when the declaration of war was issued. Steiner thought that if the world learned of the confusion in German politics before and at the time war broke out, it would seek for other causes of the war: the question of guilt would be formulated anew, and unjust peace terms would not be imposed on Germany, as seemed likely and as was indeed implemented in the form of paragraph 231 of the Versailles Treaty, which spoke of Germany's 'sole guilt'.

Moltke's account was printed in Stuttgart in May in an edition of 10,000 copies, so that it could be sent to the German delegation in Versailles and help avert the threatened actions with all their dire consequences.

Emil Molt, who helped fund the publication, went to the printers, got hold of the first copies of the book without authorization, and, with great excitement, took them to a nephew of Moltke's in Stuttgart, legation councillor Adolf von Moltke. His pleasure was premature. Hans-Adolf von Moltke sounded the alarm to his uncle, the older brother of Helmuth von Moltke, along with the army's chief officers and the Foreign Office. The Moltke family's most senior member issued a veto on the publication. A military friend of Eliza Moltke's husband, General von Dommes went to see her, and they agreed that von Dommes should go to Stuttgart to discuss the matter with Steiner in person and give him cogent reasons for halting the publication.

The conversation of 1 June 1919

Wilhelm von Dommes recorded the details of his conversation with Steiner in a journal. It lasted five hours altogether, from 2.15 to 3.15 p.m. and then again from 4.30 to 8.30 in the evening.

Dommes explained to Steiner that the account contained three factual errors and could therefore not be published. The first related to the invasion of and transit through Belgium. According to Moltke, this action aimed to steal a march on the French and make it possible to conquer them quickly in open battle rather than getting entangled in a long-winded defensive war. Dommes stated that this had not been the real motive. It was a matter only of trying to prevent the *French* from passing through Belgium. Secondly, the transit through Belgium had been planned in advance, since otherwise the right flank of the German army would have been blocked by the English. And thirdly, the Schlieffen Plan had not, as Moltke claimed, originally envisaged a transit through southern Holland too.

Steiner noted down these three points during the discussion, but he was unable to check there and then whether these objections were correct or not. To dispute them he would have had to provide Dommes with hard documentary evidence. To refute them through esoteric perceptions, even if Steiner could have done so at that moment, would not have been a legitimate course of action.

Instead, Steiner explained to Dommes what considerations had led him to publish Moltke's text. Von Dommes noted in his journal that

> he [Steiner] wished to publicize truths unpleasant to us in order to influence Germany's enemies. Then they would have had to say: If they admit and acknowledge this, then it must also be true that Germany was not warmongering. He had wanted to show that the German people were so badly led that that the latter could not be the case.[56]

One of the most unpleasant truths was the Kaiser's unthinking and naive conduct, his assumption on 31 July, after a dispatch was received from London, that due to supposed British neutrality the whole army needed only to mobilize in the East. He instructed Moltke accordingly, thus breaking a non-interference promise which the Chief of the General Staff had made in 1906 as the express condition for taking this post. A few hours later, this dispatch was revoked and Moltke was again given a free hand.

Von Dommes was unimpressed by Steiner's views. Instead he stressed that Moltke's account, quite apart from its 'errors' also gave a 'completely false picture of the pure and unsullied character of his majesty'. What might Steiner have to say in opposition to *this*? In reply, he restricted himself to the question of whether von Dommes would give a sworn declaration that the three points he had raised were indeed mistaken. 'I gave this assurance,' his journal tersely states.

All Rudolf Steiner's efforts to publish the text had thus foundered, and he consented to it being pulped. What, after all, would have followed if he had gone ahead with publication? Germany's officialdom would have done its best to destroy him: he would have become the target of mockery and ridicule, and the whole affair would have done irreparable damage to the progress of spiritual science. No other course of action remained open to him.

Whitsun and German 'guilt'

After they had 'resolved' the main point of dispute, the conversation continued after an hour's break. Steiner 'spoke very interestingly about the threefold social organism, [...] his own political development, and the Moltke family, etc.' They even touched on what the 'soul' had urged [publication of Moltke's account], which Eliza von Moltke had likewise indicated to von Dommes. Dommes drew Steiner's attention to the 'great conflict of interest' to which Eliza von Moltke had succumbed due to the '"soul" of her husband urging publication'. And Steiner explained to Dommes that 'Moltke's soul [...] had believed subjectively that his account was correct'.

While the first part of the conversation was to have dire consequences for the German nation, the second part was to be significant for Wilhelm von Dommes's own personal development and destiny. Altogether his picture of Steiner is a remarkably positive one: 'I gained the impression of a very fine and utterly decent man, of great loyalty and good will.' However, he finds it 'odd that he has formed such an unfavourable view of

H[is] M[ajesty]'. He considers sending him some 'material' that will help him 'revise his opinion'. At the end of his journal entry on Steiner he remarks, with satisfaction, that 'we spoke in full confidence and parted from each other on friendly terms'.[57]

Von Dommes ended his account of this matter, written over a period of two weeks, on Whitsun Monday, 9 June, with the remark: 'Beautiful Whitsun weather on both days. Contrast with the world situation.'

Whitsun as a matter of lovely weather and sunshine! Here lies the world-historical importance of this tragic meeting in Stuttgart: the representatives of Germany's officialdom had lost all real *trust in the spirit*. If Germany was (and remains) guilty, the fault lies here. Love of appearance outweighed 'the true reality' of the German nation. While Dommes did sense something 'fine and utterly decent' in Steiner, his high regard for the Kaiser — who, according to Moltke wanted to live his life as if 'every day was Sunday' — blinded him to anything else.

The German spirit is a Whitsun spirit par excellence. On a previous Whitsun occasion Germany had faced another moment of destiny, the choice between spirit and spiritual development or glorious appearance and power. This was the moment when the unknown Kaspar Hauser appeared as if from nowhere in the market square at Nuremberg, on Whit Monday 1828.

In the Whitsun discussion in Stuttgart, the spirit of the age and the concerns of the German spirit, embodied in Steiner, came face to face with the representative of German military thinking. While the latter had a faint, dull sense that beautiful Whitsun weather should be matched by a different world situation, no spiritual fire burned in him to realize this.

In this scene therefore we see a foreshadowing of the dire rejection of the spirit which was soon to pull all Germany into disaster. As yet this denial of the spirit bore a seemingly harmless visage. But soon enough a 'puppet' would rise from the abyss to drag down a nation deprived of its good spirit and its most important advocate. The article in the Versailles Treaty relating to Germany's guilt, which Steiner had sought to prevent up to the last moment, became the stirrup on which the 'puppet' would rise to his ascendancy from the abyss.

'He noticed nothing of what went on in me'

And how did Steiner himself experience this discussion? He gave an account of it in a letter to Eliza von Moltke written two months later—two months which had been a period of the greatest inner trials for her. For the first time she had doubted whether her teacher had perceived correctly, *in this instance* and therefore perhaps in others. Due to the adversarial influx from all sides, Eliza von Moltke had to undergo a period of inner tumult, a fuller account of which is beyond our present scope.[58]

The thread of her inner confidence in Steiner might have broken here. That it did not resulted from her inner spiritual victory, which enabled her to receive further ongoing revelations from Moltke's soul after death, communicated to her by Rudolf Steiner.

On 6 August 1919, Steiner wrote that

> ... it was very sad that it thus became impossible to publish this account. What legation councillor v. Moltke undertook in regard to the Foreign Office, as you will be aware, is not something I could ever have consented to.

Then he continues in the same letter:

> Herr von Dommes's intervention inevitably had a decisive effect. He came to see me and explained that he was able to *prove* that three points in the account did not correspond to the facts. He spoke at great length about these three points.

As we saw, Steiner had noted down these three points, which we cited above.

> I was now in the most difficult position imaginable. I asked v. Dommes if he could swear on oath that the three points were incorrect, and he confirmed this unreservedly.

In Steiner's next words we can see that a third, invisible person—the soul of Moltke—was present in the discussion, and that

Steiner also had to attend to what it was experiencing of this Stuttgart conversation beyond the threshold:

> These circumstances were very difficult for the soul. It was not aware of any error, and was therefore still in full agreement with publication. It only became restless when the reflection of Dommes's view reached it, a view opposite to its own. It was not permissible for a conflict to arise between a person here and the soul beyond the threshold; and thus it happened that, though the soul felt no opposition to publication, nevertheless a difficult situation had to be avoided in which, through dissemination of Dommes's view here on the physical plane, other beliefs than those of the soul might become widespread. There is no doubt that the soul still believes the account was correct. I am not going to ask directly whether it is indeed true or not.[59]

Instead, other, exoteric means had to be used. Steiner gave his handwritten note of the three supposed errors in Moltke's document to Juergen von Grone, who as both airforce officer and anthroposophist had the right background for checking them. Von Grone showed that von Dommes's 'errors' could not be substantiated, and claimed that they were only advanced as a way of concealing the original intention of the Schlieffen Plan, which included violating Dutch neutrality, inflicting a devastating blow on France in open battle, and sparing Germany public loss of face — though at the cost of the whole fate of the German nation. Whether von Dommes knowingly lied or believed in his 'errors' himself is not something that can be resolved here. He was, at any rate, a useful tool in the hands of the powers of darkness.

On 28 June 1919 the German delegates signed the Versailles Peace Treaty.

Steiner commented to Polzer:

> Germany is in ruins. It was wrong to sign this treaty. Acknowledging guilt for the war and signing the 'sole guilt' article is tantamount to signing its own death warrant, and the beginning of its ongoing exploitation and domination.[60]

But, as Steiner later expressed it on one occasion, despite the fact that publication of Moltke's account was prevented by 'such devious means', all was not lost in this key moment: the strength of the spiritual bridge with the soul of Moltke, forged by Steiner and Eliza von Moltke, was preserved. It was vital that it should not also rupture, and this was the second, spiritual reason why Steiner had to submit to the intervention:

> Precisely to preserve the peace of the soul we had to suppress publication at Dommes's behest. These were very difficult moments I spent with a man who thought only in military terms. While he was speaking he noticed nothing of what I went through: every word spoke of prejudice, but rigidly, judging with an inflexibility that took no account at all of the global catastrophe.[61]

'The signature of humankind today'

Prevention of the publication of Moltke's account fell in the second phase of the threefold social order movement, which was now again on the wane. It had been initiated with an 'Appeal to the German People', which Steiner had published in the biggest daily papers in Europe in February 1919, signed by 90 prominent individuals. This appeal made it clear that the ruined empire had lacked a goal truly commensurate with the intrinsic mission of Germany. It urged Germans to leave all small-mindedness behind them and turn instead towards new 'strong ideas' that could be found in the elaboration of a really new form of social organism which, in accord with humanity's current state of evolution, must be organized in a threefold way. This appeal was also included as an appendix to Steiner's book *Towards Social Renewal*, which gave a detailed, in-depth account of the principles of threefolding.

The pamphlet containing Moltke's account had been published by the Social Threefolding Alliance in Stuttgart. But the second phase of the threefolding movement also waned, despite lively interest from workers. The 'small-minded' thinking of political and government leaders kept the upper hand. On 28 May 1919, Steiner wrote down the following impressions he gained at a threefolding lecture given by him in Ulm, conveying the general atmosphere predominant in ordinary people at the time, and their narrow views:

> The day before yesterday I was in Ulm, and thus once again on very unprepared ground. One sees that every day new abysses open up, new moods of conflict which 'threefolding' must bridge to find new social forms. In such gatherings one sees what is kindled everywhere: mistrust, no belief that anyone is well-motivated. And these most 'unsocial' conditions are the foundations upon which we must try to 'socialize' everything. There is such a lack of any capacity to understand in these people. *They simply do not hear* things of the greatest importance. It is as if they were only capable of understanding what they've been used to hearing for 30 years. Their brains are hardened, their ether body lame, their astral body empty, and their I greatly dulled. This is the signature of humankind today.[62]

This letter was written on the same day that, to his horror, Steiner learned that 'anthroposophists' had already collected copies of the von Moltke publication. Emil Molt's unfortunate action later came to light. Johannes Tautz, historian and supporter of the school movement, indicates that Molt suffered greatly from his action and that his inner relationship to Steiner became more difficult thereafter. In consequence he put all his energies into founding the first Waldorf school in Stuttgart, which Steiner had earlier proposed. After the failure of the publication and of threefolding initiatives, it seemed wise to start to work upon the *foundations* of an education that had led to the state humanity was now in. On 7 September 1919, in the presence of a thousand people who had gathered there for the occasion, the Free Waldorf School in Stuttgart celebrated its opening. Steiner spoke there of a 'festive deed by universal powers'—a further key moment in anthroposophy's unfolding upon earth.

The publication initiative and accounts of anthroposophical history

Steiner's initiative of publishing Moltke's document did not arise from some personal whim or any 'chance' connection with the

Moltke family. In fact we can see it as one of the great, tangible examples that the author of *The Philosophy of Freedom* adhered rigorously in his own actions to the criteria he had formulated for free action: *free* actions, he said, must always be informed by knowledge and perception. Steiner perceived the increasing tendency to lay all blame for the war at Germany's door, and wished to counteract it. That this action, quite literally, came to nothing due to the eagerness of leading personalities in Germany to see themselves in a flattering light does not alter the fact that Steiner acted out of insight into what was needed. A free action cannot be directly measured in terms of how the world responds to it; and yet it is precisely this view that has been circulated in accounts of the history of anthroposophy. Christoph Lindenberg, whose chronicle of Steiner's life is very useful in many places, writes as follows in volume 2 of his biography:

> This idea [of publishing Moltke's document] was rather unfortunate for various reasons, since his account ended with the words: 'I recorded this account in some haste without notes to hand or any other material. There may therefore be errors here and there in respect of dates and so forth. I was also ill at the time I was writing it. The record is only intended for my wife, and should never be published.'

But whether something is 'unfortunate' or not does not relate directly to the intuition for a free action! One might of course speak of a fortunate or unfortunate 'idea', for instance the idea of letting copies of this important pamphlet fall into the wrong hands, or that of presenting Steiner's world-historical initiative for Germany as something 'rather unfortunate'. The 'misfortune' certainly does not lie with Steiner's free action but in something responding to it outwardly in the form of unclear will (Molt) and unclear thinking (Lindenberg). Lindenberg's appraisal must conclude in the view that it would have been 'more fortunate' for Steiner to have relinquished his intention of publishing the document. He measures this action by its success; yet this can never be a criterion for an action's freedom or necessity. Success is governed by factors that do not depend solely on its instigator.

Lindenberg also claims that the three objections raised by von Dommes were not passed on in a reliable form, and therefore their truth cannot be verified. This means, firstly, that either he was unaware of the notes of the conversation by Steiner which were published back in 1992 or did not think them reliable; and secondly, that he had taken no account of the refutation of these objections by Juergen von Grone, likewise published in 1992.

Ultimately there is no getting round the fact that Lindenberg conceals a fact known to him: that the soul of Moltke after death altered its original view that the account should be kept secret. Such changes of intent are not unusual. In Scene 7 of the second Mystery Play, *The Soul's Probation*, the spirit of the deceased Benedictus seeks to inspire his closest pupil to change his mind in this way. Accord with the modified will of Moltke after death is intrinsic to the whole tenor of Steiner's action in seeking publication: a fulfilment of the prompting by Moltke's soul itself, in response to the nature of the times, that in consequence of the war people should again give serious credence to the spiritual counterpart of all physical reality. The posthumous communication of 22 June 1918 states:

> Humanity must increasingly be prepared to believe that the happiness they seek cannot exist on the physical plane alone. They must cease to search for *this* kind of happiness, and must recognize that into everything they experience on earth must flow what comes from the world of spirit. Only when earthly experience merges with spiritual experience can there arise what is desirable for the human being on earth. But as yet this cannot be made comprehensible for people today. And the task confronting us will be connected with the acquisition of powers through which the spiritual-corporeal can also be rendered comprehensible in social and political life.[63]

It is clear that such a need of the times went beyond the horizons of a man like von Dommes with his 'small-minded' thinking. But that an influential and supposedly anthroposophical study of history responds with such lack of understanding to one of Steiner's most important initiatives must give us pause for thought. In this matter, the historian displays a one-sidedly materialistic outlook based only on external facts and documents, but without even taking these fully into account. Here therefore his account is firmly in the tradition of pragmatic historical research as propounded by Ranke; and ultimately this is an offspring of the anti-Michaelic impulses originating in Francis Bacon's mode of thought.

*

As 1919 came to an end, Steiner spoke about the forthcoming incarnation of the being that had taken possession of Friedrich Nietzsche.[64] In doing so he was also drawing attention to entities who had instigated the deeper spiritual obstacles to publication of the Moltke document and the threefolding initiative, and were ultimately responsible for the failure of both. At the same time he showed that the threefold social order is nothing other than the social expression, required by our times, of the differentiation that arises between our three soul faculties as we cross the threshold to the world of spirit—a passage in fact that all humanity has been making unconsciously since the last third of the nineteenth century. The question therefore is this: How many people can resolve to raise what is happening unconsciously with them into thinking awareness?

16. Art, Science and Religion

The date of 27 September 1920 was a further distinctive mile-stone. On this day Steiner initiated the first anthroposophical schooling course in the still unfinished Goetheanum building. In chapter 8 we referred to this course because, during it, Steiner made a profound and significant remark about Nietzsche as a symptom of the awakening of a new capacity for inspiration. Here, as we continue to study Steiner's development, we will examine further aspects of this milestone.

The course began, in storm and tempestuous weather, seven years to the week after the building's foundation stone had been laid. This first School of Spiritual Science course ran in the new building from 27 September to 16 October. The evening before it began, 26 September, an opening celebration was held. No such celebration was ever held for the building itself. After a musical prelude, Marie Steiner—now Steiner's wife—recited a slightly modified version of Hilarius' speech from the Mystery Play *The Guardian of the Threshold*, first performed in 1912. Hilarius speaks before a group of people who have been allowed to cross the threshold of the mystery temple for the first time. Hitherto the work of the temple has been accomplished only in hidden ways. In the second part of the opening celebrations, Marie Steiner recited the Egyptian scenes of the fourth Mystery Play, *The Soul's Awakening*.

This artistic celebration shows us that serious efforts in tune with the needs of the times were being made to reconnect art, religion and science. These of course had become increasingly sundered over the millennia. The Munich Congress marked a first step in this direction (see chapter 11). The underlying intention of the Goetheanum building was not to pursue and present science, even a science of the spirit, separately from artistic and religious experience. It was instead itself a living archetype of this new union of art, science and religion from which a new civilization could emerge after the old had foundered in the tumult and catastrophes of war.

Steiner, very deliberately, gave three lectures on recitation and declamation during the almost three-week conference, accompanied by demonstrations and presentations by Marie Steiner. He also gave three lectures on the ideas underlying the Goetheanum building. Marie Steiner published these six lectures in 1928 and 1942, but so far they have not been included in the Complete Edition (GA) of Steiner's works.

There were several eurythmy performances, with introductory addresses.

The chief cycle of lectures, given over eight days, was entitled 'The Limits of Natural Science' (GA 322). Bursting the normal bounds of the 'scientific', Steiner showed how its limits can be overstepped. He spoke here of moral imagination, social issues, and the stages of higher knowledge. And here too he referred to Nietzsche as the contemporary symptom of a newly emergent capacity of human Inspiration.

During the whole School of Spiritual Science course, around 30 pupils of Steiner offered their own contributions, some of which were discussed and evaluated. It became apparent that the tenor of many of these talks did not yet correspond to the 'total artwork' of the building. The completed Goetheanum should have become a mirror that showed people their own intellectual one-sidedness and thus offered a means to educate those who spoke there. Like the laying of the foundation stone in 1913, the course was held during Michaelmas. And like the whole building itself, it aimed to respond to the time's urgent needs.

The opening address

It was a festive and one might even say holy moment in anthroposophy's development when Rudolf Steiner first spoke before an audience of around a thousand in the not yet finished Goetheanum. He stood at a lectern before the drawn curtain in the large domed hall. The intention eventually was for the viewer's gaze to fall upon the statue of Christ under the smaller cupola, but as yet this did not occupy its place in the East end of the building. In guided tours that took place during the conference, the small domed hall was of course opened.

Guenther Wachsmuth gives a striking picture of the expectant mood in the full hall:

> I have an unforgettable memory of the moment of expectancy as an organ and orchestra played a prelude. The serious and festive mood amongst around a thousand people gathered in this hall for the first time, the mighty, artistically sculpted columns rising organically into the sphere of the cupola's painted ceiling, the shimmering light streaming through the great, artistically shaped windows, laying its coloured brilliance upon this world of sculptural forms: it was a noble unity which, like a living being, seemed to absorb the expectant audience into it. All this was infused with a current of mutual receiving and giving that unfolded like a first life-giving breath between each person present and the enveloping building in this festive moment. And in this 'House of the Word', which gave expression in its sculpted forms to an inner connection between the spiritual power creatively at work in it and its outward embodiment, Rudolf Steiner now spoke to humankind for the first time.[65]

Steiner's own introductory words can best give an impression of this distinctive moment:

> My dear audience, it is with deep emotion and seriousness that I now speak these words, the first that will be dedicated to spiritual science in this hall. The mood is inevitably a serious one. The dire needs of our time underlie what we do here, along with everything negative in cultural life that has led to these dire conditions. Yet today I also perceive everything that has been done in these times by various souls inspired to cultivate a spiritual future for humanity, making it possible for this building in which we now begin our first School of Spiritual Science course to reach at least this initial stage of completion.

The core message: in view of the decline of civilization, we must now work towards a new union of art, science and religion.

Current developments have already contributed very greatly to the dissolution of these three realms. Art has become 'acosmic', religion 'atheistic' and science 'agnostic'. Specifically in this first address in the 'House of the Word', Steiner coined entirely new terms such as 'acosmic', to try to lead his audience away from all their old habits of thinking and speech. People, he said, must work towards a newly 'visioning art', a science of 'spiritual comprehension' and a new religion that 'experiences rebirth in the supersensible realm'.

The first School of Spiritual Science course, intended primarily for university students, who attended in good numbers, sought not only to show the limits of the traditional sciences but also how they could be overcome and how one-sided academic thinking can be enlivened. Lectures on the Goetheanum's architecture, on art, and the artistic presentations, also served this aim.

The idea was to show not only that anthroposophy is not in conflict with science but that it is capable of enriching a wide range of academic domains. Steiner hoped that his audience of young academics would come to see that 'lectures in academia must be drawn from *new, spiritual sources of research* in all the various disciplines, to engender a new spirit in science'. The 33 speakers included a practical businessman, since economic and social questions were also in need of a new direction inspired by spiritual science.

In 1918 there had been much interest in Oswald Spengler's work *The Decline of the West*. The new Goetheanum building was intended to be the locus of a new upward momentum. Steiner ended his address with the following words:

> It would run counter to the spirit of spiritual science to think in immodest terms. Yet true will springs only from true conviction, from conviction founded on true perception. It is therefore not perhaps immodest but simply something that flows from the powers naturally accruing from spiritual science if, in studying dire contemporary circumstances, and the currents of decline in our society that illumined minds have discerned, we see that we must counter

all that leads to the downfall of western civilization through a will infused with art, knowledge, inner religiosity and social commitment, so that a *new civilization can begin to develop*. For this reason, in modesty and yet at the same time with a conviction drawn from spiritual science itself, I would like to speak the following words to all those whom we are so glad to welcome here today, who wish to share in our work — words that express the spirit in which we wish to unite here:

> To turn towards the light
> In times of dark affliction,
> To send our inner gaze towards
> The dawning sun of spirit:
> Here let this be our human will
> And remain so evermore.

The journey from the everyday to the higher self

At the end of the conference Steiner reviewed the previous weeks, once more emphasizing in his 'words of farewell' why the plight of modern life required spiritual science and a new union of science, art and religion. It was necessary, he said, to see

> that humanity has reached a point in its development when, simply through the powers intrinsically driving this development, it is inevitable that mankind will prenetrate to far more conscious conditions in its religious feeling, its artistic work and its scientific endeavours than was previously the case.

The opening address and the words of farewell in which Steiner referred to the work of the other speakers have not so far been included in the Complete Works, nor have the three lectures on the Goetheanum building which Steiner gave during the conference, and which Marie Steiner published in 1942 under the title, 'The Idea Underlying the Dornach Building'. Those who have noticed the distinctive style and atmosphere of these lectures and addresses which Steiner gave on this occasion in the Goetheanum building itself, and thus in a place where he was quite literally 'at home', will feel the need to see all these lectures united in one volume. If this were to happen one could discern a unity of form and content, quite irrespective of whether this is more scientific, artistic or religious in nature, of a kind that testifies to the fact that they could only have been given in this building itself.

To end this chapter, therefore, I would like to highlight the fundamental idea underlying this new and unique building in humanity's history. In the first building phase in 1914, already, Steiner made clear in a lecture in Dornach that it would seek to be an image of world evolution as well as an awakener of the human being's soul-spiritual development. The double cupola was based on two circles, the larger of which comprises the auditorium, entered from the west. From this point, when the curtain was open, one's gaze would penetrate the circle of the smaller cupola at whose east end the statue of the Representative of Humanity was intended to stand. The large cupola was supported by seven columns whose architraves reflect the sevenfold planetary evolution of the earth, from which the human body and human soul were born. The small dome was supported by twelve columns, indicating the twelvefold zodiac which endures beyond all temporal evolution. It is in this sphere that the human I is rooted, our spiritual aspect. In consequence, the construction of the circle of each cupola was completely different: the large dome was based on the ordinary circle formed in relation to its central point, while that of the small dome is based on the circle of division. What is the difference? Steiner describes this as follows, first in relation to the circle of the large cupola:

> If one looks at the circle [...] one sees it is a very ordinary little fellow, quite banal really; and yet the circle has a mysterious quality. We can also understand it by taking two points, dividing them and then the circle arises by always obtaining the same results of division. Thus the circle is something very remarkable: the most ordinary form, easily surveyed and at the same time the outcome of an occult division, as we can become aware. The same is true of the human self: we have our ordinary self, our mundane daily existence; and then the higher self, much more mysterious, which rests in the depths of the soul and has to be sought by departing from ourselves

first of all and considering the world to which it relates. Just as the circle is the same whether it is the simplest form, quite ordinary and mundane on the one hand, or the result of the division of two points — we still obtain the same circle after all — so we have two things in one in ourselves: what belongs to everyday existence, is easily grasped; and then something we only understand if we depart from ourselves and enter the wider world, and then see this self in a sense as the most complex outcome of the great universal conflict in which Ahriman and Lucifer carry out the division process. In the face of this division, our higher self has the task, in seeking to come to expression, of maintaining itself as quotient.[66]

And now Rudolf Steiner applies what he says here to the human being entering the building:

After describing this double significance of the circle, you will be likely to ask this: If I enter the building from the west I feel myself encompassed by the circular structure and the spherical ceiling. This is simple to survey and is a reflection of the human self. But now I look towards the adjoining building, which is somewhat smaller, and I will not immediately understand it. One will have a sense of something mysterious. And this is due to the fact that it is also circular in form, but must now be pictured as the result of division, and as only outwardly identical with the other space. So we have a circle and a circle; but one is a circle adapted to daily existence while the other relates to the whole world. Just as we bear our lower, ordinary self in us, and a higher self, and just *as these are also in turn a unity*, so our building had to be a double structure. In its intrinsic form — not just symbolically — it expresses the two aspects of human nature. When the curtain is open we will sense in the building an image of the human being, not just as he exists in daily life but his *whole* being. The forms of the building, as we saw, express something like a movement from west to east, and *thus the passage of the ordinary self to the higher self comes to direct expression in this form.*

Visitors to the building could thus simultaneously experience the defined, limited earthly self they have become during world evolution, and also gain a view of the higher self, and the great mission of uniting with it in the course of our future evolution: both these in one and the same building!

We find a correspondence to this in the architecture of Steiner's verses, specifically in those for each week of the year. Here for instance is a verse from the Soul Calendar first published in 1912:

> I feel as if enchanted
> In shining World of Spirit-weaving
> It hath ensheathed my Selfhood
> Within the dulling senses
> To give to me the strength
> Which powerless is mine I to master
> Encased within its straitened bounds.

This is a verse that evokes the experience in the large domed hall. We can add to this its complementary verse which can lead us into an experience of the smaller cupola space:

> I feel the spell as lifted
> From Spirit-child in womb of Soul
> Within the heart's bright radiance
> The Holy World-Word has begot
> The heavenly fruit of Hope
> That grows with joy to cosmic distance
> From my own being's ground divine.[*]

The assassination at Sarajevo, which was to plunge humanity into the First World War, occurred on the same day that Steiner spoke of *this* aspect of the double cupola. As millions of people were dragged into the abyss of outward warfare, with great loss of life and devastation across much of Europe, Steiner was constructing a building in Dornach that could offer an experience of how, as befitted the times, humankind could undertake a journey from the ordinary, mundane self—in which all anti-social impulses were also rooted—towards the higher self.

---

[*]Both verses translated by Mabel M. Cotterell (*Calendar of the Soul*, Rudolf Steiner Publishing Co., London 1948).

17. Comrades-in-Arms in the West

The First World War was not 'incited' or even caused by the central European powers as many believe and as, just a hundred years after it began, is again being trumpeted across the globe. Rather it was something that had long been envisaged and planned by western secret societies. Such brotherhoods are guided by an overriding impulse: a conviction founded on common egotism that the world must bear the stamp of Anglo-American interests for centuries to come. To achieve this, central Europe was politically marginalized and the Slavic East, where the sixth cultural epoch is to unfold from the year 3573, had to become a target of influence. In this region a large-scale 'socialist experiment' was carried out for 70 years; and without the First World War such experiments in eastern Europe could never have become reality. Decades before the First World War began, these secret societies were planning and intending this.

To find confirmation of this one need only read what C.H. Harrison wrote in 1893 in his book *The Transcendental Universe*. According to this author, western interests with a strong economic orientation were and are battling for global dominion. Or one can study a brief account by Steiner entitled 'Battle for the Core of Russian Culture' which was first published in the journal *Der Europäer* in March 1999. This account is a kind of essence of the utterances made by Steiner during the First World War in his historical observations[67] on the vested interests of western brotherhoods, and their resulting actions.

The Anglo-American West was therefore inevitably and increasingly opposed to the *universal impulse* of spiritual science, and this opposition was further intensified by the fact that there were people in the English-speaking West who were capable of supporting and cultivating this universal impulse.

One such figure, Daniel Nicol Dunlop, encountered Rudolf

Steiner in England in April 1922. The first moments of this meeting, as well as Steiner's farewell from Dunlop in August 1924, testify to the extraordinary nature of their connection.

The first meeting took place in London. Steiner scarcely spoke English and Dunlop next to no German, so they needed an interpreter. This was the prosperous Dutch textile businessman and later timber trader Joseph van Leer, a patron of important anthroposophical activities. For instance, he funded publication of the 'Austrian Messenger' periodical, for which Ludwig Polzer-Hoditz was responsible, and the West-East conference in Vienna which took place at Whitsun 1922. In the USA he founded a branch of Weleda, as D.N. Dunlop intended doing in Great Britain.

Steiner and Dunlop sat a table whose tablecloth hung down from the sides. Van Leer began to speak to introduce the two people to each other. But unnoticed by him, Steiner reached under the tablecloth, took Dunlop's hand, and held it in his for several minutes.

Since his time in Dublin and his intense preoccupation with the works of H.P. Blavatsky, whom he did not know in person, Dunlop had wanted to meet a real master, a modern initiate. This wish had long remained unfulfilled since neither Annie Besant, Charles Leadbeater nor any other leading figure in theosophical circles came anywhere near his conception of a modern initiate. At the time of his meeting with Steiner he held a leading position in British business. He was director of BEAMA, an umbrella organization of the British electricity industry. Besides his demanding professional obligations he cultivated theosophical activities of various types. He had started and organized regular theosophical summer schools and before the First World War he edited the important journal *The Path*, and was director of the Blavatsky Institute near Manchester. During the war he was active in the Light on the Path Lodge with Mabel Collins.

He had caught a glimpse of Steiner as long ago as 1905 or 1906 at a theosophical conference in Paris, and the impression of him remained unforgettable. He invited Baron Walleen to give a talk on Steiner and his Christology in the Light on the Path Lodge, and during the war he began to study his books. But he was not someone who quickly fell under the spell of a personality, still less so after his repeated and painful experiences with the personality cult in the theosophical movement. He reserved 'final judgement' about Steiner for the moment of their actual meeting, in accordance with the good old British motto 'the proof of the pudding is in the eating'. On that day in April he saw for himself what he was seeking, as the elderly Simeon had once seen in the temple the person he had so long sought. The difference here was that Dunlop still had a couple of years left to collaborate energetically in the great work.

The most apparent fruit of the encounter was the organizing of summer schools at Penmaenmawr and Torquay which, in Steiner's words, were inscribed in the 'golden book of the anthroposophical movement'. Dunlop was familiar with both locations through the planning of previous summer schools. They gave Steiner new insights into this western Celtic region and its spiritual atmosphere. During the course in Penmaenmawr, for instance, he stated that it was easier to grasp hold of imaginations in this region. It was not by chance therefore that the karma between Ita Wegman and Rudolf Steiner was 'fully revealed' in this particular area. And here too the question of a new mystery medicine was born in her. One fruit of these days was the medical work Steiner undertook with Wegman, as recorded for instance in the little volume *Fundamentals of Therapy* (GA 27).

The conference in Torquay gave Rudolf Steiner the chance to visit the nearby Arthurian centre at Tintagel, where he spoke of Richard Wagner's connection with Merlin and was able to bring to some conclusion his research into the karma of the painter Arnold Boecklin.

It was not accidental that both courses dealt with the theme of developments in initiation through the ages. It was clear that Steiner enjoyed being able to lecture in such places and at such well-organized events. It was as if he breathed more freely here than elsewhere because there was a person present who knew how to bring these conferences to fruition: someone who was there to help and not to ask for help. This could only be a person who had already undergone esoteric spiritual development in a fully self-reliant way, which, in Steiner's eyes, enabled him to have his own spiritual pupils. Eleanor Merry had become acquainted with Dunlop a few months before the latter met Steiner; and when, on meeting Steiner soon afterwards she asked him for a meditation, he said to her: 'But you met Mr Dunlop first.'[68]

Thus, in his view, she needed no additional instruction. He even added this: 'Make as firm a bond as you can with him. He was connected with all ancient mysteries.' And on another occasion he indicated to her that Dunlop had been active in an 'inner circle' of the Templar Order.

In 1923, Steiner remarked to Ita Wegman that Dunlop possessed ancient western esoteric knowledge and was the right person to lead the Society in England. 'Ancient western knowledge' refers to Saturn mysteries as these lived on in native American traditions in North America. It does seem that Dunlop had a connection with these mysteries from a former incarnation. Friends described their impressions of him in terms of an 'Indian medicine man' with a great fund of healing knowledge. It is surely not accidental that he was committed to getting the book on medicine by Steiner and Wegman translated into English, and oversaw the founding of the British branch of Weleda. On several occasions when Wegman stayed in London he also studied *Towards Social Renewal* with her.

Shortly before the summer school in Torquay Dunlop had reached the apex of his professional career. On 30 June 1924, the Prince of Wales opened the first World Power Conference in London, initiated and organized by Dunlop. It was the first post-war gathering to try to survey and make purposeful use of international energy resources without the sway of vested national interests. In the following years further such conferences were held. An international economic conference was planned for 1936 but this did not happen because of Dunlop's death on 30 May 1935. The organization he instituted remains the leading (and only non-governmental) body for collecting and coordinating global data in the field of energy resources. It is now called the World Energy Council. Its website refers to its founder Dunlop as a 'Scottish visionary'.

Dunlop had an international outlook in relation to economics and this informed his thinking, planning and—in so far as circumstances allowed—his actions. Similarly he had an international perspective when it came to developing the activities of the Anthroposophical Society. Here he supported and cultivated everything that deserved it, rather like a gardener whose green fingers can make even frail shoots flourish. He almost stopped giving lectures himself, stopped writing his own books and articles, and instead tried to help others find their proper realm of work. In this respect anthroposophy made him into a real genius of social benevolence. In 1928 he launched the first anthroposophical world conference in London, which to this day remains unique in anthroposophical history. The plan for it was discussed with Rudolf Steiner back in the autumn of 1922, and the latter recommended holding such conferences every few years in all the great cities of the world. The list of contributors is, to an astonishing degree, a compendious list of central European anthroposophists, ranging from Friedrich Rittelmeyer, the agriculturalist Alexander Mirbt (Later Mier) through to Walter Johannes Stein and Eugen Kolisko. The two latter both emigrated to England a few years later, in a sense going into exile, and became close collaborators with Dunlop. Karl Koenig was also one of the speakers on the list, and later described the conference as a 'quietly resonating motif' that was influential in his founding of the Camphill movement ten years later.

*

Despite these and many other anthroposophical activities, Dunlop did not for a minute lose sight of the fact that there were and would continue to be great and growing obstacles to the spread of anthroposophy in the West. It was all the more important therefore that in the West particularly anthroposophy should develop and be presented to the world in a *pure*, open-minded and cosmopolitan form. Dunlop knew that opposition to anthroposophy ultimately originated with actual beings, specifically Ahriman. He himself once put it like this:

> Ahriman knows the strength of his weapons; he knows the stupefaction which the senses have brought about in the spiritual life of man; he works consciously in the fear human beings have in face of concrete spiritual revelation. We should realize that the opposition to spiritual science is only just beginning; it will grow stronger and more insidious … Therefore for us there must be no compromise with materialism in whatever form it may be; we have to assert a wisdom that is 'not of this world' and therefore in its pure form inaccessible to the darts of Ahriman.[69]

These words show Dunlop to be fully cognizant of spiritual hindrances to the spread of spiritual science. The brotherhoods described earlier were *one* vehicle for this opposition. However, Dunlop was also aware of their originally benevolent and universally human intent, as we can see from his lecture, 'The Masonic Examination' which he gave at the Blavatsky Institute in 1912.[70]

Following the summer course in Torquay and several lectures in London, Steiner took his leave of Dunlop at Victoria Station at the end of August 1924. This farewell is no less distinctive and illuminating than their first meeting. According to George Adams-Kaufmann, who acted as interpreter for most of Steiner's lectures in England, Steiner said as they parted, 'We are brothers.' One gains the sense that they were comrades-in-arms in the battle to further the impulses of the Michael age.

*

Originally a Scot, Dunlop loved Walt Whitman and Emerson, having lived for a while in the USA, and was a friend of the poets W.B. Yeats and George William Russell ('AE'). He felt a strong connection therefore with the best elements of the Anglo-American West, but at the same time central Europe was very dear to his heart. In the early twentieth century he once took a trip through Thuringia, and in the account he wrote of it offered a kind of survey of European mystics such as Meister Eckhart and Wolfram von Eschenbach. His interest in the character of central Europe was deepened through his relationship to anthroposophy, and not least of course also through his encounters with Steiner or some of his pupils such as W.J. Stein and Ludwig Polzer-Hoditz.

A comment by D.N. Dunlop about the German nation stands in sharp contrast to all partisan interests such as those living in the brotherhoods described earlier, and testifies to his profound understanding of this people's true mission. He said: 'The German nation stands amidst other nations as the I stands at the centre of the soul.' We will later return to this comment.

*

At this point let us turn to a further milestone in Rudolf Steiner's development. It fell in May 1922, one month after his first meeting with Dunlop in London, and occurred in Germany. It shows us that many Germans had themselves completely lost sight of the real nature of German culture as this lived in the soul of the British Dunlop.

18. A Light in the Darkness of German Nationalism

On 9 November 1918 the old empire lay in ruins. On that evening Steiner had given a clear-eyed account of the new situation, and organized the premiere of Fercher von Steinwand's 'Chorus of Primordial Dreams' (see chapter 15). Drawing on these 'primordial dreams' by one of the greatest poets and thinkers in the German language would, he believed, offer new reflections on the true nature of Germany.

In Fercher's poem 'Awakening Call' he writes:

> Blindness and confusion cease
> Where the spirit starts to rise.

Since the day of defeat, Rudolf Steiner's efforts had been focused on finding new forms in which this spirit could make headway. In the spring of 1922 the same spirit led him through German cities, on one of the two biggest lecture tours of his life. The tour was organized by the Wolff and Sachs concert agency, and began in January already with public lectures in 12 German cities. The second cycle began in May, on the theme of 'Anthroposophy and Spiritual Cognition'. Munich was one of the places where he lectured. In both tours Steiner spoke on one and the same theme — unusually for him, and by no means making his task easier since in every city his talks met with a different spiritual atmosphere. The one in Munich had a particularly antagonistic charge. Nationalist groups had planned to disrupt Steiner's lecture, and there was the possibility of an assassination attempt. The lecture took place on 15 May in the Four Seasons Hotel where Steiner was staying.

Hans Buechenbacher, a former army officer and at that time the director of the Munich branch of the AS, considered the danger a serious one, and took corresponding security precautions. He was aware of the fact that Steiner figured as number 8 or 9 on a list of targeted individuals, alongside Walther Rathenau who was later murdered in June 1922. He told his teacher this in Stuttgart before he arrived in Munich, at which Steiner asked in a friendly tone, 'I see, so you think they want to bump me off?' When Buechenbacher replied that this was so, Steiner calmly responded, 'I'm sure you're right.' In Dornach too the potential danger had been discussed. Edith Maryon, who was helping Steiner complete work on the 'Representative of Humanity' sculpture, cautioned Steiner of the danger in a letter, specifically warning him about Munich.

Since only inadequate police protection was available, Buechenbacher organized a group of boxers and wrestlers, and also put together a bodyguard of ten anthroposophists, posting the latter at strategic points such as the lighting control room and the stair entrance. As well as Buechenbacher himself, the body-guard consisted of Eugen Kolisko, Herbert Hahn, Hermann Beckh, Ludwig Noll and the young Andreas Grunelius. Before the lecture began the latter saw that the speaker's lectern was badly lit. He installed a simple lamp and connected it to a separate electrical point in the green room.

The lecture was sold out. Herbert Hahn reported that Rudolf Steiner himself seemed to 'find it hard to speak, as if he had to wrestle his way through something with great effort'.[71]

But things seemed to be going so well that the guards in charge of the hall lighting crept into the hall after a while so as to hear better. Suddenly the lights went out. 'Those who planned the attack had helpers who gained entry to the lighting control room.' Only the lamp at the lectern continued to shine. 'The mood in the dark hall was impenetrable,' said Hahn. 'In retro-spect it seems to me that most people were merely alarmed and anxious, but one could also sense a heavy, ominous element.' Steiner did not pause for a moment:

In a carefully enunciating voice he calmly continued to speak. And this complete self-possession clearly nonplussed the attackers in the hall and kept them in check. No one moved. He spoke powerfully in the purest sense, and with inner conviction. He spoke of the spirit and his voice had a wonderful, resonant timbre, like a bell. Speaking each word clearly, he said: 'And so the spiritual researcher knows the spirit. But he who knows the spirit also safeguards and protects it.'

What a picture! Rudolf Steiner in a spirit-obscured atmosphere and in physical darkness, illumined by the light of a small lamp beside him and speaking most tranquilly of the spirit!

The next moment the light in the hall came on again. The guards had gone back to their posts and set things to rights. After a tumult of applause, Steiner continued his lecture to the end. But in the middle of the final applause the attack proper began, with a real fight breaking out in the hall. The lectern was stormed. 'But members threw themselves around Rudolf Steiner like a living wall.' He was able to reach the green room without hindrance, and from there his hotel room. Hahn and the others prevented anyone pursuing him by closing the door to the green room and 'using all our strength to keep it shut as others in the hall tried to force it open'. Eventually the official forces of law and order succeeded in escorting the attackers from the hall.

After the lecture demonstrators marched through Maximilian Strasse singing the war song 'We will prevail and vanquish France'.

The same night Steiner asked Grunelius to send a telegram to Edith Maryon which stated: 'Survived Munich — Steiner.'

Astonishingly, a report by a special correspondent, with the headline 'Riot at Munich Lecture', written in an almost derisory tone, appeared in the *New York Times* just two days after the incident. Steiner's public activities were clearly being followed closely on the other side of the Atlantic — for what motive is another question.

'The demon's grimace'

Where this riotous opposition originated became clear in, among other things, a report published 12 days later, on 27 May, in the

Völkischer Beobachter ('People's Observer'), an organ of the Nazi party that had been founded in February 1920 in Munich. The anonymous writer stated:

> It is a waste of ink to spare serious words on such an anti-German charlatan. But one's hair stands on end to think that this man was able, unhindered, to give a lecture in Munich last week without any intervention from the government. Or is it possible that, even if it had wanted to put a stop to this national pest, the Bavarian government had its hands tied by familial relations with a certain Herr Otto von Lerchenfeld [whose uncle was a Bavarian MP], a co-founder of the anthroposophical joint stock company 'Der kommende Tag'? That would hardly surprise us, since the Foreign Office in Berlin also boasts a whole number of Steiner's worshippers and patrons.

The *Völkischer Beobachter* goes on to describe the aims of Steiner's spiritual science as follows:

> Mr Steiner's doctrine has aims almost identical with those of all enemies of our national and state independence. It is just that he calls it by a different name. Under the names 'anthroposophy' and 'threefold social order' he pursues his dark intent. He has access to millions of Deutsch Marks to help corrupt our nation with his teachings, and this far-reaching influence has made him a danger to our current and future progress. As far as I am concerned, Mr Steiner can go and spread his poison in some other country — in Dornach near Basel for instance, where he has erected his temple, and sullied the name of our Goethe in so doing.

Munich, the same place that had once refused permission for the Goetheanum to be built, thus pursued him with these tirades. The hate-filled dismissal of his spiritual message in the Bavarian capital did not bode well for the future destiny of Germany.

Herbert Hahn also experienced something of the dark storm brewing at this key moment. The members who had accompanied Steiner to Munich travelled with him back to Stuttgart, from where he drove on to his next lecture in Mannheim. Hahn reports:

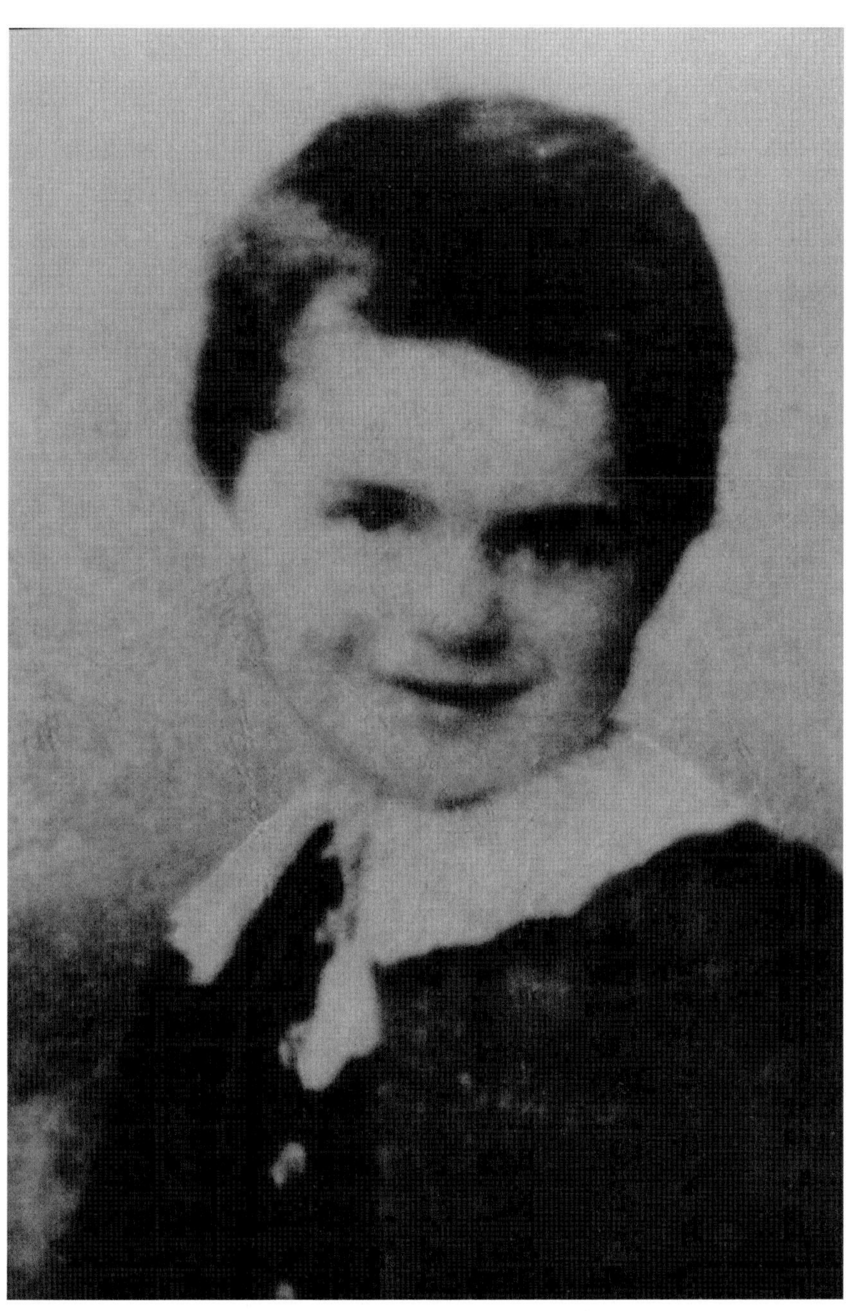

Rudolf Steiner as a child

Rudolf Steiner's death mask (Perseus Verlag Archive)

As we took our leave there from Rudolf Steiner, he continued to look at us for a long time from the carriage window. I will never forget the expression on his face, which conveyed much that cannot be put into words. One could discern what he had intentionally avoided expressing aloud: Never forget this moment—it was more incisive and of graver consequence than you can realize at present! Over a decade later I began to understand what had occurred. On that evening, as if through a cleft, we had glimpsed the grimace of a demon who was later to bring nameless obscurity and endless misery over central Europe.

*

Rudolf Steiner never again set foot in Munich. On 9 November 1923, his abysmal adversary marched on Munich's Feldherrn-halle ['Commander's Hall'] with a troop of fanatic supporters. His rise as a speaker was associated with his rage against the 'shreds' of the Versailles Treaty. Here it can only be mentioned in passing that this power from the abyss drew support from the same western circles we referred to earlier. A growing oblivion to the spirit and hatred for it had lured the demon from the depths, and yet his work of destruction would not have been possible without the help of the West. As representative of other literature on the subject, let me cite here the pioneering work by American economist and academic Antony Sutton, entitled *Wall Street and the Rise of Hitler*. The German spirit only began to suppress and extinguish *itself* after the German nation had been marginalized with outside aid. The first signs of this growing tendency became apparent in Munich.

'Fercher, leader of the Germans' White Lodge'

A little known and yet reliably reported event must be included in our picture of these key moments in Munich, and I will describe it briefly now to end this chapter. Heten Wilkens, for many years the General Secretary of the Anthroposophical Society in Germany, reported in an article in the periodical *Die Drei* that, after tumult broke out in the hall, it was 'possible to conduct Steiner through a dark passage to a side street at the rear of the building'. As he was being led along this passage, he

> calmly spoke a few sentences about Fercher von Steinwand. Those accompanying him, younger members of the Society, could make nothing of the name. One of them later recalled Steiner saying, 'Fercher, this leader of the Germans' White Lodge.'

Thus the name Fercher von Steinwand emerges at the very moment of the attack upon Steiner. This is of great significance. On 9 November 1918, Steiner had spoken of Fercher in relation to the destiny of Germany. And now, at the darkest moment of Steiner's work as the guardian of true German culture, the name of Fercher is uttered just as the latter seems about to be trampled underfoot and consigned to the abyss.

Fercher von Steinwand was aware like few others of the spiritual, cosmopolitan mission of the essential Germany. A qualified astronomer among other things, the lofty constellations of German culture were inscribed in his poet's heart, and he had intimations of much that lay in the future destiny of this people. In a lecture he gave to the King of Saxony and a selected audience in 1859, he expressed some aspects of his prophetic vision. He spoke about the gypsies, but then, at the end of the lecture, transposed what he had said of them to the whole German nation as a prophetic warning of its future. He foresaw the danger of this nation forgetting its mission towards all humanity and succumbing to spiritual degeneration. It is surprising that Fercher's genius cast its light upon Steiner's soul at this dark hour in Munich, and it speaks volumes about this individuality's inner connection with the real aims of Germanhood. That Steiner saw in Fercher the 'leader of the Germans' White Lodge' is no less surprising, for he had never previously spoken of such a 'White Lodge'. We will return to this phrase, and the question connected with it, at the end of this monograph (see p. [198ff.]).

19. The West-East Congress in Vienna: the Adversaries Take up Arms

If, in passing from this spiritual presence of Fercher von Steinwand in Munich we now look towards Vienna, we find ourselves on the originating ground of Rudolf Steiner's work and the place where, exactly 33 years earlier, he had made the inestimable acquaintance of Fercher and won his friendship.

Like the Munich Congress of 1907, the West-East Congress also took place at Whitsun. There are many accounts of this event, but here I wish only to trace, once again, certain threads in Rudolf Steiner's creative work. In a sense it was the high point of his public activities, He was speaking to an audience of around two thousand. His evening lectures were published in volume 83 of the Collected Works (GA) as *West and East, Contrasting Worlds*. Ludwig Polzer-Hoditz was responsible for preparing and organizing the conference, along with Joseph van Leer and Eugen Kolisko.

The whole building belonging to Vienna's *Musikverein* was rented for the occasion. Steiner and his wife stayed in the nearby Hotel Imperial, in which one can still find the café frequented by Friedrich Eckstein, an important figure and friend of Steiner's youth. Richard Wagner had also stopped at this hotel and — many years afterwards — Hitler would stay there too.

On 1 June Polzer gave the opening address — a high point in his own life. Once again numerous students and pupils of Steiner spoke about a range of different disciplines as illumined by anthroposophy. There were also musical offerings and recitation. On 9 June Fercher von Steinwand's 'Cosmic Choruses' were recited to eurythmy. In general the Viennese press reviewed the event favourably.

Marie Steiner highlighted the special nature of this congress:

It was as if this home ground radiated welcoming powers to him, in joy and admiring acknowledgement of what one person has accomplished, which the whole nation of Austria has been unable to achieve: to overcome the standpoint of warring nationalities and, resolving these problems out of the spirit, embody a full, all-embracing humanity. Public recognition of Rudolf Steiner's importance became apparent during this congress. When he entered the large auditorium, which was full to overflowing, all stood up from their seats and accompanied his coming and going with thunderous, serious, deeply respectful applause lasting for several minutes. [...] There was a Palm Sunday mood infusing these days.[72]

Gladys Mayer, an English painter who, despite her lack of knowledge of German, took part in the congress on the recommendation of George Adams, was all the more open to observations of a moral–visual nature and made several sketches of Steiner. She found that 'The power of his gestures was so mighty that it could only have emerged from utter authenticity and the full dedication of his own person to the huge importance of the task assigned him.' Mayer gained a lasting sense

> of Rudolf Steiner, one since increasingly confirmed, that here was a man with a global mission that would only be fully revealed in future centuries [...] I was told that at this time Rudolf Steiner was at the height of his powers as a lecturer. And one could feel that the earth's future was here at stake.[73]

The adversaries take up arms

In his last evening lecture Steiner spoke of his efforts to kindle understanding of the threefold social organism, tracing the course of events from the date when *Towards Social Renewal* appeared to the current day. He spoke about the need to overcome the omnipotence of the 'centralized state', and concluded with the following words:

> Only when people see that a social organism structured along threefold lines is needed if we are to bring about freedom, equality and fraternity will it be possible to shape social concerns in the right way. Then our present time can properly respond to demands in the

> eighteenth century for freedom, equality and fraternity by saying:
> Freedom in spiritual and cultural life, equality in the life of rights
> and state, and fraternity in economic life. This will accomplish much
> in relation to the social question, and it will be possible to delineate
> how the three domains in the social organism, arising in freedom,
> equality and fraternity, can interact with each other to heal today's
> chaotic cultural, legislative and economic conditions.

This was to be Rudolf Steiner's last public lecture on three-folding.

Steiner was insistent that the successful congress should lead to follow-up work, but no such activities arose except the founding of a bi-weekly journal to which Steiner gave the name 'Anthroposophy—Austrian Messenger from Human Spirit to Human Spirit'. This was the initiative of Ludwig Polzer, and Steiner made regular contributions to it, initially in the form of a series of West-East aphorisms

But already new stormclouds were gathering over Austria. Following the 'Palm Sunday mood', Marie Steiner said that an 'organized counter-attack' was 'arming itself for renewed conflict'.

When Steiner left Munich, Nazism was gaining ground and this spark also later caught in Austria. When so little further work was undertaken by anthroposophists following the very successful congress, in Vienna the void was filled by a man who had absolutely no understanding of the need for social three-folding. His Austrian-Japanese descent gave him the appearance of cosmopolitanism, but his thinking could not get beyond the construct of a centralized state. In his head a Kantian, in his heart a Catholic and in his will an agent of *political* Freemasony, he was a member of the Austrian Humanitas Lodge. This man was called Richard Coudenhove-Kalergi. On 17 November 1922—the anniversary of the founding of the Theosophical Society—a 'Proposal' by him for a Pan-Europe appeared in Vienna's *Neue Freie Presse*, and excited much interest. Ludwig Polzer immediately responded in his journal by outlining this proposal's complete inadequacy. But in vain. The adversaries were on the move, and by 1924 Coudenhove was able to found his Pan-Europe movement, which Churchill later promoted and controlled, and which threw the luke-warm water of conventional, formulaic pseudo-social ideas on the fire of a really new social impulse.

After the very hopeful congress, Ludwig Polzer wrote: 'The adversaries of spiritual renewal drew their own consequences. They saw something emerging that could pose a threat to them, and in Austria, in particular, were intent this should not happen.' Coudenhove was exactly the right man to oppose Steiner's impulses of renewal.

*

A week before Coudenhove's Pan-Europe proposal was published, the Hamburg pupil of Steiner, Dr Max Kaendler — who was also a Freemason in a lodge with scarcely any political orientation — wrote to Steiner (in a letter dated 7 November 1922) to say he had heard that 'the regional Grand Master in Berlin has issued "word" against you to the Provincial Grand Master. In particular it seems he objects to rituals that he says are no longer reconcilable with Freemasonry.'

To issue 'word' against someone means, in the language of Freemasonry, that a person is declared an outlaw because he is hindering certain aims. The 'rituals' referred to no doubt relate to those instituted by Steiner in the autumn of 1922 when he founded the Christian Community in Dornach.

Clearly Kaendler wanted to warn Steiner and protect him, and asked him whether he should undertake to meet the Provincial Grand Master in Hamburg with another anthroposophical Freemason to discuss this. No reply from Steiner is extant, but he always distinguished rigorously between Freemasonry of a harmless, non-political kind and other lodges run for more egotistic reasons. The fact that 'word' was issued against Steiner by a 'benevolent' lodge shows either the decadent character of the lodge to which Kaendler belonged or a passing merger, at least, between the two types of Freemason groups. Though it is hard to settle this question, Kaendler's letter is an important testament to a concealed campaign by Freemasonry against Steiner behind the scenes of more blatant opposition such as that in Munich. It is the only document known to us which indicates opposition *from this quarter*, whereas clerical attacks were far more open.

Predictions of the Goetheanum fire

A seemingly unimportant scene that took place during the West-East Congress, and was later echoed in Dornach, shows that Steiner himself had no illusions whatever about growing opposition to him. Julie Klima, a pupil from Prague, who possessed certain clairvoyant powers, travelled to Dornach with her husband and daughter two months after the Vienna congress. Rudolf Steiner led them into his studio, as he did many visitors, and showed them the figure of Christ he was working on:

> After a while he said, pointing to the sculpture: 'That is how I see him, as he walked amongst us.' Then, on a board, he showed us the head of Ahriman which he had modelled, saying: 'He had to sit for this. He didn't want to, but he had to.' I asked the Master why the fingers of Christ's hand were so curiously divided, and with visible pleasure he replied, lifting both his own hands in the same way: 'This is how Jewish initiates gave their blessing.'
>
> As we took our leave, the Master turned to my husband and asked whether he had nothing further to ask? We looked at each other and did not know what to say. And again the Master turned to me and asked, insistently: 'Is there nothing more you wish to ask?'

Only later did the veils fall from Julie Klima's gaze:

> Now I know what I should have asked him. At the West-East Congress the Master was sitting very close to me. Although I had never yet seen the Goetheanum, during my teacher's lecture I suddenly saw one of its columns veiled in thick smoke. After this experience I saw the Master's gaze fixed upon mine. Now I had asked nothing. This tragedy still weighs heavily on my soul.[74]

There is another clear pre-vision of the fire reported by Anna Samweber, Marie and Rudolf Steiner's Berlin secretary. Worried that she could not visit the building, which she had never yet seen, for financial reasons, she said to Steiner, who reassured her she could visit at Easter: ' "If I cannot come at Christmas time, I will never see the building. It will burn down and no longer be there at Easter." Herr Doktor looked at me in surprise, did not remark on what I had said but again reassured me I might come at Easter.'[75]

Edouard Schuré's night-time experience

A further presentiment of coming disaster should be mentioned here also, and comes from the pen of Edouard Schuré, who has figured frequently in this volume. After a self-inflicted estrangement from Rudolf Steiner and his wife during the war, he came to Dornach for the first time in September 1922 where Steiner was giving the 'French Course', which later formed the basis for his book *Philosophy, Cosmology and Religion* (GA 215).

Camille Schneider, who wrote a monograph on Edouard Schuré and his meetings with Richard Wagner and Rudolf Steiner, reported what Schuré told him:

> I saw a plant growing with a double blossom. It seemed that this plant was standing upon a building that I clearly recognized as the Goetheanum. The two flowers touched each other closely, but were however different in kind: one seemed hardened and was the colour of wood while the other was delicate, almost etheric, its blue colour finely grading into red. Both blossoms grew quickly, opened into the infinite and suddenly vanished, leaving a deep opening in the earth. Around the opening I recognized Europe. I woke up with a sense that the rapid upward sprouting of the plant into the infinite would leave a hole in Europe that the latter could not fill. The following day I read in the newspapers that the Goetheanum had burned down.[76]

20. The Night of the Fire

New Year's Day 1923 fell on a Sunday. On Christmas Eve Steiner had embarked on a course of scientific lectures, dealing with the 'Origins of Natural Science' (GA 326). On 31 December at 5 p.m. a eurythmy performance took place in the Goetheanum to accompany a recitation of the 'Prologue in Heaven' from Goethe's *Faust*. In the evening Steiner gave a lecture on general anthroposophical themes, towards the end of which he described the nature of a modern, thought-imbued act of worship culminating in a spiritual communion. He recalled his book on Goethe's world-view (GA 2) where he described thinking as the 'reality of the world'. (And in his very first work, 'An Introduction to Goethe's Scientific Writings' (GA 1)[*] we find the important sentence, 'Perceiving the idea in reality is the human being's true communion.') In this last lecture of the whole year of 1922, therefore, Steiner points back to his earliest philosophical beginnings. The day before this he had spoken about certain problems arising in the Christian Community, founded in the autumn of 1922, for which, at the request of the priests, he had initiated a distinctive rite and act of worship. The *knowledge-*informed cultus he pointed to on New Year's Eve was therefore foundational in *his own* development and that of anthroposophy. In his actual words: 'Thus spiritual knowledge and perception is a true communion, the beginning of a cosmic cultus appropriate for humanity today.'

This was the last lecture Rudolf Steiner gave in the new Goetheanum building. A short time after the lecture ended, smoke was seen in the White Room, the place where the Christian Community had been founded. The alarm is sounded and members rush to the building. The architect Ernst Aisenpreis

---

[*] *Nature's Open Secret*, Anthroposophic Press 2000.

hurries with the site foreman Max Schleutermann to the room on the upper floor of the south wing. Schleutermann is overcome by smoke. As Rudolf Steiner arrives, Schleutermann is lying unconscious in front of the south entrance. Steiner attends to him until he is out of danger, and then takes part in the painstaking search of the building to discover the source of the fire. All electricity fuses are intact and there has been no short circuit. The fire has been laid behind a partition wall. To locate it a wooden wall is knocked through, but this lets in a flow of air that fans the flames. I have intentionally described these events in the present tense, and their sequence is important as we will see below.

Musical instruments and stage items were saved from the flames. At an instruction from Steiner that the joinery workshop should be protected from the fire, the same Andreas Grunelius who had rigged up a lamp at the lectern in Munich (see chapter 18) climbed up on the roof of the workshop and spent hours spraying the tarred roofing felt despite increasing heat from the fire. In this way the sculpture of the Representative of Humanity in the studio was saved and was initially carried outside into the open air. Around midnight a ghastly and beautiful scenario unfolded. In Grunelius's words, as he stood on the roof he saw

> ... both cupolas collapsing together around midnight, revealing the burning columns; I saw wreaths of flame winding and dancing around the capitals ... From my position on the roof I had a direct impression of the living elements of this double circle of columns upon which the cupolas had been resting. This showed me the archetype of sustaining strength that underpinned the whole building, and was now streaming out into the cosmos in a sea of flame.[77]

Many stood and watched the shocking drama in silence. People from the nearby village also gathered to watch, among them a ten-year-old girl who observed Rudolf Steiner standing there quite still. The girl suddenly felt great compassion for this dear man who had always smiled in so friendly a way and had often given the children sweets as they passed by. Now he was suffering such pain. Fifty years later she could still vividly recall the painful sympathy she had felt for him.[78]

Ita Wegman was also standing by his side that night. Vague memories rose in her then of another fire long ago at Ephesus. Only a few words passed between them. 'This is terrible for us,' she said. 'Yes,' he replied, 'now everything is inscribed in the cosmic ether.'[79]

> In these hours the decision ripened in her to serve his task utterly.
>
> Marie Steiner was suffering from a leg condition which kept her at home, and consequently she had to observe the tragedy from the distance of Villa Hansi.

Gethsemane

Somewhat later, in the early hours of the morning, 23-year-old Ehrenfried Pfeiffer encountered Rudolf Steiner in the eurythmy building where Edith Maryon lived. Exhausted, he had gone to rest there. What now occurred between the teacher and his pupil is one of the deepest mystery scenes of Rudolf Steiner's life. Pfeiffer only hints gently at it in the memoirs which he recorded for his friend Lexie Ahrens:

> The thousands of people wandering around the fire and the ruined building looked like ants whose ant-heap has been disturbed. The crowd regarded R. St. as the great teacher of spiritual wisdom, the creator of new arts, the esoteric teacher or initiate [...]. No one seemed to recognize that he was also a *human being* capable of suffering, of feeling, someone with a heart who might need comforting at this moment of greatest despair, whose heart had been broken during this night. In these hours I saw and experienced the human being R. St., and added myself to this small group (R. St., Miss Maryon). *The few words which the Master spoke expressed this great suffering and sorrow, and the young man spoke consoling words to him.*[80]

Pfeiffer had perceived Steiner *the man* on a previous occasion, during a lecture to workers in a Stuttgart tavern, in fierce heat. Drinks were given to everyone except Steiner himself. Pfeiffer noticed this and brought him a drink. And now, on the night of the fire he once again saw Steiner the human being:

> The pupil perceived the spiritual loneliness of a great man, and in his heart rose a solemn vow never to leave his Master — neither his work nor the *human being* accomplishing it, and especially not the latter. This forged a link that still holds strong today and will remain active through all future eternity.

It is clear that Pfeiffer is struggling for words here and is para-phrasing. He continues: 'When it became apparent that there was nothing left apart from the smouldering ruins, R. St. with-drew, exhausted and broken, into a nearby building, and appeared again shortly before dawn.' And now he formulates the core of what he has experienced and has been struggling to express:

> And so it happened that this young man once again spoke to the *man* R. St., guided by an inner voice and the sympathy that enabled him to find the right, insistent words to encourage him and to point to what this moment required. The man R. St. was broken: his heart had received a fatal blow and his physical strength was failing. Miss Maryon, also a witness of these events, never recovered from the shock, fell ill and died a few months later [on 2 May 1924].

Pfeiffer does not describe more clearly what would perhaps have happened if the initiate had remained in this state for longer than just minutes — for hours perhaps or days. It is unlikely he would have recovered from this blow. The hope, and perhaps even the calculated aim of the dark agents of the arson would have been fulfilled. But it was not to be. 'Guided by an inner voice', a person appears at the moment of greatest frailty and finds just the right words that help Steiner to recover.

I will place Pfeiffer's next words in italics to emphasize their great significance, which consists precisely of what they do *not* say: '*The words which were exchanged must be veiled in silence, for they belong to the most intimate things one can experience when a great soul discloses itself.*' And he ends thus:

But the outcome was that R. St., by a superhuman exertion, succeeded in carrying on, showing no weakness when he appeared again before members in the usual surroundings. He continued his work; and the next evening gave a long lecture. It was spiritually and physically important that the continuity of work was not interrupted.[81]

If we try to enter a little into Pfeiffer's human qualities, and into what he is saying, between the lines, to a close friend, we can begin to decipher the mystery of this night. Rudolf Steiner here passed through the deepest nadir of his work. Marie Steiner had compared his glorious and outwardly jubilant demeanour during the East-West Congress in Vienna with the 'entry into Jerusalem'; and the moment described by Pfeiffer is its counterpart. It is comparable to the moment in the Garden of Gethsemane. Christ prays that the disciples will remain 'awake' but they cannot; and in deepest loneliness and surrender to destiny he turns to his Father. *'And there appeared an angel unto him from heaven, strengthening him.'* (Luke 22:43). The Christ initiate too needed strengthening in his moment of greatest frailty; and this came in the figure of the young man who found the right words to encourage him. It was as if he drew these words from the sphere in which lives the higher self and is there merged with the higher selves of others, is not sundered from them. In relation to this sphere he shared something in common with his Master: he experienced himself as one called by Christian Rosenkreutz. Could the inner voice, which he allowed to guide him at this moment, have come from *this* figure, who was also his Master's Master? I simply leave this open as a question. The nature of this moment does however make very clear that it here fell to the destiny of Ehrenfried Pfeiffer to act, in the night of the fire, as the angel of Christ for Rudolf Steiner.[82]

On the afternoon of New Year's Day the Three Kings Play was performed in the surviving joinery workshop as planned. Ludwig Polzer-Hoditz wrote that this play was

appropriate to the tragic events and their Christ-opposing and anti-spiritual nature, [depicting] Romans and Jews in alliance with the devil, and in fear of the power and strength of the spirit, who sought to kill the Jesus child protected by the archangel Gabriel.[83]

That evening Steiner gave the sixth lecture of the cycle on science (GA 322), which had been interrupted for three days.

Though the catastrophe was not entirely unexpected, there was a remarkable concordance in this: a series of lectures on science marked both the beginning and the end of his work on the building. They both heralded a new union between art, science and religion. In his introductory address before the evening lecture, Rudolf Steiner said that it was now necessary 'to find in our pain the strength [...] to work all the more intensively and energetically to achieve the aims we find to be so deeply implicit in the history of humanity's evolution'.[84]

Threats and premonitions

Did Rudolf Steiner know the fire would happen? Doubtless not, in detail and as inescapable fact. But there was some kind of premonition. In October 1912 he visited the building plot and, with Marie Steiner, stayed several days in the house of the owner Emil. After his first night there he emerged from his room in huge distress. Marie Steiner reports:

> Next day Rudolf Steiner awoke as never before. Distressed, as if crushed, benighted. There was not really any reason for this, and such a thing never usually happened to him. Despite continual rush and bustle he dwelt in infinite harmony. The mood passed; and yet I had a feeling that has often returned as time went on: that he had some prevision in that first night of things he must forbid himself to contemplate in thoughts.[85]

It seems likely during that night that he became aware of mighty enmity of a supersensible nature—ahrimanic and luciferic adversaries—increasing as his plans unfolded. Someone who risks such an undertaking must be ready for the worst and not let himself be deterred. Steiner was ready, and the worst was indeed approaching. In October 1920 a former theosophist, Karl Rohm, who had become an opponent of Steiner's for personal reasons, made threats in an obscure periodical with the highly disingenuous title *Der Leuchtturm* ('The Beacon'). Rohm's unpleasant threat was quoted verbatim in a book entitled *Ein Blick in die Zukunft* ('A Glimpse of the Future') by astrologer Elsbeth Ebertin, published in 1921, and thus gained further circulation:

> There are thus plenty of spiritual sparks which will soon strike at the wooden mouse trap [as the enemies of the Goetheanum called it], and Steiner will need all the cunning he can muster to be 'conciliatory' if he is to prevent a real spark making a miserable end some day soon of the splendour at Dornach.

Rudolf Steiner expressly told his pupils that such things were symptoms that should be taken seriously. And in the evening address on 1 January 1923, mentioned above, he recalled these words of his.

Pupils such as Julie Klima and others had premonitions whose significance was certainly not lost on Steiner. *He* saw threatening powers gathering from the very beginning, while most others perceived them only as they looked upon the smouldering ruins. Doubtless Steiner did not actually have prevision of the *fire* itself, but he did perceive all that might lead to it. For this reason he urged people to be alert, and drew his pupils' attention to the campaign waged against the Goetheanum, which grew in intensity as the building neared completion. The Goetheanum was a gift to humanity and those to whom it was given needed to protect it against the anti-spiritual powers of our age. Its destruction was not a predictable fact but reveals the lack of wakefulness amongst Steiner's pupils. In his address at the Easter general meeting in 1925, Ludwig Polzer-Hoditz said:

> The First Goetheanum was built as a mystery centre. It was taken from us because we spoke within it in a merely intellectual way. No one was there who could have protected it. Rudolf Steiner himself might not do so because he had given it to humanity as a trial of its maturity.[86]

Occult machinations during the fire

During investigation of the causes of the fire, a scene occurred that was witnessed again by Ehrenfried Pfeiffer. As far as we know he was the only one to do so.

As described above, on arriving at the burning building Rudolf Steiner stayed with the foreman Max Schleutermann, who was overcome by fumes, until his life was no longer in danger. He was therefore delayed from approaching the fire itself. In relation to this delay, the responsible insurance agent posed the following impertinent question: 'It is common knowledge that you are clairvoyant. Why did you not use these powers to discover the source of the fire and direct the fire brigade there, instead of wasting valuable time?'[87] Steiner replied: 'If one serves spiritual principles, as I do, one is obliged to do all one possibly can to save an endangered human life, even if one's own work and life be destroyed in consequence.'

This exchange can remind us once again of a phrase spoken during Christ's sufferings: the moment when he stands before Pilate and the latter likewise asks him, in an entirely external way, about his spiritual authority.

Pfeiffer continues:

This is the ethical code to which R. St. adhered. *But afterwards he mentioned that this incident [with the man overcome by smoke] had been part of the machinations of dark powers who knew that he must abide by that code. It was they who threw this man in his path as a hindrance. The author of these lines himself witnessed this incident.*[88]

The lines above that I have put in italics open up questions that can lead us into the real occult background of the fire. If it was possible to employ occult means to ensure that the foreman Schleutermann was overcome by smoke and was brought to the 'right' place at the 'right' time to hinder Steiner, then the whole series of events must have been very closely observed from moment to moment, possibly with the aid of one or more mediums. But not just observed. Where necessary these powers intervened to keep Steiner away from the source of the fire for as long as possible. Here therefore we find a specific occult attack of great and, in a negative sense, remarkable scope.

The new cultus as the 'bone of contention'

Are there any further and perhaps more tangible indications from Rudolf Steiner of the occult background to the fire? Yes indeed; they are only infrequent, but highly significant for all that.

We saw in the letter quoted above which Max Kaendler wrote to Steiner on 7 November 1922 that the Freemasons had issued 'word' against him. Kaendler believed that Freemasonry objected most to the rites and rituals of the 'Act of Consecration of Man' celebrated by the Christian Community. Steiner had given this service to the priests of the Christian Community in September 1922 (see GA 344). The service was inaugurated by Steiner in the same 'White Room' in which smoke was first discovered on the night of the fire.

In human history so far there have been and continue to be two streams whose representatives consider they have the right to establish spiritual rites and acts of worship: the Abel stream that lives on in the Catholic priesthood, and the Cain stream perpetuated by Freemasonry. Christian Rosenkreutz, the reincarnation of Lazarus-John, tried to unite and reconcile these two in a higher element. For centuries the two warred with each other. Since Schiller's death, though, they have increasingly collaborated in hidden ways.

In one of their grimmest acts of collaboration they attacked Rudolf Steiner and his work. The conservative representatives of *both* streams felt themselves threatened by 'his' new Christian rites. They could not countenance loss of their authority over ritual and worship. As early as 1911, ecclesiastical and especially Jesuit opposition to Steiner emerged, when, in the Karlsruhe lecture cycle *From Jesus to Christ*, Steiner revealed the dubious methods of Jesuit schooling and their aim of securing and consolidating power. The Catholic Church had been vilifying anthroposophy for many years, eventually also issuing threats to set fire to the Goetheanum, as did Rohm—though he was Masonic in outlook. The letter from Kaendler remains, however, the only documentary proof that the Masons were also in fierce opposition to Steiner.

Dual enmity

Six months after the fire, in an esoteric lesson in Oslo, Steiner made some important remarks about the background to the attack. His comments are only extant in one participant's transcript. This runs as follows:

> In the gathering he recounted the Temple Legend again in very striking terms. And then he began to speak of how the sons of Abel had reconciled themselves again with the sons of Cain when the theologians asked him to create a new act of worship. This intensified enmity from the sons of Abel and Cain in the outer world. (He meant, or at least that's how I understood it, the Jesuits and the occult brotherhoods.)
>
> He went on to say that the fire that destroyed the Goetheanum had been started [should be 'discovered', TM] in the same room where the new act of worship was given to the theologians.[89]

These notes were written from memory by Helga Geelmuden, who for many years was General Secretary of Norway's Anthroposophical Society. The lesson in Oslo, on 18 or 20 May 1923, which referred to the rites celebrated in gatherings held before the First World War, was often afterwards given in Dornach. In the brief transcript by Maria Roeschl-Lehrs there is confirmation of the above:

> ... two directions—in John [Lazarus–Christian Rosenkreutz, TM] lies the centre. Perceiving what comes from the two directions. Fire, because the two streams were united against the centre. Be awake! Be awake to these two streams, but also in general. Grow wakeful [...] through proper meditation![90]

With these few hints Steiner pointed to the two adversarial streams behind which, ultimately, stand the activities of Lucifer and Ahriman. The priest stream is more susceptible to the luciferic influence, and the Masonic more to that of Ahriman. Apart from the beginning made with the 'new cultus', the two streams have not yet fully reunited as Christian Rosenkreutz and his pupil Rudolf Steiner sought to achieve. Instead of a peaceable union in a higher element inspired by spiritual science, hatred continued against this third stream of the centre. And this hatred was born of envy of the new element that was independent of both streams *in their old form*.

Starry perspectives

As we saw in chapter 12, Max Benzinger, in describing the laying of the Goetheanum's foundation stone, spoke of the raging of the elements and the clear starry heavens that suddenly became visible beyond them. He wrote:

> ... the stars were shining as if they were far closer than usual. Venus [Arcturus? TM] and Jupiter stood close together in the south-west, and twinkled down, and it was one of the most beautiful starry nights that I have ever witnessed ...

The other such beautiful starry night was 'in the early morning of New Year's Day 1922/23, after the building had burned to the ground'.

Thus two starry vistas encompass the period from the laying of the foundation stone to the night of the fire. In 1913, despite elemental opposition, anthroposophy was as it were to be incarnated from starry heights into the Goetheanum building. In the first glimmer of dawn after the fire, it was lifted out again into the heavens. Would human souls try to follow it? And how would its creator now seek to embody it on earth? What would come to replace the 'forms that awaken karma vision'? The great series of karma lectures of 1924! In these lectures return the architectural forms which can prepare an artistic sensibility for karma vision—but now in outwardly invisible and therefore also *indestructible* thought forms, serving the same end. But before he could embark on these karma revelations, Steiner, in his sacrificial path, had to accomplish a further step towards 'his Golgotha'. Later we will return to this new form of spiritual-scientific karma revelation.

According to a comment which Rudolf Steiner made to Adelheid Petersen, the building should have 'stood for several hundred years', or in other words at least for the whole of the rest of the Michael period which will pass over into the age of Oriphiel in 2230. It did not last on earth for even a thirtieth of that time. It will therefore be all the more important for humanity's future evolution that anthroposophy's *spiritual* karma revelations can increasingly be taken up and integrated.

21. The New Foundation Stone

The whole of 1923 was devoted to a review of where things stood, and to the rebuilding of the Anthroposophical Society founded in 1912. Steiner was not a member of the Society but, as teacher, had an independent relationship to it. Could things continue in this way?

The fire was also a metaphor for the state of the Society, which likewise lay in ruins in many respects. Steiner's young and old pupils were divided and had little to do with each other; the anthroposophic activities of offspring movements risked fragmenting and losing their connection with the mother source, the being of Anthroposophia. In Dornach and on his travels, Steiner tried to reconfigure the spiritual emphasis. National societies were formed in order to reconsolidate the work. In particular, it was important for there to be clearer awareness of opposition and enmity, which had come to most extreme expression in the Goetheanum fire. Despite the New Year tragedy, even serious pupils who practised meditation succumbed to illusion in this regard. How *not* to proceed was vividly illustrated in the summer of 1923 in the 'Lempp affair'. In the internal journal *Anthroposophie*, the Protestant priest Lempp was allowed to publish defamatory remarks about Steiner, framed by the well-meaning, Christian phrases of Friedrich Rittelmeyer. No one told Steiner, and he was furious when he read the issue.

His reaction was a relatively rare expression of holy anger at such well-meaning naivety. 'Our opponents no longer need their own periodical, since now they can use "anthroposophic" journals for their purposes,' he said, before crying out: 'Everything is unravelling.'[91]

In August the first international summer school took place in Penmaenmawr, Wales. It was organized by D.N. Dunlop and Eleanor C. Merry, and, through the wide-ranging nature of lectures on the theme of 'initiation science' it fully and fittingly accorded with the year's developmental and restructuring work. We described this course in chapter 17. It was the first summer school of its kind, and important discussions between Rudolf Steiner and Ita Wegman also took place there. The latter asked Steiner about the possibility of a new mystery medicine. This was a question of a kind similar to the one Marie Steiner had asked at the 'chrysanthemum tea party' in 1901 (see chapter 10). As mentioned, in 1923 a full revelation was also granted Wegman of her karma with Steiner. During the night of the fire, Wegman's connection with Ephesus and a life lived there alongside her teacher had dawned upon her; and thereafter she was ready for an encompassing insight into this. Not only the time this occurred but the place too is significant. In the sequence of Twelve Holy Nights, August relates to the eighth. According to Steiner these nights are a micro-organism of the whole succeeding year. The fire took place on the eighth of these nights, and in August of the following year, as Wegman noted, 'karma was fully revealed'. We will soon encounter a similar connection in *Steiner's* life between one of the Holy Nights and an event of the following year.

On the tenth anniversary of the laying of the foundation stone, in comments made in Dornach, Steiner referred to the need to pay greater heed not only to outward but also inner opposition. By inner adversaries however he did not mean any specific people but rather three invisible, yet no less influential 'personalities': Mr Failure of Discernment, Miss Naivety, and Aunt Illusion. Certain actual spiritual beings naturally live behind these three figures, and we need to try to perceive them. In relation to the Lempp affair, Steiner illustrated the *wrong* way of dealing with outward opposition. Now it was time to initiate ways—almost completely lacking hitherto—of dealing with inner opposition. Steiner resorted to humour in relation to these serious matters, leaving his audience quite free and inviting their serious response without treading too much on their toes. The comments he made in this regard, on 21 September 1923,[92] are a key part of Steiner's efforts to lend firmer consistency to the *spiritual* structure of the anthroposophic movement before a new physical building should be erected, and a new foundation stone laid.

17 November 1923

The decision to refound the Anthroposophical Society, and for Steiner himself to become its president, only gradually ripened. In November 1923 Steiner was still wondering whether it would be best to leave the Society to its own fate and to withdraw entirely from it, instead founding a kind of order with a very few people chosen by him, and achieve more in the world by this means than through a collective plagued by lack of discernment, naivety and illusion. He made his decision in Holland, on 17 November — the anniversary of the founding of the Theosophical Society. This 'coincidence' of date is symptomatic of the decisive importance which this day was later to have for the future of the anthroposophical movement in the world, born as this was from the theosophical movement. As the crisis culminated, the turning point came on the evening of 17 November in a hotel in The Hague. According to eye witness Daniel van Bemmelen, in response to the likely prospect that Steiner might actually leave the Society to its own devices, Ita Wegman spontaneously came out with these words: 'But Herr Doktor, you can't leave the Society in the lurch. It was only this summer that you were telling me you were thinking of rebuilding and redeveloping the Society under your leadership.' At this Dr Steiner stood up, went towards her, took her hands in his and said: 'Yes, Frau Doktor, if you help me I will risk it!'[93]

In this way Ita Wegman played as decisive a part in the new founding of the Anthroposophical Society, resolved upon at that moment, as Marie Steiner had done in encouraging Steiner, on 17 November 1901, to take over the post of General Secretary of the Theosophical Society, which he did in October 1902.

*

The last and in a sense most important preparation for this refounding of the Society followed now in a series of lectures in Dornach, in which Steiner described the great ancient mystery sites of humanity and the content of their teachings and rituals. These mysteries were among the most carefully hidden in human history, and were scarcely known to anyone.

The lectures aimed to awaken in their audience the question of new mysteries that would accord with the age of Michael. Overall, events and Steiner's activities in the year following the fire testify to the endeavour to work towards a new inwardness in the Society. They have the character of *involution*.

The decision was made to refound the Society as the General Anthroposophical Society at New Year 1923/24. This gathering became known as the 'Christmas Foundation Meeting', and it was to instigate a new impulse of *evolution* of anthroposophic work in the world.

The ritual opening—an encapsulation of human evolution

The Christmas Foundation Meeting began on 24 December, and the 'founding meeting of the international Anthroposophical Society' opened on the following day, a Tuesday. On the dot of ten in the morning, the doors to the joinery workshop were shut.

Those who arrived too late could only stand there in vain. This alone was a sign that Rudolf Steiner was in the process of accomplishing a ritual act. An eyewitness reports:

Expectant silence reigned when he entered the room at exactly ten o'clock. As usual he came up onto the stage from a corridor to one side of it, through an entrance closed off by a curtain. Arriving in the hall itself he turned to the left and walking to the middle of the room came to a stop below the lectern. After resting his gaze on the audience he turned around a little and, using a small instrument in his hand, beat thrice upon the wood of the stage floor or the bottom of the lectern standing on it. The first and third strikes were louder than the middle one, his instrument then touching the wood only briefly whereas on the first and last blows it rested somewhat longer. This produced a 'long-short-long' rhythm.

Others likewise reported these three strikes at the opening meeting, but only Ernst Lehrs clearly describes their rhythmic nature. Moreover he says that many years later, after he had given an account of the Christmas Foundation Meeting during a lecture tour, an American anthroposophist approached him and asked to hear the three strikes reproduced. Before meeting anthroposophy she had belonged to another esoteric movement. She related that another eyewitness of the Christmas Foundation Meeting had previously told her that the three blows were of equal length, but that this made no sense to her. She was visibly relieved to hear Lehrs's account, and, when he asked her what this signified to her, she replied: 'Humanity has compressed itself out of the cosmos, and will arise anew into the cosmos again.'[94]

This comment resonates with Steiner's analysis of the trochee (also called 'falling rhythm', in which, he says, a high-toned syllable is followed by a low-toned one), and the iamb (also called 'rising rhythm', where a low-toned syllable is followed by a high-toned one). The first is a trochee, the second an iamb. The trochee describes a movement from above downwards, and the iamb from below upwards. The descent from spiritual heights into earthly depths is trochaic, therefore, while the ascent from earthly depths to spiritual heights is iambic. Ancient poetic epics, sustained by spiritual awareness, are almost invariably trochaic, whereas poems centred on individualized feeling are iambic.

In the third lesson of the Michael school launched in February 1924, Steiner gives mantras in correspondingly trochaic and iambic metre.

We can encapsulate all this by saying that humanity's descent from heavenly heights took place trochaically while our reascent into these heights occurs iambically.

In the three blows given in a long-short-long pulse to mark the opening of the founding meeting of the new Society, we find both descent and ascent, encompassed together in a differentiated rhythmic movement. Descent is not sundered from reascent *but the former passes into the latter.*

In opening the meeting with these three ritual blows, Rudolf Steiner gave ringing utterance to the secret of the evolution of all humanity, as well as that of every single human being.

The new foundation stone

This threefold signature encompasses everything that was then developed through the following eight days in the resonant words of the threefold meditation which Steiner called the 'foundation stone' of the new Society.[95]

Here efforts made by Steiner over many years to gain insight into the threefold nature of the world, of the individual human being and also of the future social organism were condensed into succinct mantric form. The foundation stone meditation is a symphony of diverse triads composed throughout with the utmost precision: body, soul, spirit / space, time, eternity / Father, Son, Spirit / first, second, third hierarchy.

All these triads are held together in and encompassed by the overarching 'spirit light of worlds' which, 'at the turning of the times', 'entered the onward stream of earthly being': the 'Christ sun' that warms the hearts of shepherds and illumines the heads of kings.

If we regard this 'foundation stone' as a meditative vehicle, and practise it so that it carries us in meditation into the 'spirit's flowing ocean', the fourth part which turns to the events in Palestine can then be discerned as the truly sustaining and stabilizing aspect of the whole—if you like, the keel of the whole vessel.

*

We could say that the foundation stone's 'destination' was self-knowledge of the human being as a threefold being originating in a threefold world.

Each of the three parts is divided into *twelve* lines, in accordance with the twelvefold cosmic-spiritual principles, as these come to expression in the zodiac and actively underlie the structure of the world and the human being.

No doubt this is also why Steiner calls the meditation 'dodecahedral', thus at the same time connecting with the first foundation stone which, as described earlier, had the form of a double pentagonal dodecahedron. Yet here a difference also emerges: the foundation stone of 1913 was material in nature, and was lowered into the earth by just a few representatives of the old Society who *stood for all other members*. According to Max Benzinger, its solder points would have lasted for about 70 years. The foundation stone of the new Society, by contrast, was created from incorruptible thought material. Its spiritual solder points are formed by a meditant's will for cohesion. It will therefore live on for as long as human souls carry it in their hearts and work meditatively with it.

A mighty inward deepening is apparent in the transition from the first to the second form of the foundation stone. Here we see that the evolutionary momentum of anthroposophy, or in other words its outwardly manifesting substance, first fell into ruins and then had to be reborn involutionarily from its inmost nature in order for anthroposophy to emerge into the world again in a more resistant form. But in this second emergence it would depend on each and every individual whether the new Society's foundation stone could preserve its capacity to form, guide and sustain. Through the Christmas Foundation Meeting, each and every member was called upon here as labourer to erect the new edifice of the Society. No longer do a few represent the rest of the members, as was true of the laying of the foundation stone in 1913.

Rudolf Steiner had not been a member of the old Society. In the new one he went so far as to take on its chairmanship. Trusting in the members' intensified capacity to guide and govern themselves, he himself takes up the reins of the world Society. This was a sacrifice — and a risk for continuing pursuit of his spiritual research work. But we will say more about this below.

Gabriel and Uriel mood

Whereas the foundation stone meditation is rooted in the events in Palestine, the eight evening lectures had a different, and as if complementary character. They were entitled, 'World History in the Light of Anthroposophy, as a Foundation for Knowledge of the Human Spirit' (GA 233). They included wide-ranging reflections on the evolution of memory since Atlantean times, the appearance of key individuals such as Gilgamesh and Eabani at the beginning of the third post-Atlantean epoch, and of Alexander and Aristotle in the fourth. They concluded with a penetrating account of the situation of humanity at the threshold to the world of spirit, over which the grave Guardian of the Threshold keeps watch. In his lectures on the cycle of the seasons, Steiner referred to the awakening of a capacity for 'historical conscience' as something which Uriel, the earnest spirit of St John's, seeks to inspire in humankind. It is precisely this Uriel mood that the great evening lectures during the Christmas Foundation Meeting invoke.

In comments Steiner made on 13 October 1923 (GA 229), he shows how the four archangels Gabriel, Raphael, Uriel and Michael 'pass each other golden vessels'—as Goethe puts it in *Faust*—and during the course of a year migrate from the northern to the southern hemisphere, not only working in from the cosmos but also *through the earth itself* into the sphere of the respective antipodes. Gabriel is guardian and supporter of births, including of a spiritual nature. These reflections are in the finest accord with the Christmas Foundation Meeting itself. Whereas Gabriel here acted as guardian for the renascence of the anthroposophic impulse, awakening a mood of new birth, Uriel, in complementary interplay with Gabriel in a sense, worked into these evening lectures to awaken historical consciousness. Thus the Christmas Foundation Meeting is also exemplary for a future shaping of the year's festivals, in which the influences of the complementary archangel working from an opposite hemisphere of the earth must always also be taken into consideration.

In this sense the gathering was not merely a local event occurring in the world's northern hemisphere.

In the last of the evening lectures, Steiner picked up on comments by Willem Zeylmans, General Secretary of the Dutch Anthroposophical Society—whose founding on 18 November 1923 coincided with Steiner's decision (the evening before) to refound the whole society—about a worrying tendency among some anthroposophists to acquaint the public first of all with the 'fruits' of anthroposophy such as medicines or eurythmy, initially 'sparing them' any encounter with anthroposophy itself. This was a 'softly softly' approach employed in the hope that people would then gradually find their way to anthroposophy by the back door as it were. Steiner's response to these comments by Zeylmans clearly shows his expectations for anthroposophy's new influence in the public domain: 'We must have the courage to regard such an approach as deceitful and to repudiate it inwardly; and then anthroposophy will find its way into and through the world.' Only by such means, he said, could the impulse of the Christmas Foundation Meeting be more than a celebration of the start of a new year, instead becoming 'the dawn of a new age in the universe'. This too was an appeal to 'historical conscience'. We should never forget this commentary by Steiner on a tendency that repeatedly surfaced after his death and today remains a very widespread and characteristic outlook.

The poison attacks during New Year festivities

It is close to a miracle that Steiner could hold this final evening lecture at all, concluding it with a last sounding of the foundation stone meditation. This is because he had been targeted only a few hours before in an attack that aimed to end not his life but his *active work*. Clearly the destruction of the Goetheanum by fire had not sufficed. The new attack had evidently long been in preparation, and employed the occasion of a convivial gathering on the afternoon of New Year's Day, which Steiner had not proposed but merely assented to. There were various eye-witnesses to the events which I will now describe, whose details remain shrouded in uncertainty. Their testimony has certain aspects in common, and certain points of difference. They included Ilona Schubert, Guenther Wachsmuth and Marie Steiner. There is also a witness — Ehrenfried Pfeiffer — to the true motives of those behind the attacks.

The celebration took place in the joinery workshop's large room, and included tea, coffee and cake. A tea kitchen had been set up in one of the cloakrooms. In her memoirs, eurythmist Ilona Schubert-Boegel reports on this incident as follows:

> I was coming through the corridor with a cup of tea in my hand when the curtain which shut the corridor off from the hall opened suddenly, and Dr Steiner approached me on unsteady feet, white as a sheet and moaning loudly.[96] I quickly put down my cup and found him a chair in the nick of time. He said only: 'I am feeling so unwell.' I wanted to fetch Frau Dr Steiner and Dr Wegman, but he kept a firm hold of my hand and said: 'No, stay with me — please fetch me water, water.' Fraeulein Mitscher, who came up at that moment, ran quickly to fetch it. I could not leave him as I was supporting him with my arm. He drained the glass of water that Fraeulein Mitscher gave him. We asked him what had happened and he said: 'I have been poisoned.' It was clear that he was in terrible pain: he was ice-cold and covered in perspiration. Fraeulein Mitscher, Frau Turgeneff, who had by now joined us, and I decided to get help. Frau Dr Steiner came from the hall and asked what had happened. Dr Steiner said to her, 'I have been poisoned — how are the other Vorstand members?' Frau Doktor told him they were all conversing calmly; it was only she who had been worried that he had stayed away so long. With some difficulty we then took Dr Steiner to his room and put him to bed on the sofa. Then Frau Turgeneff fetched Frau Dr Wegman [...] After a while Frau Doktor emerged from the room and said Dr Steiner was asking us to say nothing to anyone. Dr Steiner was then taken home to Villa Hansi, and after medical treatment and a milk cure he soon felt better.

An additional, undated account of the incident comes from Anna Gertrud Huber, who related that the roll (cake) was baked at the

'Sonnenhof' and served by a 'garden boy' from the Sonnenhof who had 'shot at an American lady'. Huber also relates that, according to Erich Schwebsch, who attended the Christmas Foundation Meeting, 'a highly poisonous substance had been inserted into a very small coffee bean, and the latter then hidden in a sandwich' (in other versions, in a carrot).

Another account, though somewhat contradicting the others, appears in a note by W.J. Stein:

> A lady who then disappeared to America, poisoned Dr Steiner with arsenic, the poison of the Borgias. She fed the poison to a pig, prepared the poison from the pig's blood, and put it into the cream filling of a pastry.

This is in a handwritten marginal note by W.J. Stein to Marie Steiner's foreword of the first book edition of *Die Weihnachtstagung zur Begründung der Allgemeinen Anthroposophischen Gesellschaft* (1944). We do not learn where Stein got this information. He concludes his note with the words: 'Dr Steiner forbade any pursuit of the lady.' In the same foreword Marie Steiner states: 'On 1 January 1924 he fell seriously ill all of a sudden. It was like a mortal sword blow in that convivial gathering, a festivity accompanied by tea and other refreshments.'

Finally we must quote a remark by Guenther Wachsmuth, which the latter made to W.J. Stein, who in turn entered it in his diary on 8 October 1924:

> Wachsmuth said that the Doktor had been poisoned at the tea party on New Year's Day: 'It was an oriental poison that affects the ether body, and causes a crisis every Wednesday. In karmic terms it represents for him an expansion of initiation.'[97]

But the same Wachsmuth, in the second edition of his biography, *Rudolf Steiners Erdenleben*, concealed this poisoning incident which he had referred to in the first edition.

These reports, either direct or indirect, tell us the following: 1) There *was* a poison attack on Steiner, which he was not expecting, and which had a grave effect on him; 2) he was able to counteract it within a short time; 3) he had reasons for keeping the whole incident secret.

Because of this last point, the immediate eyewitness Ilona Schubert could only state at the end of her account: 'However much Fraeulein Mitscher, Frau Turgeneff and I thought about it all, we were never able to work out what had happened and how it could have occurred.'

A testimony by Ehrenfried Pfeiffer, not published until 1999, casts clearer light on the evidently dark and obscure background to the incident. As we recall, Pfeiffer had already reported some very significant facts about the night of the fire too.

'Surmounted the attack with the aid of spiritual powers'

At the end of the 1950s, after a long illness, Ehrenfried Pfeiffer was staying in Dornach for the last time. During an internal meeting in the foundation stone room, attended by 30 to 40 people, Pfeiffer, no doubt aware of his imminent death, offered the gathering a kind of 'general confession', a survey of his whole life and endeavour. One of those present, Paul Gerhard Bellmann, who died in 2011, had collaborated for many years on the publication of Rudolf Steiner's lectures. He took notes of this address, which were included in the biography of Pfeiffer, *Ein Leben für den Geist – Ehrenfried Pfeiffer (1899–1961)*. Below we cite the key passage relating to the events of 1 January 1924:

> He [Pfeiffer] had sought a meeting with people who had real knowledge of mechanical occultism—and this was one of the reasons why he had gone to America. He found one such person fairly soon and a close relationship developed. One day they started talking about various phases in Rudolf Steiner's life, and touched on the poisoning incident after the Christmas Foundation Meeting (1 January 1924). At this, Pfeiffer's interlocutor made the following surprising and dramatic statement: 'Please forgive me, I must now unfortunately tell you something that will greatly alarm you and quite possibly sunder us completely, although if this were to be so I would very much regret it. *I* was the one commissioned to poison Rudolf Steiner! There was no intent to kill him, but instead to render

him incapable of employing his great esoteric capacities so masterfully. These capacities would practically have been extinguished. One could then have pointed to Rudolf Steiner and said something like this: 'You see, those who seek an esoteric schooling along such lines—as he described, say, in *Knowledge of the Higher Worlds*—will end up as he has.'

Ehrenfried Pfeiffer did not say whether he maintained his connection with this grim occultist. He indicated only that Rudolf Steiner surmounted this attack 'with the aid of spiritual powers. The brothers of the left-hand path were not victorious.'

Of all testimonies on this matter, Pfeiffer's is the most significant, telling us not only about the dire aim of the attack but also enabling us to compile various details from other accounts, otherwise hard to comprehend, and form a whole picture of the incident.

First of all it confirms the line of enquiry that points to the USA, although the American lady mentioned by Stein seems only to have been the 'messenger' or carrier of the poison. It also sheds new light on Wachsmuth's statement that the poison 'affects the ether body, and causes a crisis every Wednesday'. Here perhaps we should add that the four aspects or levels of the human being each have their own differentiated rhythm. The I follows a daily rhythm, the astral body a weekly one, the ether body a monthly rhythm and the physical body is subject to the rhythm of the whole year. If we give proper credence to Pfeiffer's testimony, then we must include the astral body in the poison's effects: in order to achieve a lasting disruption of consciousness the attack had to intervene in the interplay of ether body and astral body. Processes of consciousness are bound to this interplay, which determines ordinary waking life. It seems in fact that the astral body was directly targeted in the attack. This would have considerably disturbed its engagement with the ether body in the weekly rhythm, and called forth pathological states of consciousness. Wachsmuth's statement is only comprehensible in the light of Pfeiffer's explanation of the *aim* of the poison attack.

Wednesday was the day following the attack. Biographical and medical research of a subtle nature might discover whether, in a series of subsequent Wednesdays, Steiner did in fact suffer health problems or any indications of relapse. Many have testified to the fact that after the Christmas Foundation Meeting, Steiner's state of health did begin to seem more frail, and that he only succeeded in repeatedly suppressing these symptoms through the alchemy of spiritual activity. The poison attack seems, at least, to have been partly responsible for his increased frailty, although the attackers apparently did not have this aim in view any more than they directly intended to kill him.

The intention that becomes apparent in Pfeiffer's testimony was therefore something much 'worse' than causing his death: he himself was to be brought to a state where he could serve as an alarming example of the harmful and irrational nature of anthroposophy! This aim opens up broad, albeit very negative vistas. A dead Steiner could have become a martyr for his cause, whereas signs of mental illness would have discredited it most effectively.

While Pfeiffer reveals nothing in his last 'address' in Dornach about the motives for this truly diabolical attack, he did give hints about it, at least, on other occasions. In one of his lectures on the heart[98] he speaks of an American physican and occultist who told him that in the view of certain occultists Steiner 'was revealing too much about the spiritual function of the human heart'. If one considers that a certain development of the heart is a prerequisite for perception of Christ's appearance in the etheric, this opposition acquires a graver context. The occultists in question, according to Pfeiffer, invoked powers opposing Rudolf Steiner, 'which he could not defend himself against, and therefore fell ill'.

This does not necessarily mean that those responsible for the poison attack are identical with the aforenamed occultists. The real, terminal illness of Steiner's began only in the autumn of 1924. And yet some connection is likely. Certainly there is a connection between the tea party attack and the beginning of Steiner's illness at the end of September 1924 (see the next chapter). Perhaps these occultists only set to work after it became evident that Steiner had been able to ward off the effects of both the arson and the poison attack.

The presence of Christan Rosenkreutz's spirit

According to Pfeiffer, Steiner was able to do so with the 'aid of spiritual powers'. He does not say which spiritual powers in particular intervened with both their inspiration and protection to undo at least the worst aspects of these attacks. But in this context there is a noteworthy comment by Rudolf Steiner himself, quoted by Margarete and Erich Kirchner-Bockholt in their book *Die Menschheitsaufgabe Rudolf Steiners und Ita Wegman*. We have already seen that taking over exoteric chairmanship of a global society posed a danger for Rudolf Steiner's spiritual research activities. But the spiritual powers standing behind anthroposophy not only accepted the sacrifice involved in taking on this office, with all it involved, but responded to it with an unreserved opening of the spiritual floodgates. The two authors above write as follows:

> The world of spirit had accepted his action and replied with ever new revelations, as he himself expressed it. In addition, a spiritual stream of decisive importance for the task of modern humanity, and its originator, bound themselves to these events. This, surely, is how we must understand Rudolf Steiner's comment *that Christian Rosenkreuz and his hosts moved into the joinery workshop during the Christmas Foundation Meeting*.[99]

'But he who knows the spirit also safeguards and protects it,' Steiner had said during the lecture in Munich disrupted by right-wing extremists (chapter 18). Now too, in the terrible poison attack, the worst of its effect was kept at bay. The spiritual presence of Steiner's teacher, Christian Rosenkreutz, must surely have played some part in protecting him.

Nothing in the mode or manner of the evening lecture which concluded this whole Christmas Foundation Meeting betrays the least signs of disturbance or disruption.

Thus the few hours between the late afternoon of 1 January 1924 and the evening lecture of that day are another milestone in Steiner's life, which, if we reflect carefully enough, reveals things of deep significance. First and foremost this moment was significant for Rudolf Steiner himself. Wachsmuth had said to Stein, 'In karmic terms it represents for him an expansion of initiation.' Was Steiner at this moment granted sudden new insights about the devious enmity he faced, and ways he was protected?

In the last phase of Steiner's life, a uniquely creative wealth and power of revelation became apparent. But the attack of 1 January 1924 itself, and the protection he received against it, remained shrouded in secret. If this had been divulged the members would have grown excitable and Steiner could scarcely have spoken to a calm auditorium. But today, those who seek deeper understanding of the attacks to which anthroposophy's originator was exposed on his inner path can and must learn to endure more.

22. The Floodgates Open

The Christmas Foundation Meeting was a 'success' in so far as
the spiritual powers that stood and stand behind anthroposophy
affirmed it and in response showered still greater spiritual
wealth upon Steiner. It remained to be seen, though, whether the
members would, as Steiner hoped and expected, engage with the
sacred cause with still deeper seriousness.

This seriousness was called for by two things in particular.
Firstly, by the path of meditation involved in the newly opened
Michael school whose First Class was held by Steiner on 15
February 1924 in Dornach. Here the previous esoteric schooling
was raised to a new level for all members who not only pursued
anthroposophy for their own personal development, but also
sought to cultivate, protect and support it as a concern of
humankind. According to Ludwig Polzer, the initiative for this
Michael school came from Ita Wegman, who of course had
already asked Steiner about the possibility of a new mystery
medicine.

Steiner gave a total of 19 lessons of this kind, and the same
number of repeat lessons, although only eleven of the latter were
taken down in writing. The texts of these lessons are now generally and publicly available. Membership of the Michael school
was conducted with great rigour, and by the nineteenth lesson a
total of nineteen exclusions had been enforced.

The second impulse was given in the form of the karma lectures which, as we have seen, in a sense aimed to replace the
karma vision-awakening physical forms of the destroyed Goetheanum. They did so as indestructible 'thought substance', in
the same way as the second foundation stone related to the first.
Only in this way could the karma revelations intrinsic to Steiner's
core mission be safeguarded against ahrimanic resistance, at
least in as much as they were placed *objectively* into the world for

all times. How these revelations would continue to live in members' awareness was an open, albeit very decisive question.

On 16 February, in Dornach, Steiner embarked on the first of an extensive series of karma reflections which he would hold in various European cities through to September. That this was just one day after he had given the First Class lesson already shows the close connection between these two spiritual impulses following the Christmas Foundation Meeting.

Steiner likewise expected these karma reflections to instigate in their listeners a greater spiritual seriousness. He urged such seriousness directly, both during the karma lectures and in the Class lessons: not least by repeatedly stressing the danger for his continuing spiritual research of his action in taking on chairmanship of the GAS, and the fact that the spiritual world had responded to this move by opening new spiritual floodgates to him, as an act of grace.

*

Many observers have described the exemplary intensification of Steiner's activities in the nine months following the Christmas Foundation Meeting. The 82 karma lectures run like a golden thread through all these activities. They contain the long-ripened fruits of Steiner's 'core mission' which had already appeared in two preliminary phases in 1902 and 1910, but as yet had met with little understanding. Back then, too, as Steiner himself put it, anti-Michaelic demons who repudiate all karma revelations were still able to put a lock on his tongue. This spell was broken by the Christmas Foundation Meeting.

The karma lectures of 1924 offer an almost inconceivable deepening and realization of the motif on which Steiner embarked in the evening lectures of the Christmas Foundation Meeting, entitled *World History in the Light of Anthroposophy*. Countless human destinies are revealed here in their karmic continuum through several earthly lives. To name but three, Steiner explored the karma of Goethe, Nietzsche and Schroer, figures who had played such an important role in his own development. He also shed profound light on the threefold social movement, which had failed initially, by presenting the karmic background of figures such as Karl Marx and Friedrich Engels. He unveiled the underlying Arabic context of modern science and education in his lectures on Francis Bacon, Charles Darwin and Amos Comenius. And last but not least he illumined the similar spiritual origins of Woodrow Wilson, with his misguided global ideals so unsuitable for the reality of Europe.

One especially vivid strand in this golden thread of karma lectures is his exploration of the great school of Chartres and its leading minds, such as Bernhard of Chartres, Alanus ab Insulis, John of Salisbury and Bernard Silvestris.

Larger and smaller conferences and courses during the spring and summer of that year can seem like distinctive islands of the spirit set amongst this current of karma revelations.

In Koberwitz at Whitsun, Steiner gave the great Agriculture Course (GA 327). Here the spirit was, literally, made fruitful within earthly conditions, giving birth to a new agriculture. Yet the stream of karma revelations was not interrupted. On 11 June Steiner writes an important letter to Ita Wegman from Koberwitz, with reminders about their association during the time of Alexander. He reminds her, too, of the Munich Congress when she had decided to throw in her lot with him rather than with Besant.[100]

Between the lines of the Agriculture Course it also became apparent how anxious Steiner was about Europe's future. Ludwig Polzer-Hoditz reports:

> One day when we were having lunch at the mansion's great dining table, the conversation turned to the general world situation. Rudolf Steiner spoke with terrible seriousness about the great catastrophe towards which humanity was heading, saying that factory chimneys will topple in central Europe and only a primitive form of agriculture will survive. From this moment on it was clear how greatly he was suffering in both body and mind, and yet how humanity's suffering drove him on to tireless exertions.[101]

Did Steiner here have a vision of the devastations of the Second World War, or was his gaze looking further ahead?

Steiner was also worried about whether members were taking up the Christmas Foundation Meeting in the right way. The priest Rudolf Meyer reported as follows in a letter:

> He was concerned that members were not really taking up what had been intended with the Christmas Foundation Meeting despite the enthusiasm which that event had elicited, and the many very innovative things they were engaged in. For instance, he expressed this worry in Breslau (and Koberwitz) in our daily encounters with him during the agriculture course.

Meyer also reports another of Steiner's comments: 'People are not taking up the Christmas Foundation Meeting. There is still time. But if this does not happen by the autumn, *the ahrimanic powers will fill the void.*'[102]

*

At the end of June, in Dornach, Steiner started a curative education course (GA 317) and a little while later, in Arnheim, Holland, he gave the great Michael lectures in which he first drew attention to the sub-earthly counter-school of Ahriman (GA 240). Nietzsche's destiny plays in here again when Steiner reveals the real author of the latter's late works to be the spirit of Ahriman. And he offers a far-reaching future perspective, far beyond our day, of times when Ahriman will figure as an author in all kinds of domains. We have already indicated some of the fields in which he has already authored works (see chapter 8).

In August, in Torquay, as mentioned in chapter 17, the great summer school took place, again organized by D.N. Dunlop and E.C. Merry. The theme was similar to that of the previous year: 'Initiate Consciousness—true and false paths in spiritual research' (GA 243). Here Steiner presented significant findings about the great figure of Brunetto Latini, Dante's teacher and inspiration.

In Torquay Dunlop, like others before him, was anxious about

Steiner's state of health. When he mentioned this, Steiner took him aside and said in clear, insistent words, that no ordinary concepts of illness could be applied to his condition. This 'clarification' inevitably remained a mystery.

Before he returns to Dornach Steiner gives two Class lessons in London and further lectures, among other things on the karmic connection between Ignatius Loyola and Swedenborg, and between Laurence Oliphant and Ovid. Both Swedenborg and Oliphant died in London, and are therefore connected with the city's spiritual atmosphere.

Something very surprising happens in the second Class lesson in London, on 27 August. For the first time Steiner makes the Michael sign and the Rose Cross seal, according to a reliable witness as protection against a betrayal of the Class mantras which has occurred in England.[103] From now on both the sign and the seal will be retained until the last repeat lesson in September.

We have already mentioned Steiner's unusual words of farewell to Dunlop at the railway station in London (see chapter 17).

In Dornach, in the last days of September, the Drama Course (GA 282) began. During this same period (!) Steiner gave to the priests his reflections on the Apocalypse of St John (GA 346).

*

The miracle of these last nine months of intensified activity, only a fraction of which we have mentioned here, culminates in the last karma lecture on 23 September and the last address of 28 September 1924 (GA 238).

In chapter 7, especially the section on 'The birth of systematic karma research', we explored the last karma lecture in detail. In this lecture on 23 September, Steiner reveals Schroer's Greek incarnation as well as the one in the medieval era, falling at the time when Fulbertus founded the Platonist School of Chartres. Here all Steiner's karma reflections came full circle: in this last karma lecture he reveals the karmic individuality of the individual who, 30 years previously, had first given the impetus for systematic karma research.

A conversation with Ludwig Polzer-Hoditz

Ludwig Polzer was present at the karma reflections in Dornach that began on 12 September. He also heard the very last full lecture on 23 September. On the following day he received a telegram which called him away to Vienna to attend his mother's deathbed. Before he departed, Steiner received him in his studio on what must have been 24 September.

On this occasion Steiner made significant remarks about Polzer's father Julius Ritter von Polzer, who had brought his son with him to attend the first lecture he heard by Steiner, in 1908. After the death of Polzer's father in July 1912, Steiner often remarked on him and the help he was giving from the world of spirit. On one occasion he indicated that his individuality had absorbed impulses from the School of Chartres in the eleventh century.

In his conversation with Polzer on that day in September, he revealed something new to him. Polzer reports as follows:

Never had Rudolf Steiner communicated to me something of such significance as in that conversation. He said: 'In spiritual vision I saw a great board upon which your father had drawn a kind of cosmic geometry in great clarity. But then he erased what he had drawn with a great sponge, writing over the board a short sentence, like an admonition.' When Polzer published his reminiscences of Steiner in 1937, he added a note here which stated: 'I can only communicate what this sentence was to a few friends [members] verbally since it could so easily be misinterpreted in the public domain.' In the reminiscences he later recorded in 1943, which were only post-humously published in 2000, he writes: 'But then he [Polzer's father] took a sponge, erased what he had drawn, and, in sharp accentua-tion, said that there was now no time for this. Over the erasure he wrote that "the Church knows no progress".' And, according to this later transcript, Steiner commented: 'Yes my friend, this does indeed have significance for the near future. People are sleepwalking while grave destiny approaches.'[104] This sentence, 'The Church knows no progress' is tantamount to saying that the Church has lost all Christianity, since Christianity is precisely a trust in progress and in its ceaseless, transformative dynamic. The Christ impulse entered the world as the greatest evolutionary factor in world history, which anthroposophy seeks to serve. By contrast the powers of the established Church—though not individual believers—do not wish this and cannot approve it.

In the same conversation Steiner gave Polzer permission to read a Class lesson in Vienna, which he did at Michaelmas, as the first person to hold this Class in Austria.

To Polzer, Steiner seemed tired and disappointed:

> When I mentioned that the Society's future was now assured by the executive council he had appointed, he made a gesture with his hand which betrayed dissatisfaction—as if he had been expecting something else, and was now expecting various kinds of hindrance.

The fears and anxieties Steiner had expressed in Whitsun already, at Koberwitz and elsewhere, did not seem to have grown any less. And the decisive moment of the autumn was at hand, which he had referred to in a letter to Rudolf Meyer.

In their conversation Steiner urged Polzer 'to remain vigilant in the face of events, so that no opportunity was missed to speak a good word for the threefold social organism and anthroposophy in places where those in power might hearken to it.' Polzer took this very much to heart, as we can see from the later course of his life.

The last address

The address which Steiner gave a few days later, on the eve of Michaelmas, was to be his last. He walked with difficulty to the lectern and had to break off the address before the end. This speech too contains new things, such as his incomplete comments about the spiritual interpenetration of the two 'Johns' during Lazarus's awakening. According to Marie Steiner's notes of the address, he also gave a last karmic indication that Schroer's father had been the individuality of Socrates.

This occasion marked the end of Steiner's work as a lecturer. He spent the remaining six months of his life on his sickbed in the studio, and during this period produced, among much else, two things in particular: the Michael reflections which were later included in the posthumous work *Anthroposophical Leading Thoughts* (GA 26) and the autobiography he had published in weekly instalments since 1923 (GA 28).

23. Taking Leave of Life

Rudolf Steiner had never before had to break off a gathering in this way. His illness seems to have broken suddenly upon him, similar to the way in which he had been suddenly struck down on 1 January 1924, as if by a sword stroke, as Marie Steiner put it. September is the month corresponding in the year's whole cycle to 1 January in the micro-organism of the Twelve Holy Nights. It is therefore noteworthy that Steiner's last, and in a sense also the first long illness of his life, broke out in the month corresponding to 1 January.

While some may consider this mere 'chance', it is worth considering whether this word expresses anything more than ignorance of the laws underlying phenomena. There is a real inner connection, at least, between the Christmas Foundation Meeting as the prelude to the karma revelations of 1924, and Steiner's illness in the autumn of that year. According to Meyer, Steiner stated in the letter to J. Waeger, from which we have previously quoted, that 'unreserved revelation of karma truths is what Ahriman most greatly fears'.

The Christmas Foundation Meeting was the prelude to such unreserved revelations, and as such a provocation to the ahrimanic powers. It was not only the old Goetheanum that should have been better protected by the members who received its gift, but also the developing organism of tangible karma revelations. In the same letter Rudolf Meyer said of the ahrimanic powers 'that their counter-attack could only have been endured and powerfully averted if Dr Steiner had not stood there "alone", but if, instead, his pupils had succeeded in creating a kind of safety barrier to defend him.' This was lacking.

'The impulse of the Christmas Foundation Meeting lies in ruins!'

'The Christmas Foundation Meeting has failed!' said Steiner to the eurythmist Ina Schurrman as early as the late summer of that year. At almost the same time he cried out to the solicitor Bruno Krueger: 'The impulse of the Christmas Foundation Meeting lies in ruins!'[105]

On 11 November Polzer, whose sons had informed him of Steiner's illness, was in Dornach again. Steiner summoned him. The studio had been turned into a sick room, and Steiner sat in an armchair to talk to people. He spoke again of Polzer's father, and then of matters relating to the Michael School, giving Polzer full freedom to structure Class readings as he wished: 'Do it as you like.'

Polzer was able to speak to Steiner on a third occasion, on 3 March 1925. This time he was lying in bed and 'found it a little difficult to speak'.[106]

To Ita Wegman, who lovingly nursed him to the end, Steiner remarked on one occasion, 'My illness is peripheral in nature.' This phrase, too, suggests that the real causes of his illness lay, on the one hand, in the social environs he had so intimately allied himself with through his decision to take over leadership of the Society, and on the other in the lack of 'defensive barriers' that members should have formed to properly absorb the new spiritual wealth flowing to them.

*

'My dear friend Count Polzer,' read the addressee in a letter he received on 30 March 1925 in Prague, where he was giving a lecture. This was at 10 a.m., the same moment that his beloved teacher died in Dornach.

If we can compare Steiner's appearance at the West-East Congress with the entry into Jerusalem, and the dark hour of the Goetheanum fire with Christ's loneliness in the Garden of Gethsemane, then his death was comparable, too, with Christ's sacrificial death on the cross.

Departure from the earthly Anthroposophical Society

Steiner had named no successor. And Polzer, along with Marie Steiner, was one of the very few to immediately draw the relevant conclusions both from this fact and from Steiner's death. In his memoirs, written at the request of W.J. Stein and first published in Prague in 1937, we read about Steiner's final sacrifice:

> When Rudolf Steiner saw that the Society could only continue if he made the sacrifice of taking on its leadership himself, as he did at the 1923/24 Christmas Foundation Meeting, he bound his earthly destiny with that of an *earthly* society. When his further work on earth was made impossible soon after this, he died. He cannot remain bound up with an earthly organization in the world of spirit. And therefore it was also clearly apparent that the anthroposophic movement has to be carried through the catastrophe by certain of his pupils.

These are words of great clarity and importance, and in the last part of this book we will return to them.

A true image at the funeral

The funeral took place in the Goetheanum's joinery workshop where Steiner had given most of his lectures. At the wish of Marie Steiner, Friedrich Rittelmeyer held the service with the rites of the Christian Community, and during this

> a drop from the scattered water fell in the middle of Steiner's forehead and shone there like a luminous diamond throughout the service. The light of many candles was reflected in this radiant diamond, an image of the luminous revelations of higher worlds that had been reflected in this mind. Adorned with this precious jewel upon his forehead, the body sank down in the coffin. It seemed to me that higher spirits had given us, in an earthly picture, an indication of what we had experienced.[107]

This 'precious jewel' can also point us to the two-petalled lotus flower, initially activated through the sense-free thinking of spiritual realities. It renders visible 'the spiritual beings of higher worlds' and enables the human being 'to connect his higher I with superordinate spiritual beings' as Steiner writes in his schooling book *Knowledge of the Higher Worlds*.

This true image witnessed and recorded by Rittelmeyer shows

Steiner freed of all earthly suffering. It is a metaphor for the eternal in him, shining beyond all temporal confines: a reality in which he had begun to root himself fully consciously from the moment of his night-time I experience in January 1881. Now he entered this eternal realm with his whole being, as if drawing a deep breath.

Christ's sacrificial death was followed by his Resurrection. The image Rittelmeyer records bears in it a resurrection atmosphere.

Anthroposophy's liberating impulse

To conclude, let us turn back once again to that very first milestone: the idiosyncrasy we identified in chapter 1 of Steiner's insistence, as an infant, that things were to be used only once. Let us recall his own account of this trait:

> From the moment I was able to eat unaided, people had to watch over me carefully since I had formed the view that a soup bowl or a drinking cup was only to be used once. Each time, therefore, that I had finished eating or drinking I would, if not watched, throw the bowl or cup down on the floor so that it broke into pieces. When my mother came up to me I would shout out to her: 'Mother, I've finished now.'

And Rudolf Steiner commented immediately: 'This cannot have been rage or destructiveness on my part since I treated my toys with painstaking care and kept them safely for ages.'

A mysterious characteristic. Steiner himself considers it important to make clear this had nothing to do with rage or anger. He tells us what this trait is *not*; and he is concerned to describe it. But he offers no actual explanation for it.

In terms of spiritual science, all materiality is condensed spirit. Densification into substance occurs for the sake of *human evolution*. Only within 'dead' substance can we become free beings. To engender the necessary solidification, lofty beings of the hierarchies must guide certain other beings into dense substance and there hold them under a 'spell of enchantment'. In a sense they are exiled. This is a path of sacrifice accomplished for the sake of human evolution, and the beings in question are elemental beings who thus serve us so that *we* can make use of the realm of substance. This realm is set aside for our use. Our sensory gaze falls only on the solid *outcome* of this process of densification. The clairvoyant gaze knows that beings underlie this process.

The higher purpose of this process of consolidation and densification will be fulfilled once the human being has to some degree concluded the evolutionary development facilitated by it; and then substance can be resolved again into spirit. The beings banished within substance or, as Steiner says, spellbound there, can be liberated once more and released into their spiritual homeland. This will happen in a later planetary epoch. Densification into mineral substance is something that belongs to our present Earth stage, and is *unique* within the overall seven-phase sequence of planetary evolution from Saturn to Vulcan; and thus for 'one use only'. Knowledge of a long-gone, immaterial embodiment of the earth and of its immaterial embodiment in the far future is something that anthroposophy has brought to human culture. It is a clairvoyant knowledge which Rudolf Steiner brought with him into his latest earthly incarnation. He knew that all dense substance is a unique condition within overall planetary evolution, and will come to an end in the same way that it first began. Through a self-spiritualizing humanity the beings 'enchanted' within substance will be freed again. The young boy Steiner experienced this in relation to things that specifically served mundane human use. *And ultimately, the earth condensed entirely into substance is something that serves mundane human use in the fullest sense.*

The boy's breakage of plates and cups is, in reality, an unconscious gesture of liberation.

The beings who have served us 'once only' within all substance must, after this usage — in other words, after we have attained self-aware freedom — be liberated themselves. The destruction of substance is the liberation and redemption of the spirit spellbound or enchanted within matter. This liberation of spirit beings starts with *knowledge* of the spiritual reality underlying all matter.

In grandiose miniature, this idiosyncratic trait of the young Steiner points to the 'idiosyncrasy' of all anthroposophy: the impulse to knowledge-borne self-emancipation of the human being, which will ultimately lead to the liberation of all the world's beings. Only when the beings who have helped us towards our own freedom have themselves been liberated will the end of cosmic evolution be attained.

Twenty-eight years after his own I was born, in the second lecture in his cycle on the hierarchies given in Dusseldorf in 1909 (GA 110), Rudolf Steiner described a primary aspect of this process of the liberation of other beings.

The Development of Anthroposophy Since Rudolf Steiner's Death

An outline, and perspectives for the future

On one occasion I was prompted to ask him this: 'Where, really, are the "initiates" of humanity committed to furthering work such as yours?' And he replied: 'The important thing now is for people to grasp higher truths through their thinking.'

Friedrich Rittelmeyer: *Rudolf Steiner Enters My life*

From Steiner's death until 1935

After Rudolf Steiner's death, the first difficulty faced by many of his pupils was to determine how anthroposophical work within the General Anthroposophical Society should continue and progress. As Ludwig Polzer-Hoditz made clear, Rudolf Steiner could obviously no longer be regarded as connected to an *earthly organization*. In Polzer's view,

> certain *individual* pupils will have to carry the anthroposophical movement safely through the impending disaster [of the approaching Second World War World]. He [Steiner] can reach these individual human souls. He can help them and guide them if only they have good will towards him. Earthly communities can only develop slowly, with difficulty and in accordance with individual karma. His work upon earth will be maintained in many diverse groups, perhaps soon continuing, until powers arise that can once again reunite all these groups with one another.

Marie Steiner and others also thought in a similar fashion. But this realistic view of things was opposed by the idea that Rudolf Steiner had appointed an 'esoteric' executive council (Vorstand) and that he himself would continue as its leader. For a while Ita Wegman wrote Leading Thoughts—essays whose title, being identical with that used by Steiner, inevitably gave the impression of a spiritual succession. Yet Polzer was clear:

> Even ordinary common sense must see that direct continuation of what only he [Steiner] could keep united is impossible. Lamentations about the impossibility of this have been detrimental to anthroposophy's public reputation. It would have been necessary to come to terms with the fact of a great teacher's death, and draw the right consequences from it; and this would have been less harmful to his life's work than frantically refusing to accept it and vainly hoping for miracles.

These consequences would have involved the Society becoming a quite ordinary administrative association. The affairs of the Michael School ('Class') and its meditative path, which Steiner handled very rigorously, could only have been governed by agreements based on trust and never by a central executive. This administrative executive body should have *elicited* trust and not demanded it. At most, people should have sought their own individual spiritual connection with anthroposophy and its founder, and have borne the *fruit* of this striving into the Society, rather than elevating the Society itself to some hallowed spiritual status, as became the norm over centuries in the Catholic Church.

These realities and consequences described by Polzer, and many people's difficulties in coming to terms with the first, and drawing the second, were at the root of many unproductive conflicts and disputes during the ten years following Steiner's death.

These conflicts culminated in 1935. There is no scope here to detail the complex entanglements that led up to those events. Such accounts have often been given elsewhere, albeit usually without drawing conclusions relevant to the *subsequent period*. Here I propose only elaborating the salient and sometimes tragic developments and fractures in the development of anthroposophy after Steiner's death.

Two of the executive council members appointed by Steiner (Ita Wegman and Elisabeth Vreede), and a series of other prominent officials—including Eugen Kolisko, Willem Zeylmans and D.N. Dunlop—were expelled from the GAS alongside thousands of members of the Dutch and British branches of the Society.

Polzer, as a result of his meditative work with the mantras of the Michael School, was knowingly and repeatedly graced by spiritual experiences that maintained his connection with his deceased teacher. He had two experiences during the hours of night that called on him to intervene in the unfolding events. He heard his teacher ask him: 'Do you know the Jesuit who seeks to introduce Jesuitical methods into the Society?' Yet he did not search for a single 'guilty party' but rather sought to expose the dogmatic, Catholic-Jesuit outlook which had gradually spread through the Society, and which had led to the expulsion motions. He rejected these and drafted a speech which he wished to give in Dornach at the annual general meeting at Easter to warn against the threatened step of expulsion and if possible avert it. A few weeks before this decisive meeting a fanatical *Memorandum* had been published, whose repellent attacks focused among other things not least on certain karma revelations relating to Ita Wegman. One can see this publication as one in a series of more or less ahrimanically inspired, or at least co-inspired, writings that had appeared since Nietzsche's *Anti-Christ*. This is scarcely surprising if we recall the comment by Steiner, cited earlier in this book, that 'Ahriman most fears a forthright disclosure of karma truths'. Readers who regard this view of the *Memorandum* as incomprehensible or even unjustified should form their own judgement by studying it with an open mind. We can be grateful to Emanuel Zeylmans for reprinting it in the third volume of his biography of Wegman.

A Michaelic speech at the 1935 Easter general meeting

In the mood primed in this way, Polzer gave his speech in a hall largely filled with advocates for expulsion.

He warned against succumbing to the illusion that the expulsions might solve deeper social and spiritual problems. The only means of averting the impending catastrophe, in his view, was to wholeheartedly embrace a decentralized mode of thinking for all spiritual concerns within the Society. Above all, Dornach should not seek to issue authorizations for reading the

Class lessons of the Michael School's meditative path, as Rudolf Steiner had done. 'Issuing authorization [for reading the 'Class'] in recompense for diligent 'achievements' or for great erudition would be unacceptable to me,' he said, 'since we would then soon find ourselves in an entirely superficial, authoritarian mode.' And in relation to the new Foundation Stone of the Christmas Foundation Meeting, which should be cultivated inwardly, he said:

> The Foundation Stones that rest in strong hearts are no longer tied to a particular location and a single building. They must become the Foundation Stones for the mystery centres of the future at diverse locations. Those who will sow the seeds for these mystery centres can only be called to do so by their destiny, directly by the world of spirit. This however requires esoteric courage above all, rather than paternalism and restrictiveness.

Lasting almost 40 minutes, Polzer's speech is truly infused with a Michaelic spirit. In the same way that Steiner, in his evening lectures at the Christmas Foundation Meeting, introduced a Urielic impetus into the Gabriel mood, so Polzer introduced a *Michaelic dynamic* into the Raphael mood of Easter. Yet most of the 1700 people present were left unmoved by the speech. Instead, after he sat down, a leading representative of the Society revoked his right to continue working in the Michael School—a task which, as we have seen, Rudolf Steiner had personally conferred on him and others. Polzer spoke of a 'wooden sword of Michael' here wielded against him.

He spent the following evening and night in a guest room at the clinic in Arlesheim, and there once again had a remarkable experience during the night. He woke up feeling 'as if I had been consecrated'.[108]

George Adams-Kaufmann translated Polzer's speech into English so that D.N. Dunlop, General Secretary of the British Society, could read it. Dunlop decided, like many others similarly affected, to stay away from the Dornach assembly after the expulsion motions were announced. Polzer's speech, in full accord with Dunlop's own outlook, must surely have warmed his heart. He died soon afterwards, unexpectedly, on Ascension Day, 30 May 1935.

The impact of the Dornach catastrophe on contemporary history

The most important aspect of the expulsion catastrophe, in Polzer's view, was not that it revealed tremendous weaknesses in the internal state of the Society but that it would inevitably give an impetus to the anti-spiritual powers that had been casting their ever-darkening shadow over Germany since the 20s. Ita Wegman and Elisabeth Vreede felt and thought likewise. The banning of the Anthroposophical Society by the Gestapo on 1 November 1935 in a sense provides symptomatic confirmation of this view.

The real significance of the Dornach tragedy of 1935 actually lies in this negative power shift, with its disastrous impact on the whole contemporary situation. Monica von Miltitz, someone deeply connected with the being and work of Novalis, felt similarly. In an unpublished essay entitled '33 Years After the Ban' she writes:

> I must start with a report of the Annual General Meeting of 1935, which was one of the most difficult experiences of my life. Two individuals, Frau Dr Wegman and Frau Dr Vreede, whom Dr Steiner had appointed to be members of the Society's esoteric executive council, were expelled by the general meeting, along with 40 of Dr Steiner's closest friends, the truest of the true.[109]

As she continues, she reveals a deeper glimpse of the real significance of these events:

> At the end of the meeting, an older member stood up and said: 'What has occurred here will have grave consequences in the public domain.' In the autumn of that year, the Anthroposophical Society was banned. Superficially, this had nothing to do with the general assembly of course, but in terms of higher causality perhaps, after all, it did.

On the other hand, we could no doubt also ask whether the anti-spirit of Nazism, first repulsing the voice of spirit then descending on central Europe like a dark cloud, may also have influenced the souls of numerous members of the GAS, and have metamorphosed into all kinds of fanatic impulses of dismissal, expulsion and eradication. This is not to minimize what happened, but is a question that might aid deeper understanding of the Dornach catastrophe.

Miltitz was also one of the very few to consider the meaning of the events in Dornach from the perspective of the 33-year cycle:

> Only later did I realize that this general assembly took place 33 years after Dr Steiner had begun his anthroposophical work. He, of course, pointed out that the cycle of 33 years is significant, as the period during which an impulse can unfold. It can also, however, provide us with a verdict, like a court of law. And here the verdict is this: 'You have not taken up what I gave you.'

Monica von Miltitz wrote these words 33 years after 1935, at a time when the after-effects of the Dornach catastrophe could again be observed, as we will consider below.

Polzer's deeper analysis: the shadow cast by the Council of 1869

Like Miltitz, Ludwig Polzer-Hoditz saw the Dornach tragedy against the backdrop of broad historical perspectives, and like her related it to the year 1902 when Steiner began his public spiritual-scientific work. He went a step further however. Pursuing a suggestion by a friend of his, a journalist, he began to study the origins and nature of the Vatican Council of 1869/70, which declared the Pope's *ex cathedra* utterances to be infallible.

These explorations led him to the following conclusion:

> The way in which the majority view formed in Rome back then was strikingly similar to what was done in Dornach. At the time of the Council, Church dignitaries with their large, peripheral ecclesiastical dioceses were not considered, nor the deeper religious mood and disposition of northern peoples. Instead, ascendancy was asserted by

the imperialistically minded peoples of the Mediterranean, with their more outward form of Christianity. The majority vote was obtained by calling upon a great many ecclesiastical authorities without dioceses, along with a large number of bishops close to the centre of Rome, who were primed beforehand by strictures both spiritual and material in nature. *What happened at the general assembly at the Goetheanum was very similar.*[110] [...]

Then also, in a memorial after Ita Wegman's death,[111] he revealed his own destiny connection with the year 1869 in the following words: 'Easter 1935! Twice 33 years since I was born, and since the last Vatican Council in Rome.'

It would be possible to draw further parallels. When Polzer came to Dornach on 11 March 1935 to ask Albert Steffen, the chairman of the GAS at the time, not to publish the exclusion motions that had so far only been circulated internally, Steffen described these motions as something he was not responsible for, but which he must nevertheless pay heed to. In all seriousness, he advised Polzer to speak to the authors of the *Memorandum*. In a similar though far crasser fashion, whenever necessary Pope Pius IX hid behind those who, while promoting his aims, seemingly expressed their independent views at the Council of 1869.

Polzer stated:

The warning Rudolf Steiner gave me during the night six weeks before the general assembly was one I increasingly understood. This was indeed the spirit of Jesuitism at work! And that is why I think that, from then on, Rudolf Steiner no longer regarded the Society as a suitable form for the anthroposophical movement. I feel sure this is connected with its prohibition, and the potential destruction resulting from this.

Did the Easter assembly at Dornach produce something comparable to the dogma of infallibility? It did indeed. The individuals working for expulsion sowed the seed of a conviction that reared its head once again in the last quarter of the century: that, despite everything, Rudolf Steiner was still connected with the earthly Society as such, and not only with the strivings of individual pupils. In this view, the Society was still identical with the movement, in a unity presided over by an 'esoteric' executive council, in organic, unbroken succession from the original executive council.

This conviction flies in the face of reality. From 1935 onwards there were, all of a sudden, thousands of anthroposophists who were no longer members of the GAS, besides those who had never belonged to it. Rebuilding of the Society ought to have fully recognized this fact. Ludwig Polzer-Hoditz himself felt it necessary to leave the Society in order to pursue unhindered his work on the meditative path of the Michael School, although his right to do this was revoked by the Dornach executive council.

He left the Society in full deliberation on the day D.N. Dunlop died, a man he greatly esteemed. Henceforth, as he expressed it, he considered the Goetheanum to be located wherever people were working as Rudolf Steiner intended.

A new start after the war: the Waldorf School movement
There is no doubt that the Second World War with its traumatic experiences led to a new spiritual deepening in many of the anthroposophists who survived it. The great catastrophe swept many petty sectarian concerns away with it. In other words, the war induced much healthy inner self-scrutiny, or spiritual *in*volution. After the war a pioneering spirit of renewal prevailed amongst many spiritual pupils, some of whom had been personally instructed by Rudolf Steiner. This wind of renewal was primarily apparent in the flourishing and expansion of the Waldorf School movement, starting in Germany. A new phase began in which anthroposophical substance and dynamism could evolve outwards and unfold. The Stuttgart Waldorf School was symptomatic of this new flourishing, alongside the Christian Community and, somewhat later, endeavours in the field of medicine. Some of the teachers who worked at the school when it opened again after the Second World War had taught at the first Waldorf School at Uhlandshoehe. According to Johannes Tautz,

whom we can regard as the school movement's biographer, around a third of the original teachers rejoined the newly opened school, including Herbert Hahn, Karl Schubert, Max Wolffhuegel and Erich Schwebsch. The founder, Emil Molt, was no longer alive, but his spirit still seemed to infuse the place. His portrait hung in the rebuilt school hall. Partly inspired by sitting with the bodies of deceased colleagues prior to their funeral, Tautz, assisted by Gerbert Husemann, later put together a valuable photograph collection of all the teachers whom Rudolf Steiner had appointed to the first Waldorf School, along with biographical sketches of each. As the first teacher of German and history after the school's reopening, he wanted to pick up the thread of his predecessor's experiences and insights at the original school. Thus at the beginning of the fifties he sought out W.J. Stein in his exile in London, later becoming his biographer. Tautz compared the encounters he had with Stein over three days with Trevricent's instruction of Parzival.

Much of the school's original spirit thus lived for a while in the second Stuttgart school, initially little touched by the tragic events which had split the Society in 1935. Figures such as Emil Bock, who helped the Christian Community to a new, powerful resurgence after the prohibition was lifted, and Juergen von Grone, who had intimate knowledge of the Moltkes and their destiny, helped set the mood and tone in Stuttgart. Grone was one of those expelled in 1935; and thus deep, living, and destiny-creating connections were formed with important anthroposophists outside the Society.

Tautz had many pupils who later became well known in some way or other, including Michael Ende, the popular children's author. He came to be a lively mediator between the first generation of teachers and a younger, post-war generation.

In 1947, in Stuttgart, the first issue of the anthroposophical newsletter in Germany was published. Initially edited by Emil Bock, this periodical appeared quarterly and contained high-quality articles. Juergen von Grone and Fritz Goette later took over as editors. A big Whitsun conference, organized by the

Anthroposophical Society, was held the same year. Training courses for priests and teachers were established, and later the Eurythmeum. This period can be regarded as a 'golden age' of energetic anthroposophical renewal in Stuttgart, and of warm, spirited work in the public domain.

The literary estate dispute

But in Dornach things were not developing in such promising ways.

In 1948, Marie Steiner did describe the expulsions of 1935 as a mistake, but this of course could not resurrect key figures in anthroposophical endeavour such as D.N. Dunlop, Eugen Kolisko and many others.

And at the same time a new conflict was brewing, about how best to manage Rudolf Steiner's literary estate. Steiner's will could not have been clearer; but soon after his death its validity had been questioned by some of his pupils, including W.J. Stein—who did however later alter his stance.

At this point Albert Steffen and Guenther Wachsmuth became opponents of Marie Steiner, seeking legal control of the literary estate for the GAS. A few months before her death (27 December 1948), therefore, Marie Steiner founded the Estate Association (later called the Rudolf Steiner Estate Administration). Encouraged by Ehrenfried Pfeiffer she was still able to plan publication of Steiner's complete works (Gesamtausgabe or GA), whose first volumes started to appear in 1961, the centenary of Steiner's birth. In other words, Marie Steiner had to battle against resistance from her former executive council colleagues to ensure the Collected Works found their way into the world.

Entirely without authority, and ignoring Marie Steiner's copyright, the GAS executive started to publish Rudolf Steiner's lecture cycles and books, refusing to acknowledge the position of the Estate Administration. Eventually the latter had to resort to legal action to enforce its rights. In the course of the lawsuit, the court magistrate in Dornach developed great esteem for Marie Steiner's person and achievement, stating: 'Frau Steiner was central to the movement, if not its very heart.' He kept his own council as far as the actions of the GAS leadership were concerned, but made the following perspicacious statement: 'It is tragic that a Society whose task is to bridge divisions in the world, such as those between East and West, cannot even reconcile differences of view within its own executive.'[112]

In June 1952, Solothurn Supreme Court determined that Marie Steiner had been entirely justified in founding the Estate Association.

Appraising the deed of Willem Zeylmans

At Easter 1960, Willem Zeylmans van Emmichoven, who had been expelled from the Dornach GAS in 1935 along with the Dutch Society over which he presided, decided on an unusual step. In a conversation with Albert Steffen he re-affiliated the Dutch Society with Dornach. Some of his friends were surprised, others even horrified, since he did this without insisting on conditions that had previously been agreed for such a move. These would have included concessions from Steffen over the literary estate question. To Steffen he simply said: 'This is what we wish.' Lovingly and with a sense of responsibility for Rudolf Steiner's work, Zeylmans wished to prepare the ground for the end of the century with this gesture of unconditional trust in the good powers of striving anthroposophists. His deed was doubtless significant, not least because it was accomplished by a man in whose presence, on the evening of 17 November 1923, Steiner took what was perhaps the most difficult decision of his life—that of refounding the Anthroposophical Society under his chairmanship.

Whether Zeylmans's action had a 'positive' effect was not solely dependent on this action itself but still more on the way in which it was received in Dornach. It would have been desirable if Zeylmans had been invited to join the Dornach executive council, making impossible, or at least very difficult, a relapse into the centralist customs and spiritual pretensions that had led to the split in 1935. The Society could at last have become what Polzer and others had regarded in the thirties after Steiner's death as the only appropriate vehicle: an earthly administrative association that would serve Rudolf Steiner's work in an appropriate and humble way. While, as Steffen noted in his diary, he believed he 'had gained a friend' through Zeylmans's unexpected step, he then added the following: 'But if he were to become a member of the executive council, this friendship would soon be lost again.'[113]

The re-affiliation of the Dutch (and later also the British) Society did not bring the desired benefits: no new tasks or responsibilities were assigned within the Society. Zeylmans gave numerous lectures, and worked on the new edition of his important book *The Foundation Stone*, also writing a monograph on Rudolf Steiner which was published in 1961 to mark the centenary of his birth. 'The world of spirit no longer gives me any tasks,' he said to a friend. In October 1961 he travelled to South Africa, and on 18 November he died in bed, and was found lying with folded hands and closed eyes. All his papers were in order. He died on the day of the founding of the Dutch Society, which he had re-affiliated with Dornach over a year earlier.

*

Besides Zeylmans's book on Rudolf Steiner, the centenary of his birth was also marked by monographs by Rudolf Meyer and Herbert Hahn. Emil Bock's studies of Steiner's life, which he had first given as lectures, also appeared in book form. Shortly afterwards the monograph by Johannes Hemleben was published in the Rowohlt series. Significantly, therefore, three priests, one physician and a teacher engaged with Steiner's biography in this centenary year.

1968: 33 years since 1935

At the end of the 60s a wave of protest and awakening surged through the students' movement in the West. This movement was rooted in a rejection of the power politics of the West and America, with its strong hold on Europe, and to a certain degree on a clear and truthful sense of the occult background to such political manoeuvering. Western cities witnessed waves of demonstration against the terrible and no longer winnable war in Vietnam. But protest largely remained an emotional reaction, while the energies underlying it either degenerated into violence and terrorism or were diverted into any of three directions: psychoanalysis, Marxism or drugs.

In 1965 an important book by anthroposophist and political commentator Renate Riemeck, entitled 'Central Europe — Survey of a Century', was published in Germany. Alongside its scholarly account of historical facts it also offered broad perspectives and insights into European history over the previous century, and included evidence of how secret western societies planned the First World War. It also referred to Rudolf Steiner's ideas on a threefold society. Riemeck was the foster mother of Ulrike Meinhof. Her book appeared at the right moment to provide the European protest movement with a deeper awareness and foundation, and to offer it fruitful ways forward and possible solutions. But it remained an isolated phenomenon, receiving no lasting response or support from large parts of the anthroposophical movement. Rudolf Steiner's *Karma of Untruthfulness* (CW 173, vols. I and II) in which he casts a piercing light on the intentions of the western lodges,[114] and the Roman Curia, appeared [in German] in 1966, but anthroposophists capable of doing so failed to convey its insights to the protest movement in a way that the latter could have understood.

The '68 protest movement therefore lacked any orienting impulse from spiritual science, whose strength had been senselessly fragmented 33 years earlier.

The fact that, until 1968, books published by the Rudolf Steiner Estate Administration were not allowed to be sold at the Goetheanum shows us the extent to which the Society, supposedly representing spiritual science, was again embroiled in useless internal struggles during the very decisive 60s. This was a full 18 years after the Society's executive had lost its pitiful court case against the association—quite rightly founded by Marie Steiner—to which we owe the Collected Works of Rudolf Steiner!

*

A communication received from the deceased Helmuth von Moltke on 16 February 1921 states: 'Europe had to divest itself of its old robes. Now, for a while, it is wandering naked through humanity's evolution.' This is an imagination invoking the end of the old centralized state (old robes) and the need for new social garments (threefolding) after a period of 'nakedness'.

Is Europe's nakedness now a thing of the past? Not at all. We have not divested ourselves of the old centralized state. Instead it now wears a double face, like Janus: one in which economic power seeks to be all-dominant; and the other which the Roman Church seeks to ensoul. These two impulses were already embodied in the founding fathers of the European Union, Jean Monnet and Robert Schumann. Today's EU is entirely under their sway. The first is represented by far-reaching US influences on financial dealings while the second is symbolized in the twelve stars of the EU flag, a 'Marian' emblem. The resolution adopting this symbol was passed on 8 December (1955), the same date that the dogma of Mary's immaculate conception was enacted in 1854, and likewise that of the start of the 1869 Vatican Council at which the blasphemous 'infallibility' of the Pope was approved.

Anyone who thinks that Europe is really wearing new clothes has not noticed that the emperor is actually naked. A truly renewed Europe could only have come about with the help of a science of the spirit, something almost entirely lacking in public life at that crucial period at the end of the 60s.

Pseudo-processes of involution in the last quarter of the twentieth century

In relation to social, cultural and economic affairs, Europe's outward social and political condition at the end of the 60s reveals a stark absence of any really strong anthroposophical impulse. Did things improve towards the end of the century? Sadly, the opposite is true. To cultivate more energetic public activity, a further phase of realistic internalization (involution) would have been needed. Instead of this—parallel with immoderate growth of the school movement and other initiatives—we witnessed flights of fancy in the form of misdirected internalization processes. Just one phrase characteristic of this tendency is: 'The Christmas Foundation Meeting'.

Rudolf Grosse, who revered Albert Steffen, and was chairman of the Dornach GAS from 1966, as it were fired the starting gun for these misguided developments in his book *The Christmas Foundation, Beginning of a New Cosmic Age*. Here we find sentences like the following:

> The Society, as the vessel of anthroposophy and bearer of the esoteric, spiritual impulses of the Christmas Foundation Meeting, has *remained the place* where Rudolf Steiner still maintains creative connection with his work, in accordance with his spiritual task.

Instead of looking towards the end of the century and finally drawing the proper conclusions from the 1935 catastrophe by starting to undertake a humbler administrative role, alongside healthy meditative practice, glorification of the Society as such commenced. This was allied with the very dogmatic assurance that this Society was still, as ever, the (!) vessel of anthroposophy and remained the (!) place with which Steiner was still creatively connected. This flies in the face of reason, of any 'historical awareness', of any truly spiritual-scientific outlook and, not least, of the intentions of clear-thinking spiritual pupils such as Ludwig Polzer-Hoditz, Willem Zeylmans and many others. Centralistic pretensions to 'esoteric' ascendancy again burgeoned and blossomed.

The outcome of this misguided esotericism came home to roost in the era of Manfred Schmidt, active in the Dornach executive from the mid-seventies and becoming its chairman around ten years later. He appended 'Brabant' to his name in remarkable resonance with the Belgian Catholic Duchy of Brabant, from which had sprung a figure he also esteemed, Richard Coudenhove-Kalergi, an opponent of any truly anthroposophic impulse for Europe. The following incident, witnessed by the author, clearly signalled the new, Catholic and centralizing tendency in management of GAS affairs. In 1985, when Peter Tradowsky began work on an edition of Ludwig Poltzer-Hoditz's memoirs, he also wished to include Polzer's great speech at the Easter annual meeting of 1935 as an appendix to the volume. *The chairman of the GAS at the time vetoed this intention* — scarcely surprising, since the tone of Polzer's speech breathed a very different air, that of spiritual decentralization, from the outlook prevailing once again in the executive council. This intervention left no doubt as to the new direction of the Society's upper echelons: consolidation of the spiritual centralism focused on Dornach.

Even the 'periphery' was soon infected by this outlook. In 1992, when the author gave a lecture on D.N. Dunlop in London at the Annual General Meeting of the British Society, he ended by suggesting the need for spiritual 'peripheralization' within the anthroposophical movement, while retaining central administration. He also expressed the contentious idea that advocating spiritual centralism in terms of Rudolf Steiner's ongoing strong connection with the GAS *as earthly society* (as had become fashionable again since Grosse), rather than just with striving individuals, was in fact an inhibiting and erroneous Catholic-type view. Indeed, he said that it would be very beneficial to anthroposophical work to live without such a guarantee, which was unworthy of a spiritual movement. In his concluding words of thanks, the British general secretary at the time replied that while a figure such as *Ignatius Loyola* did at a certain point after his death take leave of the order he founded, R. Steiner remained strongly connected as ever with the GAS. In other words: to conceive of Rudolf Steiner distancing himself from the Society he founded was a 'Jesuitical' idea.

The misguided 'involution' steps also include the brazen attempt in 1993 to inaugurate a 'Second Class' although Steiner did not even complete the first one.[115]

Failing to defend Steiner against accusations of racism

We must now cast a brief glance at a series of phenomena which demonstrate unequivocally the extent to which anthroposophical work has been weakened by misguided and sectarian processes of involution. These phenomena were ones which came towards the anthroposophical movement from the public domain.

During the 90s, anthroposophy, and Rudolf Steiner himself, were increasingly attacked in the media for Steiner's supposedly racist doctrines, along with hints in his work, at least, of anti-Semitism. This triggered a kind of panic reaction amongst leading anthroposophists in Holland, the starting point for the worst attacks. They believed they would only be able to 'save' anthroposophy by making admissions to their opponents. Their admissions were void of any objective basis and were thus tantamount to an attack that they themselves launched on Steiner. For instance, they claimed Steiner did not propound any racial doctrine, instead of clearly showing that no racism figures in his work. Additionally, on behalf of the Dutch Anthroposophical Society, a compilation was made of all Steiner's comments on race, national characteristics and Judaism, which — since removed from their specific context — can be very easily misunderstood. The conclusion of these efforts was to establish that 16 passages in Steiner's work would be liable to criminal proceedings under today's laws!

The compilation of these passages has become known as the Van Baarda Report. Modern opponents of anthroposophy sometimes cite it as evidence of 'recognition' by some anthroposophists that Steiner did make 'problematic' comments. This is stated, for instance, in the Steiner biography by the educationalist Heiner Ullrich.

In January 2000, in the Foundation Stone Hall at the Goetheanum, opponents of anthroposophy, who had only a passing acquaintance, if that, with Steiner's work, were given an opportunity to express their doctrinaire criticisms of Steiner and anthroposophy, based on only a few, easily misunderstood passages which they had mostly learned by heart. The discussion was chaired by a civil servant from Basel. Only a single member of the Dornach executive council was present, and said nothing. In passing, we can see this event as a kind of internal mockery of the spiritual aims implicit in the foundation stone lodged under the floor of this same hall in 1913.

A couple of years later, Rudolf Steiner Verlag halted release of volume no. 32 in the Collected Works because in one of its essays there is a defence by Steiner of Robert Hammerling against accusations of racism. The essay contains two sentences it was thought could possibly be interpreted as racism![116]

It is easy to see what has done the greatest long-term damage to anthroposophy's reputation: not the primitive attacks on Steiner from without—whose substance was not fundamentally new anyway, and will surface again in future—but fearful caving in to these attacks by 'representatives' of anthroposophy. If the decades of review and reflection on the 'Christmas Foundation Meeting', the 'Foundation Stone Meditation', the 'School of Spiritual Science', along with everlasting assurances of Steiner's 'eternal connection with the institution of the GAS' had been aspects of a genuine involution process, such weak and timorous actions, which even to some degree betrayed the spirit of anthroposophy, could never have come about. Authentic spiritual deepening and true anthroposophical work would not have led to such a shameful 'running with the pack'.

The Chantilly experiment and the Grand Orient's good favour

The Chantilly experiment—we'll call it that, since the whole way it was undertaken made it appear to be one—occurred in 1995. Clearly, ecclesiastical and anthroposophical circles wanted to find out how far the two movements could find some rapprochement.

Briefly, although the new centre of the Anthroposophical Society in Paris had just been completed, the French members were informed that the spring general assembly would take place at Chateau Les Fontaines in Chantilly, 40 kilometers north of Paris. The Paris centre, it was said, was too small. No mention was made of the fact that Les Fontaines housed the Jesuit headquarters of France and the Robert Schuman Institute. The chairman of the GAS was due to give the evening lecture. French members who felt unsure about all this asked for some explanations but no real clarification was forthcoming until an anonymous article[117] was pinned up on the bulletin board in Dornach. This clarified the nature of the location, and urged participants to conduct themselves in accordance with its spirit.

If it had really been necessary to go to Les Fontaines, this would have provided an opportunity to speak about the differences between anthroposophical and Jesuit paths of schooling. But clearly none of the organizers had such a plan in mind. The chairman of the executive council withdrew his proposed lecture, and shortly afterwards the idea of going to Les Fontaines was dropped, and the French members were informed that the general assembly would, after all, take place in Paris. The new centre was apparently suddenly big enough.

*

During a conference in the 90s for Class members, again in Paris, discussion turned to the planned French edition of Rudolf Steiner's *Texts and Documents from the Cognitive-Ritual Section of the Esoteric School 1904–1919* (GA 265) with its references to Freemason rituals. The then chairman of the GAS mentioned in this context that a publication of this nature would elicit a warm response in Grand Orient (Masonic) circles. It is known that the chairman had contacts with Freemasonry. But why state that an anthroposophical publication would meet with its approval? Was this another attempt to sound out the extent to which anthroposophists might agree to collaborate with Freemasons?[118]

It is worth remembering here that the Grand Orient Lodge is one of the Masonic groups which, since the time of the First World War, if not before, have sought to influence the course of international politics.

Thus, in a very dubious—because untransparent—way, members of the Anthroposophical Society were encouraged to ally themselves, or at least to feel themselves allied, with representatives of other movements that were spiritually incompatible with anthroposophy. This was a significant prelude to the new 'public visibility' of certain anthroposophical officials initiated at the beginning of the millennium.

In the 90s too, at the same time as the events described here were unfolding, *internal doubts* were voiced about Rudolf Steiner's competency as a spiritual researcher. They related in particular to certain comments he had made in his 'Observations on Contemporary History' (three volumes, including *The Karma of Untruthfulness*, GA 173). A representative of the AS in Great Britain wrote an article published in the Dornach Newsletter on 15 March 1992 which stated that Steiner's 'Observations on Contemporary History' reveal 'emotions in Rudolf Steiner that many have previously been unaware of', and that he had seemingly sometimes been 'influenced' by the 'national emotions' of some members of his audience.

'Occult imprisonment' as starting point for a new 'evolution'

In the period between 1994 and 2000, misguided involution processes within the GAS reached their greatest culmination.

Members were urged to focus their work on one esoteric 'mystery' each year leading up to the millennium. This began with the 'mystery of initiative' (1994) and ended with the 'mystery of freedom'. In this last year, in which anthroposophical work was supposedly dedicated to the 'mystery of freedom', the chairman suggested to members that the Society, which lacked any effective public influence, was clearly caught up in some kind of 'occult imprisonment'. This statement by the chairman, who died soon afterwards, became his highly influential legacy. It was the starting signal for an unthinking rush into the public domain, which increasingly led and still leads today—sometimes literally—to an embrace of individuals who know no more (and do not desire to know more) about anthroposophy than a cow knows about Sunday.

The first appeal to tackle and break out of this 'imprisonment' was announced by executive council member Bodo von Plato in the Newsletter (19 January 2000). In his view this 'break-out' must start from the School of Spiritual Science.

The phrase about 'occult imprisonment' marked the transition from a phase of pseudo-involution to one of renewed evolution, of work done in the public eye. There is no need to be clairvoyant to see what kind of evolution could come from so many decades of misguided involution.

Never mention Steiner

In Paris once again, at a general assembly of the French Society held exactly seven years after the 'Chantilly experiment', Bodo von Plato outlined a programme for the future of anthroposophical work. It was he who allegedly advised against mentioning Steiner, instead proposing such things as critical detachment, and the cultivation of psychological factors in members' interpersonal relations. Eight years later, in a supplement to the weekly journal *Das Goetheanum*, he stated that in relation to anthroposophy 'change and flux has become our all-determining principle', and expressly questions the imperishable spirit of anthroposophy in the following words: '... "eternal values of anthroposophy" — if such a thing exists.'

In this 'representative of anthroposophy', 'transience and change' have indeed become an all-determining principle that even overrides eternal values ... We can therefore now, presumably, delight in engaging with those who know anthroposophy only superficially at most, and attribute the worst kind of nonsense to Rudolf Steiner. Such figures include: Miriam Gebhardt, who proclaims Steiner's research to have been fuelled by cocaine; Heinrich Ullrich, who thinks Steiner did not understand Kant; and Helmut Zander, who, in his love-hate relationship with anthroposophy cannot study a single page by Steiner with an open mind or any self-detachment, and demonstrates this in thousands of his own pages. I leave it to others to list everything he accuses Steiner of, and will confine myself to his assertion that all talk of a supersensible realm is a great swindle, and that Steiner did not pay much heed to the truth—as evidenced supposedly by a *single* discrepancy relating to his date of birth.

A great change has indeed occurred since Steiner's 100th birthday. Back then, anthroposophists published thoughtful monographs about Steiner; now non-anthroposophists, with dilettantish knowledge and a slanderous intent, are doing so. But this is not the greatest cause for concern. The worst thing is that an executive council member finds such publications highly commendable. When asked in an interview with the Sunday paper *NZZ am Sonntag* (9 January 2011) whether he was pleased about the three new biographies of Rudolf Steiner, Bodo von Plato said: 'Definitely. These are three acknowledged authors and three major publishing houses.'

Shortly after this, Prokofieff, his Russian colleague on the executive council, stressed that the Dornach executive was an 'organism' despite marked differences of view between its members, especially in relation to anthroposophy's opponents. Prokofieff is the most important theorist of the 'Christmas Foundation Meeting' since Grosse, and propounds the dogma of Steiner's indissoluble connection with the institution of the GAS.

Yet from a deeper perspective perhaps these divergences of opinion are not so great. Seen in terms of the law of evolution, it is apparent that a false evolutionary process *inevitably* proceeds from a false involutionary one. In other words: a one-sided, sectarian inwardness ('Christmas Foundation Meeting', Steiner's profound connection with the GAS as institution, etc.) will induce a one-sided, superficial outwardness. Thus we can see both these types of one-sidedness—the one more involutionary, the other more evolutionary—as *two sides of the same coin*.

The illusion of clinging to the 'Christmas Foundation Meeting' and the 'School'

A certain culmination of false evolution (based on false involution) was reached in 2003. An internal 'constitution debate' that had exerted its debilitating effect through much of the 90s found a preliminary end in January 2003 with modification of the GAS entry in the Swiss Companies Register, which now ran: 'General Anthroposophical Society (Christmas Foundation Meeting).' Yet this was to be only the temporary end to a process that squandered huge spiritual and financial resources. After justified internal protests against the factually unfounded change of nomenclature by the executive—one might even call it attempted false labeling fraud—Solothurn's Court of Appeal decided in January 2005 that the supplementary description 'Christmas Foundation Meeting' should be removed, and this was done on 10 May 2005. Once again, anthroposophy's reputation was damaged considerably by these events, which were splashed all over the press.[119]

We can see from this grotesque sequence of events that deluded sectarian ideas and legal actions can go hand in glove, mutually reinforcing and in fact eliciting each other. Seen in terms of spiritual science, we find here an interplay of luciferic and ahrimanic powers.

Though opposed by Polzer, this same 'duo' was allowed to take centre-stage back in the 30s already, with very negative results. At the beginning of the 50s we had the court proceedings relating to Rudolf Steiner's estate; and 50 years later came another such action, concerned with the 'Christmas Foundation Meeting' epithet.

Anthroposophist Karl Buchleitner commented as follows on the 2005 Solothurn verdict:

> The claim to embody the Christmas Foundation Meeting has greatly hindered anthroposophical work, and condemned anthroposophy itself to inefficacy on the world stage. Something great could still arise however if this Society were to retreat from its spiritual pretentions and get down to specific tasks. There is much to be done. The Solothurn verdict could lead to an awakening.

Did an awakening occur? Let us examine this by considering two questions:

1. How was the innovative Munich conference of 1907 remembered in Dornach in 2007?
2. What is the current conception of the School of Spiritual Science founded by Steiner?

For several months in the spring of 2007, a container filled with dried banana skins stood in the entrance hall of the Goetheanum, a creation by an English student of Beuys. This 'artwork' was labelled 'social sculpture'. An exhibition entitled 'Joseph Beuys and Rudolf Steiner' was set up in the archive offices of the Rudolf Steiner Estate Administration. Both events were, by their very nature, a—doubtless not consciously intended—mockery of the healthy new anthroposophical art impulse that came to public attention for the first time in Munich, from which the Goetheanum building later emerged.

And how do things stand with the School of Spiritual Science established by Steiner, for whose members Steiner gave the 19 lessons of the First Class? In Ludwig Polzer's view, the School was killed off by the expulsions of 1935. Charles Kovacs, too, the clear-sighted anthroposophist and painter, placed the beginning of the end of the School in the 30s, and could not understand that the Dornach executive was still refusing to recognize this in the 80s. Both these figures, of course, are representative of many others who hold similar views.

Carl Unger had written as follows of the psychological and spiritual background to pseudo-esotericism, which is usually associated with secrecy or conditional, restricted access:

> Modern esotericism must be free, for only in this way can it be Christian. Esotericism bound to old traditions is something luciferic. Behind efforts to maintain secrecy stands an old, not a new impulse—the aim of securing superiority over others. And this works like a poison in human society.[120]

Anyone who today still holds and promotes the view that access to the texts of the Michael School's path of meditation (Class texts)—which have long since been published!—can only be allowed after presentation of a special members' card from a School of Spiritual Science that no longer exists, is continuing to help produce such poison.

Refusing to credit the reality of certain facts—of which Polzer already spoke—perpetuates a false involutionary process into our present time, and, as the described phenomena show, can only trigger further unhealthy evolutionary processes.

Buchleitner's twin hope, that a number of catastrophes would finally teach us to 'retreat from spiritual pretentions and get down to specific tasks', has therefore—apart from the courageous achievements of a very few anthroposophists—so far remained unfulfilled. People have been unable to decide either to relinquish the corpse of the School or to get down to 'specific tasks', such as proper tackling of opponents or energetic publication of the results of spiritual-scientific research. As regards the latter, in fact, the reverse has often happened: academic standards or qualifications have increasingly been introduced *into* or imposed *on* anthroposophic institutions.

Taking stock

The mutually inducing erroneous processes of involution and evolution in the development of anthroposophy since Steiner's death have led to a desolate situation today: an anthroposophical movement governed largely by *both* these unhealthy processes— albeit with varying emphases—and now stuck in a kind of stagnation.

On the one hand, Steiner's work is available throughout the world as never before, downloadable onto a hard drive measuring just a few square centimeters; and on the other, *thinking* engagement with and assimilation of anthroposophy has—again, apart from a few exceptions—sunk to rock bottom, as can be seen by glancing at the bibliographies of those 'acknowledged authors', as well as by perusing certain volumes produced by supposedly anthroposophical publishers.

In Helmuth von Moltke's post-death communications can be found two comments that seem particularly noteworthy in this context, both received on 26 October 1920. The first states: 'The imminent fate of the "spiritual movement" will be to stand there like a plucked chicken. All its feathers will be pulled out.' Here is a picture of the intellectual plundering of anthroposophical substance, made still easier now by the electronic Collected Works and internet search engines. Through such intellectualization, spiritual substance loses its innate impetus.

The second comment states: 'The 'spiritual movement' is spiritual substance without a reflection in human heads.'[121]

Here the Moltke individuality experiences the objective spiritual substance of anthroposophy — in a sense, its 'eternal value' — but also witnesses how humanity fails to integrate it into its *thinking consciousness*. This is certainly a radical statement, but does hold true today even amongst some sections of the 'anthroposophical movement'.

*

It could be objected that, for instance, the school movement has expanded further, into eastern Europe and even Asia. In Hungary alone 27 schools have been established since the turn of the millennium. Nearly 1000 Waldorf schools are in existence today. And hasn't the medical movement also spread internationally? Then there is the biodynamic movement too, reaching as far as Nepal. Surely the current state of play is not so negative.

Certainly, in these fields we can discern expansion, and within certain bounds this is positive — yet only to the point where we ask whether and to what extent this proliferation is accompanied and sustained by healthy processes of involution or inner deepening in an *anthroposophical sense*. Expansion alone will not be the important thing in the long term. Let me clarify this with an example. Ehrenfried Pfeiffer once reported a conversation he had with a leading Jesuit, who told him that biodynamic agriculture would be the only sound basis for a future social order. Pfeiffer asked:

'Do you realize that biodynamics originated with Rudolf Steiner, whom the Catholic Church attacked?' The man replied: 'Oh yes, we're fully aware of that.' Then I continued, 'He also taught about reincarnation,' to which the answer was: 'There's nothing in the Bible that contradicts the idea of reincarnation.'

Pfeiffer concludes this account by saying, 'I cannot dwell further on this here. All I'd like to say is that if we don't take Steiner's teachings seriously then others will.'[122] And my own addendum to this is that they will do so in *their own way*. Here Pfeiffer is suggesting that adopting and realizing something that originates in anthroposophy is not enough. It also depends on *who* does this, and *in what* spirit.

The plucked feathers can also be used by people who serve beings quite other than anthroposophy.

*

In a private conversation with W. J. Stein, when the latter asked how one could defend oneself against the mental disorders so rife today, Rudolf Steiner replied:

> There are three enemies of the psyche: vanity, ambition and untruthfulness, all of which have bad effects in daily life. But in a spiritual movement their effect is devastating. If people are on their guard against these three, they need not fear for their psychological health.[123]

He impressed the same thing, almost word for word, on the priests of the Christian Community, but also warned them against impulses to anger.[124]

These three or four fundamental vices are also what have led to false processes of involution and evolution within the anthroposophical movement. The author hopes that a history of the development of anthroposophy in the world will one day be written, or at least considered, from *this* perspective. A great deal of obstruction during Rudolf Steiner's life, and still more after his death, must be attributed to the influence of these four. Much of the inner or outer developmental distortions here described arose from vanity, not to mention the other three 'dis-graces'. A huge amount has simply been conceitedly squandered in this way.

Domes of the future

After this perhaps sobering analysis, let us turn now to the future, taking our lead from certain comments by Rudolf Steiner. One such states that domed buildings will arise everywhere in Europe in 2086. He made this comment on 7 March 1914 to a group of anthroposophists in Stuttgart. This was during the very early building phase of the first cupola in Dornach, and a few months before the outbreak of the First World War. According to a very sketchy transcript, Steiner said:

> Confusion and devastation will hold sway as the year 2000 approaches. And no single piece of wood of our building in Dornach will be left standing. All will be destroyed and ravaged. We will look down upon this from the world of spirit. But when the year 2086 arrives, everywhere in Europe will be seen arising buildings dedicated to spiritual goals, constructed in the image of our Dornach building with its two cupolas. The golden age for such buildings will have arrived.[125]

Taking the strikingly precise reference to the year 2086 in relation to 1914, we find that the year 2000 is an axis of reflection lying exactly midway between them. Anyone who was not completely asleep at the time knows of course that 2000 fell in a period of catastrophe. In 1999, thanks to NATO's illegal intervention, the bloodiest phase of the war in Yugoslavia began, followed on 11 September 2001 by the first global war of the third millennium. Thus 2000 was flanked by these two events or sequences of events. The old wooden Goetheanum had long since been destroyed of course, while the new, concrete building still stands, but we have already seen how much anthroposophy was practised within its walls around the turn of the century.

Moltke's post-death communications also contain a comment that might relate to the period Steiner referred to in 1914. Received on 8 February 1918, it runs: 'In the twentieth century much materialism will prevail, and will increase further in the twenty-first century. But everywhere there will be centres of spiritual will and action.'[126]

The communication of 1914 can lead us to ask whether the 'golden age' prophesied there will only dawn after a further global catastrophe. There is a whole series of other prophesies in fact, which should be taken seriously—for instance that by the Bavarian seer Alois Irlmaier—which speak unmistakably of a third scenario of devastation.[127]

But there is not even a need to seek out such prophesies. The fact that neither the wider world nor the anthroposophical movement, which should inform it with beneficial impulses, have drawn the necessary conclusions from the twentieth century must leave all reasonable people expecting further catastrophic lessons from world-historical powers. Moltke's comment could tell us that prior to a forthcoming world catastrophe, and even during it, anthroposophic spiritual work could be undertaken on a small scale at least, in homoeopathic dosage as it were. This would mean an emphasis on involutionary, internalizing activity, which can thereby shine out all the more spiritually into the wider world.

The era of new domed buildings will be one when the Foundation Stone laid in 1923 will enable people to undertake new, individualized, *outward-directed* work. In the same way that many cupolas will have arisen from the originating one, so the one Foundation Stone will live in many human beings in individualized form. To both phases—both the preliminary one suggested by Moltke's communication as well as the actual golden era itself of new domed buildings—the phrase of Polzer's will apply in tangible form: 'The Goetheanum exists wherever esoteric work is undertaken as Rudolf Steiner intended.'

Specifically in view of the lack of much hope in the current situation in the 'wider world', as well as in the world of the anthroposophical movement, both statements, certainly, are capable of kindling our will so that we do not succumb, as if hypnotized and petrified, to the Medusa gaze of current events.

In preparation for the not so distant future at the end of *this* century, it is clear that the involution and evolution processes of anthroposophic spiritual-scientific work must be harmonized in a way that has not yet been forthcoming since Steiner's death. While many people one-sidedly sought outward development and public recognition, others withdrew into a navel-gazing esotericism. In fact, the fundamental one-sidedness of all modern times consists in an *over-valuing of the evolutionary dynamic*, as Steiner told the priests on 2 October 1921: 'Today, in our modern civilization, we live almost entirely in adherence to evolutionary values. It is very necessary that we return to involution values once more, by nurturing sacramental qualities.'[128]

But for Steiner himself, the sacramental already began with our *thinking* and *perception*, as we showed in chapter 20.

The development of the Cistercian Order offers us an historical precedent for relatively harmonious processes of involution and evolution. The order spread by moderate degrees, and was always sustained and governed by a corresponding inwardness compatible with those times. This was the secret of its successful and really sustained growth through many centuries, and of its spread through the whole of Europe as it then was.[129]

The connection of anthroposophy with the true spirit of Germany

Below I wish to clarify a couple of grave misunderstandings, and develop a few future perspectives connected with anthroposophy's further development.

It is a historical fact that Rudolf Steiner developed anthroposophy in attunement with the intention of the Time Spirit, Michael, but at the same time also with the aims of the true spirit of Germany who is 'intimately allied' with Michael.[130]

This spirit of the nation, who is still young, and received his national tasks from Michael when the latter became the prevailing time spirit in 1879, is the guardian angel of the Bodhisattva who was elevated into Buddha. This was first pointed out by Karl Heyer in his important essay entitled 'Who is the spirit of Germany?'[131] This nation spirit still has a task that will last for over a thousand years, as Rudolf Steiner said on 17

January 1915 (GA 157). Steiner's description of this spirit can show us the true task of the German nation:

> The mission of the German people is that ultimately its endeavours must inevitably flow back with it into spiritual life. Yet this means nothing other, spiritually speaking, than that the German people is called upon to connect inwardly with what arises in the world through Michael's leadership.[132]

The rejection of spiritual science on German soil in the 20s of the last century — as symbolized starkly by the attempt on Steiner's life in Munich — obstructed real engagement with this task for decades at least. Yet everything leading in Germany to the Second World War and the Holocaust should not be attributed to the true German spirit but, on the contrary, to its utter absence.[133]

And here arises the misunderstanding that circulates even in some anthroposophical quarters: that, due to the Holocaust, the German spirit no longer has any task, and in a sense has 'come to an end'. *This spirit* has not come to an end, but rather large swathes of the German people lost their connection with it or, to be more accurate, did not inwardly connect with it. What Steiner said in a public lecture in Berlin on 14 January 1915 (GA 64), in the midst of war, remains true despite all pseudo-Germanic nationalism.

> The German spirit has not yet brought to fulfilment
> Its active work in world evolution.
> Concerned for the future it lives full of hope,
> Hoping for future deeds, and full of life;
> Within its being's depths it feels the might
> Of hidden nature that must emerge and ripen.
> How can the power of enmity allow
> An uncomprehending wish for its demise
> As long as life is manifest, sustains
> within this spirit's roots creative power?

It is essential to distinguish between German spirit and 'German' reality in the twentieth century. In a conversation with Stuttgart solicitor and anthroposophist Bruno Krueger, Steiner said:

'Anthroposophy is and remains connected with the German spirit.'[134]

Those who read anything even remotely connected with the Holocaust and world war into this phrase will inevitably remain 'uncomprehending' in the above sense. In his conversation with Krueger, Steiner then added:

> Twice the spirit of Germany descended upon its people: at the time of Walther von der Vogelweide in the Wartburg region, and again at the time of Fichte, Schiller and Goethe. Now, as a third occasion, Germans must intentionally raise themselves to this spirit.

This self-raising did not initially occur to a sufficient degree. But it must happen if the 'future deeds', for which the German spirit lives 'full of hope', are at last to become reality.

It is another question whether this has to occur in the geographical area of Germany or even whether it can any more. It is apposite here to recall the great poet and thinker Fercher von Steinwand, who appeared in spiritual form to Rudolf Steiner during the dark days when the latter was working on German soil — as if to comfort and admonish him to attend to the still uncompleted mission of the true German spirit. Steiner referred to him at that point in Munich (see chapter 18) as the 'leader of the White Lodge of the German-speaking peoples'. All talk of German culture must be rooted in this picture, and not in its opposite that was, soon afterwards, to assume tangible form.

In a presentation he gave to the King of Saxony (1859), Fercher outlined a picture of German culture scattered across the globe, albeit in the sense of degeneracy such as he perceived in Gypsies. He warned against the decline to which the German people — though not the German spirit itself — was susceptible, and which might come about precisely if they were not willing to heed the German spirit.

Another great German, Goethe, spoke of how the Germans would only work in a way beneficial to other nations once they, like the Jews, had been scattered through the world. His actual words, to Chancellor Mueller in 1808, were:

Germany is nothing, but every single German is a great deal; and yet the Germans imagine the very reverse to be true. The Germans must be transplanted and scattered through the world like the Jews, so as to develop the mass of good in them for the benefit of all nations.[135]

There is something remarkable here. Fercher, born on the day Goethe died, takes a parallel used by Goethe but alters it to warn of a possible decline, whereas Goethe emphasizes the positive aspect of such a development. At that dark moment in Munich, Fercher appears spiritually to Steiner no longer to warn but as the *guardian* of the true mission of German culture, just when this mission is being betrayed or forgotten by the German people.

An unpublished poem by Karl Julius Schroer embodies a beautiful but little known characteristic of the universal spiritual mission of the German people. Here Schroer completes a well-known fragment that Friedrich Schiller composed on 'German Greatness':

Not to momentarily dazzle
But conclude the spiritual battles
Which the world has long waged:
Reconciling all division
Thus victorious is the mission
Which sustains its coming age.[136]

In Goethe already, we see that fulfilment of the future mission of the German spirit is no longer bound to German *territory*.

Following the collapse of a great majority of the German people into the chasm of anti-Germanism, we can lead on from Goethe and Fercher to ask: Is fulfilment of the as yet uncompleted mission of the German spirit still exclusively bound up with people of German descent? Fichte already knew that one is not a true German by birth, but can only *become* one. Surely this also means that 'becoming German' in a good, spiritual sense is also possible for people of quite other national and linguistic origins. Indeed, the fact that so many 'German Germans' did not initially take up this task—to the detriment of the whole world—means that fulfilment of the mission of the German spirit can, all the more, draw on this *possibility*. All such 'elective Germans' would include those who find or will find their way to Rudolf Steiner's anthroposophy in an honest and judicious way, since the latter 'is and remains connected with the German spirit'.

In this sense, a person from Japan who penetrates the spirit of anthroposophy would actually come far closer to the German spirit than a 'German' who, if he outgrew materialism at all, turned to ancient Asian spirituality.

Anthroposophy and the German language

Anthroposophy is and remains tied to the German spirit. To what extent does this apply also to its connection with the German *language*? The spirit of the German language is connected with the German spirit in a manner similar to that in which the latter is connected with the Time Spirit, Michael. This is not altered by the fact that the German language has also been misused by the anti-spirit of Nazism. Rudolf Steiner's comments on the nature of the spirit of the German language, on 18 December 1916 (GA 173), show that in comparison with other European spirits of language it is a particularly apt vehicle for enabling us to experience thoughts inwardly prior to and independently of linguistic expression, thus nurturing our capacity for pure thinking. By contrast, the Romance languages tend to hinder this capacity by adapting thoughts to words; and in English, the thought even becomes completely subordinate to the word. Steiner says, in relation to the German language:

> It is a peculiarity of Germans that their thoughts stop short of words. And it is due to this fact that German culture has possessed philosophers who could not have existed anywhere else, such as Fichte, Schelling and Hegel. A German does not bear his thought right into words but retains it as thought.

The following basic characteristic of the German language is at the same time a core concern of the whole of anthroposophy, as expressed in the motto cited earlier: 'The essence of German is to establish a union between the spiritual per se, and the spiritual in thought.' The fact that anthroposophy also appeared in the world in the linguistic garb of idealistic philosophy thus reveals its deep justification. For this reason, a 'correct translation', especially from German, 'is not possible, and is always only an approximation or substitute'.

The spirit of the German language is, additionally, available for new, individual forms of thought in a way that neither French nor English allow. Only Russian possesses a somewhat greater creative, formative capacity, indicating the future mission of this language. However, one has to consciously and determinedly wrest new expression from the spirit of German, in the same way that anthroposophy must also be won by the thinking *I*. This is particularly apparent in Steiner's mantric verses: from the *Calendar of the Soul* through the Mystery Plays to the mantras that form part of the meditative path of the Michael School. It is not mere chance that anthroposophy's creative texts, especially the most profound of all, have appeared in the world in the garment of the German language. Likewise, it was not accidental that Homer's great epics arose in the Greek language, nor that Dante's *Divine Comedy* was written in Italian. It is clear from this that knowledge of the German language can without doubt *make it easier* for people to understand anthroposophy, and will do so also in future.

George Adams-Kaufmann, the gifted, brilliant interpreter of Rudolf Steiner's lectures in England, writes in his memoirs that almost all the meditations which Steiner gave to his pupils were in German, and adds:

Despite the fact that many of his pupils never master German for ordinary, daily purposes, it has become apparent that they nevertheless learn the language in a way that allows them to live in it in the domain of spirit, above all when meditating. And this corresponds to what Rudolf Steiner foresaw: the possibility that the German language might become to some extent universal, not only in outward communication but as a means to express the life of spirit, as was the case in former times, for example, with Sanskrit, Hebrew, Greek or Latin. I once heard him speak of this at a late-night meeting in Dornach during the time of the threefold social movement.

And Adams continues: 'However, if I have understood this possibility rightly, it is connected with matters of humanity's destiny that may not yet have been determined, and signify for the German people a sacrifice rather than outward self-assertion.'[137]

No doubt these are important future perspectives in regard to anthroposophy's further spread over the coming centuries. Today everyone, whatever their mother tongue, takes it as self-evident that international air traffic and global commerce are conducted in English. Yet a time might come when acquiring at least a few basic elements of the *language of the spirit's flight* will be regarded as equally self-evident for meditation and for easier, fuller engagement with the substance of anthroposophy. Wouldn't that be a better idea than labouring over various surrogate versions of the original, and wondering which is better? Perhaps the future here will lie with dual-language editions of Steiner's work. But such means will only become possible once a study of history that accords with the spirit has come to show that the true, spiritual nature of German culture—as exemplified in Fichte through to Steiner—can no longer be associated or even confused with the shadows of Germany and its abysmal deeds. Once the true German spirit is recognized in its indissoluble connection with anthroposophy, then the German language, too, will come to be valued as one that is especially appropriate for serving both.

The vessel of the anthroposophical movement in future

The anthroposophical movement of the future will need a vessel in the form of a Society capable of harmonizing the involutionary and evolutionary processes of anthroposophic activity that were disrupted during the twentieth century. This can only come about through authentic 'creation out of nothing', or in other words through genuinely free deeds (see the preface to this book,

p. 6). Such a vessel was envisaged already by D.N. Dunlop when he wrote to his younger friend and colleague W.J. Stein, after the latter emigrated from Nazi Germany in 1932. In his letter, written seven years after Steiner's death, he suggested the need to reflect on a future perspective for the Society.

At the time he wrote this letter, Dunlop was general secretary of the British branch of the GAS, and in this office did everything possible to nurture the Society in England. But with growing concern he could also see how the Dornach Society was increasingly heading down a sectarian cul-de-sac, with inevitable negative repercussions for the way in which anthroposophy was represented in the world. This was the period of ever more militant conflicts in the Society, which led to the expulsions of 1935 in which he too was caught up. On 16 June 1932, Dunlop wrote as follows:

Dear Dr Stein

I feel very strongly that an effort should be made during the next year or two to form an *International Association for the Advancement of Spiritual Science*. A preliminary prospectus should be prepared to circulate widely in all countries, and when the foundation is laid a Conference should be called. This should be guided & controlled by Anthroposophists who feel the call & need of humanity everywhere, and who feel how inadequate the General Anthroposophical Society (as it is now controlled from Dornach) has become. Will you think about it & see if you can get the impulse for a preliminary prospectus & we can speak of it when we meet in London.
Greetings,
Your D.N. Dunlop

No such prospectus has been found, and nothing further is known about this project. Three years later, the initiative came to an end in practical terms with the expulsions and Dunlop's death soon afterwards.

But the seed formed in deep concern about the further development of anthroposophy did not die. It continued ripening through all upheavals and in future we will need to cultivate it. We should reflect that this was not an impulse *against* the Anthroposophical Society, involving any kind of personal ambition. D.N. Dunlop was simply too great for that. Instead it was a seed, developed from insight into the current situation, for saving and preserving the anthroposophical impulse far into the future. The GAS of those days did not save it, nor can it be fully saved by the GAS of today. While it is true that, in the last two decades, much has been said in the AS about openness to the world, and worthwhile global activities have indeed been undertaken, nevertheless certain sectarian esoteric tendencies continue to operate undiminished. The most primitive opposition to Steiner and his work has for many years been met with a misguided and supposedly 'Christian' stance, or even with blindness to reality.

The association for the advancement of spiritual science which Dunlop considered necessary will have the function of including and encompassing the best parts of the GAS along with people from quite different movements: all in fact who truly connect with anthroposophy. It might well even bear a quite different name.

We still have four hundred years

Anthroposophy has come to all humanity as a new light of the spirit, not just to a group of the 'elect'. It is the Michael-Christ message *for our time*. The way it spreads can accord with human dignity and its own true nature if it finds people who want something more and different than the Pharisees to whom Christ, speaking of their stance towards his forerunner John, says in the temple: 'He was the light burning and shining, and ye wanted nothing more than to bask for a while in this light.' (John 5:35) Rudolf Steiner, the originator of anthroposophy, was similarly a preparer of the way.

In an esoteric lesson of 12 February 1911, Steiner made a significant comment about the future period during which anthroposophy—then called theosophy—can still spread to all humanity. Compared to the great evolutionary epochs of human history, this is a relatively short span of time. He says:

> Since November 1879, a small handful of people have grown mature enough to take up the teachings of theosophy. This remains just a small flock so far, while other people in modern times are as yet incapable of appropriating teachings which they regard as empty musings or fantasies, or which irritate them [. . .] We still have roughly 400 years during which we can make these teachings accessible to all, in the raiment of theosophy. And so that all will have the opportunity for this, those who have rejected these teachings in their current incarnation will be born again within the next 400 years. *But for this to happen a group must exist who represent theosophy in the right way.*[138]

This period clearly extends through the whole Michael era, lasting around 350 years, which will be succeeded by the age of Oriphiel in 2230. About 30 years had passed since the beginning of the Michael age when Steiner made this statement.

Thus anthroposophy can continue to take effect in the world, or be renewed, roughly until the end of the Michael age. And it will be of the greatest importance during this Michael era that a second, strong wave of anthroposophical work is prepared, unburdened by the false processes of involution and evolution at work in the previous theosophical-anthroposophical movement. It is only during a Michael age that spiritual *cosmopolitanism* can come into its own.

Below I would like to briefly outline how a certain tendency, at least, of this second wave of the anthroposophical movement might be prepared.

A new experience of the seasons

The future renewal of worldwide anthroposophical work will include the need to take up an impulse that so far has existed only germinally: the creation of new seasonal festivals to help human beings increasingly experience the etheric Christ, who can be found today in seasonal processes and the whole cycle of the seasons. On one occasion Friedrich Rittelmeyer asked Rudolf Steiner, 'What can one do to prepare for Damascene-type experiences of Christ?' Steiner replied: 'This is only possible by experiencing Christ in the cycle of the seasons.'[139]

However, as described in chapter 21, the cycle of the seasons takes place in polar opposite ways in the northern and southern hemisphere. During the year's process of evolution in the northern hemisphere, the antipodes are involved in the process of involution, and vice versa. The very first edition of the *Calendar of the Soul*, published in 1912, takes account of this polarity with a dual assignment of the 26 letters of the alphabet to each of the 26 weekly verses. For instance, when the Easter verse (A) begins our meditative experience of the seasons in the northern hemisphere, this corresponds in the southern hemisphere to contemplation of the corresponding or counterpart verse A', and so forth.

By meditating *simultaneously* on one verse and its counterpart, we can live our way in to the dual stream of time, knowledge of which was of such key importance to the 19-year-old Steiner. In this way, a polar sense of natural processes in which the etheric, cosmic Christ is today at work can awaken within us in relation to the whole globe.

It is clear, in fact, that Steiner's answer to Rittelmeyer also applies to an experience of the polar opposite seasons in the southern hemisphere. While the historic Christ entered the 'stream of earthly being' at a particular point in the northern hemisphere, his reappearance since the 30s of the last century is occurring in the natural processes of *both* hemispheres.[140]

The Foundation Stones for the mystery centres of the future

In a world where such global Christian sensibility can arise, new mystery centres can also emerge throughout the world from the Foundation Stones enshrined in the hearts of individual human beings. These Foundation Stones are nothing other than images living in each human soul of the meditation which Steiner laid into the hearts and souls of those present during the 'ideal, spiritual founding' of the new Society and the new building. The first 'builders' were the present members at the time, to whom he said, at the end of the Christmas Foundation Meeting and only a few hours after an attempt to poison him:

> Carry into the world your warm hearts, in which you have embed-
> ded the Foundation Stone for the Anthroposophical Society; carry
> these warm hearts into the world to work there with energetic
> healing power. And help will come to you, so that what you would
> direct with single purpose can illumine your heads. Let us undertake
> this today, with all the strength we can muster. [...] *If we prove our-*
> *selves worthy of this, a good star will shine over the will that is kindled here.*
> My dear friends, follow this good star.[141]

The history of the anthroposophical movement and Society after
Steiner's death soon revealed developments wholly *unworthy* of
these original aims. Since 1935, the 'good star' has shone, however, over *all* whose endeavours are in harmony with the
Foundation Stone meditation, whether they are members of the
GAS or not. And this is because the Goetheanum, since then, is
'wherever people work esoterically as Rudolf Steiner intended,'
as Ludwig Polzer-Hoditz wrote in December 1935. At the
Christmas Foundation Meeting, already, in the penultimate
sentence he spoke at the conference, Steiner had tied the sway of
a good star over the Society and Goetheanum building to a clear
'if'. Only when we harbour illusions can we see developments
after Steiner's death as adequate fulfilment of this 'if'. Ludwig
Polzer-Hoditz drew the consequences of this in his Michaelic
speech during the Easter general assembly of 1935, saying:

> The Foundation Stones that rest in strong hearts are no longer tied to
> a particular location and a single building. They must become the
> Foundation Stones for the mystery centres of the future at diverse
> locations. Those who will sow the seeds for these mystery centres
> can only be called to do so by their destiny, directly by the world of
> spirit.

Helmuth von Moltke, an individual significant for both the past
and future of European developments, who was never a member
either of the Theosophical or the Anthroposophical Society,
enshrined this foundation stone in his soul just a few years after
his death (in 1916, at the Uriel season). From the world of spirit,
on 13 January 1924, the individuality of Moltke gave a kind of

esoteric commentary, witnessed by his still living wife, on the Foundation Stone Meditation of the Christmas Foundation Meeting:

> There 'she' sits in the Goetheanum. Often 'her' thoughts are such that my soul can be present with her. Yes, if only this were heard: 'Practise spirit remembering', 'Practise spirit awareness', 'Practise spirit beholding'. But human beings will only hear it when the Michael spirit succeeds in finding in the astral light the trails leading to the spirit altar upon which burns the astral flame that Ahriman fears. No doubt this will take until the end of the century. For as yet the eyes are not there that could perceive the Christ walking in the ether light. Eyes filled with the divisiveness at work in humanity will not be able to have such vision.[142]

The end of the twentieth century has already passed and we stand at the beginning of the third millennium. Many Foundation Stones will be needed to establish the mystery centres of the future. Despite all diversity, these will have two founding impulses in common: knowledge that the new working of Christ penetrates the whole earth, and all humanity which it sustains; and the knowledge that Rudolf Steiner's anthroposophy is the most effective means of serving this new Christ impulse.

The Spiritual Foundation Stone for the Mystery Centres of the Future

Note: The following text reproduces the printed version of the Foundation Stone verse spoken daily by Rudolf Steiner during the Christmas Foundation Meeting to refound the General Anthroposophical Society, held from 25 December 1923 to 1 January 1924. This was first published on 13 January 1924 in the *Nachrichtenblatt* [newsletter], and can be found in GA 260, 4th edition, 1985. Perhaps the most striking deviation between this and transcribed versions are the terms 'Spirits of Strength', 'Spirits of Light' and 'Spirits of Soul' for the three groups of three hierarchical beings from Seraphim to Angeloi. Further small discrepancies from transcriptions also published in GA 260 give the impression that this authorized published version, thus no longer within the more intimate context of the conference itself, represents a slightly compromised and condensed version of the Foundation Stone verse.

Translator's note: The translation offered here draws on the work of many previous translators and in some respects represents a compilation of their work.

<table>
<tr><td>

O human soul,
you live in the limbs
which through the realms of space
carry you into the spirit's flowing
  ocean:
Practise spirit remembering
in depths of soul
where in all-prevailing
world-creator being
our own I
gains being

</td><td>

Menschenseele!
Du lebest in den Gliedern,
Die dich durch die Raumeswelt
In das Geistesmeereswesen
  tragen:
Übe Geist-Erinnern
In Seeletiefen,
Wo in waltendem
Weltenschöpfer-Sein
Das eigne Ich
Im Gottes-Ich

</td></tr>
</table>

within the I of God;
and you will truly live
within the human universal being.

For the Father spirit of the heights
  holds sway,
engendering existence in depths
  of worlds:
You Spirits of Strength
let ring out from the heights
what finds its echo in the depths;
this speaks:
From the divine humanity draws
  its being
The elemental spirits hear it
in East, West, North, South:
may human beings hear it.

O human soul,
you live within the beat of heart
  and lung,
which leads you through the
  rhythms of time
into your own soul nature's
  feeling:
practise spirit awareness
in soul composure
where surging deeds
of worlds' evolving
unite
our own I with
the I of worlds;
and you will truly *feel*
within the human working of the
  soul.

For the will of Christ holds sway
  to all horizons
bestowing grace on souls in
  rhythms of worlds:
You Spirits of Light

Erweset;
Und du wirst wahrhaft leben
Im menschen-Welten-Wesen

Denn es waltet der Vater-Geist der
  Höhen
In den Weltentiefen Sein-
  erzeugend:
Ihr Kräfte-Geister,
Lasset aus den Höhen erklingen,
Was in den Tiefen das echo findet;
Dieses spricht:
Aus dem Göttlichen weset die
  Menscheit
Das hören die Geister
Im Ost, West, Nord, Süd:
Menschen mögen es hören.

Menschenseele!
Du lebest in dem Herzen-Lungen-
  Schlage,
Der dich durch den
  Zeitenrhythmus
Ins eigne Seelenwesensfühlen
  leitet:
Übe Geist-Besinnen
Im Seelengleichgewichte,
Wo die wogenden
Welten-Werde-Taten
Das eigne Ich
Dem Welten Ich
Vereinen;
Und du wirst wahrhaft *fühlen*
Im Menschen-Seelen-Wirken

Denn es waltet der Christus-Wille
  im Umkreis
In den Weltenrhythmen Seelen-
  begnadend:
Ihr Lichtes-Geister

Let from the East be kindled	Lasset vom Osten befeuern,
what through the West takes form;	Was durch den Westen sich formet,
this speaks:	Dieses spricht:
In Christ death becomes life.	In dem Christus wird Leben der Tod.
The spirits hear it in East, West, North, South:	Das hören die Geister in Ost, West, Nord, Süd:
may human beings hear it.	Menschen mögen es hören.
O human soul,	Menschenseele!
you live within the resting head	Du lebest im ruhendem Haupte,
which from eternity's grounding deeps	Das dir aus Ewigkeitsgründen
discloses thoughts of worlds to you:	Die Weltegedanken erschließet:
practise spirit beholding	*Übe Geist-Erschauen*
in calm of thoughts	In Gedanken-Ruhe,
where gods' eternal aims	Wo die ew'gen Götterziele
bestow	Welten-Wesens-Licht
the light of universal being	Dem eignen Ich
on our own I	Zu freiem Wollen
for will in freedom;	Schenken;
and you will truly *think*	Und du wirst wahrhaft *denken*
within the human grounding deeps of spirit.	In Menschen-Geistes-Gründen.
For the spirit's universal thoughts hold sway,	Denn es walten des Geistes-Weltgedanken
beseeching light in being of worlds.	Im Weltenwesen Licht-erflehend.
You Spirits of Soul	Ihr Seelen-Geister,
let from the depths ascend	Lasset aus den Tiefen erbitten,
the plea heard in the heights;	Was in den Höhen erhöret wird,
this speaks:	Dieses spricht:
The soul awakens in the spirit's cosmic thought.	In des Geistes Weltgendanken erwachet die Seele.
The spirits hear it in East, West, North, South:	Das hören die Geister in Ost, West, Nord, Süd:
may human beings hear it.	Menschen mögen es hören.

At the turning of the times
the spirit light of worlds entered
onward stream of earthly being;
darkness of night
had held dominion;
bright light of day
streamed into human souls;
light
which warms
simple shepherd hearts;
light
that illumines
kings' wise heads.

God-filled light,
Christ sun
O warm
our hearts;
illumine
our heads:
so that good become
what we
ground through our hearts
what we
seek through our heads
to guide with clear purpose

In der Zeitenwende
Trat das Welten-Geistes-Licht
In den irdischen Wesensstrom;
Nacht-Dunkel
Hatte ausgewaltet;
Taghelles Licht
Erstrahlte in Menschenseelen;
Licht,
Das erwärmet
Die armen Hirtenherzen;
Licht,
Das erleuchtet
Die weisen Königshäupter.

Göttliches Licht,
Christus-Sonne,
Erwärme
Unsere Herzen;
Erleuchte
Unsere Häupter;
Das gut werde
Was wir
Aus Herzen gründen,
Was wir
Aus Häuptern führen
Wollen.

Chronology

Only dates especially relevant to this volume have been included in this timeline.

1861   February 27: Birth of Rudolf Steiner

1868   Clairvoyant experience in the waiting room at Pottschach

1875   November 17: Founding of the Theosophical Society in New York

1879   Autumn: Encounter with the 'unknown master' and with Karl Julius Schroer.
Rudolf Steiner passes through his first moon node
November: The Michael age begins

1881   January 10/11: Birth of the I

1888   Summer: Meets Fercher von Steinwand
November 9: Wilhelm Neumann utters the words 'Thomas Aquinas'

1889   End of January: Seemingly out of the blue, Schroer exclaims 'Nero!'
Beginning of the Weimar period and work on Goethe, until 1897

1899   February 19: End of Kali Yuga
Tumultuous spiritual experiences around the turn of the century: Steiner stands inwardly before the Mystery of Golgotha

1900   Winter: In Berlin, Marie von Sivers first hears a lecture by Rudolf Steiner

1901   November 17: Marie von Sivers asks about an esotericism suited to the West

1902   First conversation between Ita Wegman and Rudolf Steiner
October 20: Rudolf Steiner becomes General Secretary of the German Section of the Theosophical Society

1907   Whitsun: Munich Congress. Decisive conversation with Ita Wegman.
Performance of Schuré's play about Eleusis. Artistic impulse, Rosicrucianism
Esoteric revelation in Barr, 28 years after he met the 'Master'

1909   Works on *Occult Science*, which is published 28 years following birth of the I

1912   December 28: Founding of the Anthroposophical Society in Cologne. Steiner is not a member of it, only a teacher

1913   February 4: Autobiographical lecture at the general assembly in Berlin
September 20: Laying of the foundation stone of the First Goetheanum building in Dornach

1914   June 28: Lecture on architecture on the day of the Sarajevo assassination

1916   June 18: The death of Helmuth von Moltke. The beginning of his post-death communications

1917   July: First discussions on threefolding with Count Otto Lerchenfeld, Ludwig Polzer-Hoditz and W.J. Stein in Berlin

1918   November 9: Abdication of Wilhelm II. Germany becomes a republic

1919   June 1: Five-hour discussion with Wilhelm von Dommes. Moltke's pamphlet is pulped

1920   September 26: First gathering in the First Goetheanum
September 27: Start of the first School of Spiritual Science course

1922   May 15: Lecture in Munich disrupted by right-wing extremists. Fercher von Steinwand appears to Steiner in spiritual form
December 31: The First Goetheanum is destroyed by fire

1923   November 17: Steiner decides to re-found the GAS under his leadership, following a request from Ita Wegman in The Hague
November 18: Founding of the Dutch Society
December 24: The Christmas Foundation Meeting begins with three ritual knocks

1924   January 1: Attempt to poison Steiner, at around 5 p.m.
September 28: Steiner's last address

1925   March 30: Steiner dies at 10 a.m.

1935   April 14: Dornach Easter assembly, expulsion of Ita Wegman, Elisabeth Vreede and two national branches of the Society
Speech by Ludwig Poltzer-Hoditz
May 30: D.N. Dunlop dies
November 1: The GAS is banned in Germany
November 17: Letter of M. Steiner, G. Wachsmuth and A. Steffen to 'Exzellenz Hitler' (see T.H. Meyer, *The Development of Anthroposophy since Rudolf Steiner's Death*, SteinerBooks 2015)

1936   May 30: Ludwig Polzer-Hoditz resigns from the GAS

1943   March 4: Ita Wegman dies
        August 31: Elisabeth Vreede dies

1945   October 13: Ludwig Polzer-Hoditz dies
        October: The Stuttgart Waldorf School re-opens

1948   Spring assembly: Marie Steiner states that the expulsions of 1935 were a mistake
        December 27: Marie Steiner dies

1952   June 17: Solothurn Supreme Court recognizes the Estate Association (Rudolf Steiner Estate Administration) founded by Marie Steiner; this verdict is not accepted by Albert Steffen and Guenther Wachsmuth; the Society boycotts books published by the Estate

1960   Easter: Willem Zeylmans von Emmichoven re-affiliates the Dutch AS with the GAS

1961   Centenary of Rudolf Steiner's birth. Anthroposophical authors publish assessments of his life and work

1961   November 18: Willem Zeylmans dies

1963   March 2: Guenther Wachsmuth dies
        March 30: George Adams-Kaufmann dies
        July 13: Albert Steffen dies

1968   For the first time, books published by the Estate Administration are allowed to be sold at the Goetheanum

1976   Rudolf Grosse's book *The Christmas Foundation, Beginning of a New Cosmic Era* is published; also the book by Margarete and Erich Kirchner-Bockholt entitled *Rudolf Steiner's Mission and Ita Wegman*, the latter 33 years after Ita Wegman's death

1993   February 23: In advertisements published in the press, the executive council of the Dutch Society distances itself from any possible 'racial doctrines in Steiner's work'.
        Michaelmas: Experiment of a 'Second Class' with annual themes leading up to 2000 ('The Mystery of Freedom')

1995   February/March: The 'Chantilly Experiment'

2000   January: Opponents accuse Steiner of racism in the Foundation Stone Hall.
        The Society is said to be in 'occult imprisonment'

2003   January: The GAS is entered in the Swiss companies' register as the General Anthroposophical Society (Christmas Foundation Meeting)

2005   May: The supplementary designation 'Christmas Foundation Meeting' has to be removed again following a decision by Solothurn Supreme Court. The GAS has to be re-registered under the old name

2011   150th anniversary of Rudolf Steiner's birth. Opponents write biographies of Steiner and his work, which are welcomed as a positive development by many members and some people on the GAS executive

2086   Golden age of domed buildings in Europe

2230   End of the Michael age; beginning of the age of Oriphiel

Bibliography

Beltle, Erika, Kurt Vierl (eds.), *Erinnerungen an Rudolf Steiner*, Stuttgart 1979

Bock, Emil, *Rudolf Steiner – Studien zu seinem Lebensgang und Lebenswerk*, Stuttgart 1961 (*The Life and Times of Rudolf Steiner*, Vols. 1 & 2, Floris Books, 2008.)

Grosse, Rudolf, *Die Weihnachtstagung als Zeitenwende*, Dornach 1976 (*The Christmas Foundation, Beginning of a New Cosmic Age*, Mercury Press, 1984.)

Hahn, Herbert, *Rudolf Steiner – wie ich ihn sah und erlebte*, Stuttgart 1990

Hemleben, Johannes, *Rudolf Steiner*, Hamburg (rororo) 1963 (*Rudolf Steiner, An Illustrated Biography*, Rudolf Steiner Press, 2001.)

Heyer, Karl, *Wie man gegen Rudolf Steiner kämpft – Materialien und Gesichtspunkte zum sachgemässen Umgang mit Gegnern Rudolf Steiners und der Anthroposophie*, 3rd expanded edition, Basel 2008

Kirchner-Bockholt, Margarete and Erich, *Die Menscheitsaufgabe Rudolf Steiners und Ita Wegman*, Dornach 1976 (*Rudolf Steiner's Mission and Ita Wegman*, private printing, 1977.)

Krück von Poturzyn (ed.), *Wir erlebten Rudolf Steiner – Erinnerungen seiner Schüler*, Stuttgart, 4th edition, 1970 (*A Man Before Others: Rudolf Steiner Remembered*, Rudolf Steiner Press, 1993.)

Krüger, Bruno, *Leben und Schicksal – vom Weg eines Wahrheitssuchers*, Freiburg i. Br. 1993

Lehrs, Ernst, *Gelebte Erwartung*, Stuttgart 1979

Lindenberg, Christoph, *Rudolf Steiner – eine Chronik*, Stuttgart 1988

Lindenberg, Christoph, *Rudolf Steiner – eine Biographie*, vol. II, 1915–25, Stuttgart 1997 (*Rudolf Steiner, A Biography*, SteinerBooks, 2012.)

Meyer, Thomas
  Ludwig Polzer-Hoditz, Temple Lodge, 2014
  D.N. Dunlop , 2nd edition, Temple Lodge, 2014
  Von Moses zu 9/11 – weltgeschichtliche Ereignisse und geisteswissen-schaftliche Kernimpulse, Basel 2010
  Rudolf Steiner's Core Mission, Temple Lodge, 2010

Pfingsten in Deutschland – ein Hörspiel um die deutsche 'Schuld', Basel 2001

Andreas Nikolaus von Grunelius, privately printed, Arlesheim 1990

(ed.) *Ehrenfried Pfeiffer, A Modern Quest for the Spirit*, Mercury Press, 2010

(ed.) *Helmuth von Moltke 1848–1916 – Dokumente zu seinem Leben und Wirken*, vols. 1 and 2, 2nd edition Basel 2007 (*Light for the New Millennium*, Rudolf Steiner Press, 1998.)

(ed.) *W.J. Stein/Rudolf Steiner – Dokumentation eines wegweisenden Zusammenwirkens*, Dornach 1985, Basel 2010

Müller, *Spuren auf dem Weg – Erinnerungen*, Stuttgart 1970

Plato, B. v. (ed.), *Anthroposophie im 20. Jahrhundert – ein Kulturimpuls in biografischen Porträts*, Dornach 2003

Polzer-Hoditz, Ludwig, *Erinnerungen an Rudolf Steiner*, Dornach 1985

Polzer-Hoditz, Ludwig, *Schicksalsbilder aus der Zeit meiner Geistes-schülerschaft*, Basel 2000

Riemeck, Renate, *Mitteleuropa – Bilanz eines Jahrhunderts*, Freiburg i. Br. 1965

Rittelmeyer, Friedrich, *Rudolf Steiner Enters My Life*, Floris Books, 2013

Samweber, Anna, *Erinnerungen an Rudolf Steiner und Marie von Sivers*, Dornach 1996 (*Memories of Rudolf Steiner*, Rudolf Steiner Press, 2015.)

Schneider, Camille, *Edouard Schuré – seine Lebensbegegnung mit Rudolf Steiner und Richard Wagner*, Freiburg i. Br. 1971

Schultz, Felix (ed.), *Zeichen der Zeit – zur gegenwärtigen Weltlage*, Dornach 1996

Schubert, Ilona, *Selbsterlebtes im Zusammensein mit Rudolf Steiner und Marie Steiner*, Basel 1977 (*Reminiscences of Rudolf Steiner*, Temple Lodge Publishing, 1991.)

Selg, Peter, *Ich bleibe bei Ihnen: Rudolf Steiner und Ita Wegman, München, Pfingsten, 1907*, Arlesheim 2007 (*I Am for Going Ahead*, SteinerBooks, 2012.)

Selg, Peter, *Willem Zeylmans van Emmichoven*, Arlesheim 2007

Stein, W.J., *The Death of Merlin: Arthurian Myth and Alchemy*, Floris Books, 2008

Steiner, Rudolf

  Mein Lebensgang, GA 28. (*Autobiography*, SteinerBooks, 1999.)

  Selbstzeugnisse (with lecture of 3 February 1913). (*From the Course of My Life, Autobiographical Fragments*, Rudolf Steiner Press, 2013.)

Briefe I, GA 38.

Briefe II, GA 39.

Rudolf Steiner/Marie Steiner – Briefwechsel 1901–1925 (including the Barr Document), GA 262. (*Correspondence and Documents*, Rudolf Steiner Press, 1988.)

Friedrich Nietzsche – ein Kämpfer gegen seine Zeit, GA 5. (*Friedrich Nietzsche, Fighter for Freedom*, Garber, 1985.)

Geisteswissenschaftliche Menschenkunde, GA 107. (*Disease, Karma and Healing*, Rudolf Steiner Press, 2013.)

Wege zu einem neuen Baustil, GA 286. (*Architecture as a Synthesis of the Arts*, Rudolf Steiner Press, 1999.)

Menschenschicksale und Völkerschicksale, GA 157. (*Destinies of Individuals and Nations*, Rudolf Steiner Press, 1986.)

Die Kernpunkte der sozialen Frage, GA 23. (*Towards Social Renewal*, Rudolf Steiner Press, 1992.)

Die Kunst der Rezitation und Deklamation, ed. Marie Steiner, Dornach 1928.

Grenzen der Naturerkenntnis, GA 322. (*Boundaries of Natural Science*, Anthroposophic Press, 1983.)

Der Entstehungsmoment der Naturwissenschaft, GA 326. (*Origins of Natural Science*, Rudolf Steiner Press, 1985.)

Das Schicksalsjahr 1923 in der Geschichte der Anthroposophischen Gesellschaft, GA 259.

Die Weihnachtstagung zur Begründung der Allgemeinen Anthroposophischen Gesellschaft 1923/1924, GA 260. (*Christmas Conference for the Foundation of the General Anthroposophical Society 1923/1924*, Anthroposophic Press, 1990.)

Die Weltgeschichte in anthroposophischer Beleuchtung, GA 233. (*World History and the Mysteries in the Light of Anthroposophy*, Rudolf Steiner Press, 1997.)

Anweisungen für eine esoterische Schulung, GA 245. (*Guidance in Esoteric Training*, Rudolf Steiner Press, 1998.)

Zur Geschichte und aus den Inhalten der erkenntniskultischen Abteilung der Esoterischen Schule 1904–1924. GA 265. (*'Freemasonry' and Ritual Work*, SteinerBooks, 2007.)

Esoterische Betrachtungen karmischer Zusammenhänge, GA 235–240. (*Karmic Relationships*, Vols. I–VIII, Rudolf Steiner Press.)

Der Meditationsweg der Michaelschule, Ergänzungsband, ed. T. H. Meyer, Basel, 2011.

Tautz, Johannes, *Lehrerbewusstsein im. 20. Jahrhundert — Erlebtes und Erkanntes*, Dornach 1995

Tautz, Johannes/Gisbert Husemann (eds), *Der Lehrerkreis um Rudolf Steiner*, Stuttgart 1979

Wiesberger, Hella (ed.), *Marie Steiner-von Sivers — ein Leben für die Anthroposophie*, Dornach 1988

Zauner, Friedrich, Fercher von Steinwand — *Schicksal an der Schwelle*, Dornach 1989

Zeylmans van Emmichoven, Emanuel, *Who Was Ita Wegman?*, vols. 1–4, Mercury Press, 1995–2013

On the history of the anthroposophic movement and the Anthroposophical Society

In the articles listed below, published in the journal *Der Europäer*, the author has examined certain events within the Anthroposophical Society and the movement from a symptomatic perspective:

'Das Karma der Unwahrhaftigkeit — die gegenwärtige Leitung der Allgemeinen Anthroposophischen Gesellschaft: Vorstandspolitik versus Anthroposophie', *Der Europäer*, nos 9/10, July–August 1997

'In welcher okkulten Gefangenschaft befindet sich die Anthroposophische Gesellschaft?', *Der Europäer*, no. 6, April 2001

'"Keinerlei Bezugnahme auf Rudolf Steiner ..." Was will die Goetheanum-Leitung von Rudolf Steiners Geisteswissenschaft heute noch vertreten?' Special supplement to *Der Europäer*, nos. 2/3, December/January 2002/2003

'Kleine Chronik symptomatischer Ereignisse innerhalb der anthroposophischen Bewegung und Gesellschaft 1992–2011', *Der Europäer*, no. 8, June 2011, pp. 24f.

The following privately printed book was published in 1994:
Anthroposophische Gesellschaft, anthroposophische Bewegung und das Jahrtausendende — eine Fragestellung.

All these articles and publications can be downloaded from the website www.perseus.ch

Notes

1. Thomas Meyer, *Scheidung der Geister, die Bodhisattwafrage als Prüfstein des Unterscheidungsvermögens*, 2nd enlarged edition, Basel 2010. (*The Bodhisattva Question*, Temple Lodge Publishing, 2nd ed., 2010.)

2. Ekkehard Meffert, *Mathilde Scholl und die Geburt der Anthroposophischen Gesellschaft 1912/13*, Dornach 1991.

3. See *Der Meditationsweg der Michaelschule in neunzehn Stufen*, published by Thomas Meyer, Basel 2011.

4. As a Swiss national, the author may perhaps be well placed to offer a more unpartisan view of the spiritual-scientific importance of the spirit of Germany.

5. Translator's note: This book was first published in 2012.

6. See Steiner, GA 107, lecture of 17 June 1909, in relation to these basic principles of evolution, involution and creation out of nothing. (*Disease, Karma and Healing*, Rudolf Steiner Press, 2013.)

7. Currently available in *Rudolf Steiner — Selbstzeugnisse, autobiographische Dokumente*, Dornach 2007, pp. 13ff. English edition: *From the Course of My Life, Autobiographical Fragments*, Rudolf Steiner Press, 2013.

8. *Mein Lebensgang* [*Autobiography*] abbreviated henceforth as ML, p. 21. Emphasis by TM. All passages from Steiner's works have been retranslated in this book.

9. See Thomas Meyer, *Rudolf Steiner's Core Mission*.

10. See GA 262, p. 15 [German edition].

11. Printed in GA 262. German version by T.M.

12. G.W.F. Hegel, 'Lesser Logic' (§95) in his *Encyclopaedia of the Philosophical Sciences*.

13. A requirement that the 21-year-old Steiner made in his essay entitled 'The only possible critique of atomistic concepts', published in the *Beiträge zur Rudolf Steiner Gesamtausgabe*, no. 63, pp. 5ff.

14. More on Koeck can be found in the *Beiträge zur Rudolf Steiner Gesamtausgabe*, no. 55, pp. 15ff.

15. 7 March 1911, GA 124.

16. What a picture! From a spiritual-scientific perspective we owe the horse our capacity to think. At the very moment where this capacity deserts him, Nietzsche, a profound and original thinker, embraces a horse, as if in an unconscious gesture of gratitude at the outset of his madness...

17. The title of the book in German is, literally, 'Friedrich Nietzsche—a Fighter Against His Time'.

18. In relation to the problem of dating this diary entry, see David Marc Hoffmann, *Rudolf Steiner und das Nietzsche-Archiv*, Dornach 1993, p. 35.

19. Rudolf Steiner, *Nietzsche*, GA 5.

20. GA 108, 10 June 1908.

21. F. Nietzsche, 'Autobiographisches aus den Jahren 1856 bis 1869' in Friedrich Nietsche's *Werke in drei Bänden, III*, ed. by Karl Schlechta, Darmstadt 1994, p. 133. Author's emphasis.

22. GA 178, 11 November 1917.

23. GA 240, 20 July 1924.

24. GA 178, 11 November 1917.

25. GA 322, author's emphasis.

26. Steiner, *Briefe* II, pp. 238f.

27. 'Wie Theodor Herzls Werk *Der Judenstaat* geboren wurde', in Thomas Meyer, *Von Moses zu 9/11—weltgeschichtliche Ereignisse und geisteswissenschaftliche Kernimpulse*, Basel 2010, pp. 99ff.

28. August Kubizek, *Adolf Hitler, mein Jugendfreund*, Graz, 4th edition 1975, pp. 116f. Author's emphasis.

29. For example, on 31 May 1924, in Steiner (ed. Meyer), *Der Meditationsweg in neunzehn Stufen*, Basel 2011.

30. Quoted in Thomas Meyer, '"Das LSD hat mich gerufen"—Albert Hofmann, Entdecker des LSD, und der anthroposophische Erkenntnisweg', *Der Europäer*, no. 5, March 2006, pp. 7ff.

31. Heinz Mueller, *Spuren auf dem Weg*, p. 39.

32. Author's emphasis.

33. GA 262.

34. We do not know whether this required a further meeting with the unknown person, or whether this occurred in the realm of spirit alone. For more on this see chapter 4.

35. GA 262.

36. GA 262.

37. Peter Selg, *Ich bleibe bei Ihnen – Rudolf Steiner und Ita Wegman*, Arlesheim 2007, pp. 43f. For more on the Michael sign see *Der Meditationsweg in neunzehn Stufen*, ed. Thomas Meyer, Basel 2011, pp. 466ff. See also the esoteric lessons on Freemasonry in GA 265, p. 170.

38. E. Zeylmans, *Who Was Ita Wegman?* vol. 1.

39. Selg, op. cit., p. 78.

40. As witnessed by Rudolf Steiner's calender for 1912/13.

41. Much of Steiner's verbal communication to Schuré found its way into the latter's introduction. According to Schuré in a letter to Paolo Gentilli in 1922, before going to press he showed it to Steiner, who raised no objections. See also chapter 4.

42. All three can be found in GA 266a. Steiner did refer to Michael previously in Berlin on 3 November 1905 (GA 93a) but without mentioning November 1879.

43. Translator's note: a centre of Nazi activities.

44. This is according to Max Beninger, who supervised the actual making of the foundation stone. In: *Erinnerungen an Rudolf Steiner*, pp. 148ff.

45. According to a note found in the literary estate of the English anthroposophist Mabel Cotterell, to whom Pfeiffer related this. Whether the disparity—a crystal instead of two pyrites—is attributable to Pfeiffer or Cotterell must remain open, and is of relatively minor importance. The most common crystalline forms in pyrites are, interestingly, cubes and pentagonal dodecahedrons (Roempp, *Chemielexikon*).

46. In Rudolf Steiner, GA 245.

47. Ludwig Polzer-Hoditz, *Erinnerungen an Rudolf Steiner*, pp. 47f.

48. In *Erinnerungen an Rudolf Steiner*, pp. 151ff.

49. Polzer, *Schicksalsbilder*, p. 26.

50. W.J. Stein, *Merlin*, pp. 50f.

51. Thomas Meyer, *Polzer*, pp. 334f.

52. Quoted from Stein's memoir in *The Death of Merlin: Arthurian Myth and Alchemy*.

53. The thesis was later published as *Die moderne naturwissenschaftliche Vorstellungsart und die Weltanschauung Goethes, wie sie Rudolf Steiner vertritt*; and, most recently, in a new, annotated edition, as *W.J. Stein – Rudolf Steiner – Dokumentation eines wegweisenden Zusammenwirkens*, Dornach 1985, Basel 2010.

54. In: Jacob Ruchti, Helmuth von Moltke, *Der Ausbruch des Ersten Weltekriegs*, Basel 2001

55. I.e. on Russia, on 1 August 1914.

56. See Thomas Meyer, *Moltke*, vol. 1, pp. 494ff.

57. Ibid, pp. 495f.

58. Thomas Meyer, *Whitsun*.

59. Thomas Meyer, *Moltke*, vol. 2, pp. 244f.

60. Polzer-Hoditz, *Erinnerungen*, p. 108.

61. Thomas Meyer, *Moltke*, vol. 2, pp. 244f.

62. Ibid, pp. 239f.

63. Thomas Meyer, *Moltke*, vol. 2, p. 185.

64. See the lectures of October and November 1919 in GA 191 and 193.

65. Guenther Wachsmuth, *Rudolf Steiners Erdenleben und Wirken*, Dornach, 2nd edition 1964, p. 412.

66. GA 286, 28 June 1914.

67. GA 173 a–c.

68. Meyer, *D.N. Dunlop, A Man of Our Time*.

69. Ibid, p. 208.

70. Reprinted in *Der Europäer*, no. 9/10, July–August 1997, pp. 32ff.

71. H. Hahn, *Rudolf Steiner*, pp. 112ff.

72. 'Rudolf Steiner in Österreich', foreword by Marie Steiner to *Westliche und östliche Weltgegensätzlichkeit*, 1927 edition, now published as GA 83.

73. In *Erinnerungen an Rudolf Steiner*, pp. 338f.

74. In Polzer-Hoditz, *Erinnerungen*, pp. 306f.

75. Anna Samweber, *Erinnerungen an Rudolf Steiner und Marie Steiner-von Sivers*, Dornach 2009, p. 58. Samweber did get to Dornach in time. Her later experiences at the site of the fire are also remarkable.

76. Schneider, *Schuré*.

77. Thomas Meyer, *Andreas Nikolaus von Grunelius*, pp. 5f.

78. See 'Unbekannte Erinnerungen an Rudolf Steiner', in: *Der Europäer*, February 2011, p. 3.

79. Thomas Meyer, *Rudolf Steiner's Core Mission*.

80. Ehrenfried Pfeiffer, *Ein Leben für den Geist*, p. 101. Author's emphasis.

81. To avoid any unnecessary misunderstandings about assigning Pfeiffer some artificial 'special role', I include here the words that

follow after the quotation above: 'In writing this, I am not trying to say that other friends and members did not also share Steiner's suffering. In fact, all were struck by this blow and all wished to see the work continue. But there was a moment of the darkest despair that could only be surmounted through the powers of love shining from one soul to the other. After this mission was accomplished, the young man once again receded into the background or the shadows, leaving others to take the lead in the spotlight of further events.'

82. Cf. also Pfeiffer's conversation with Paul Scharff about the night of the fire, in Pfeiffer, op. cit., pp. 227ff.

83. Polzer-Hoditz, *Erinnerungen*, p. 186.

84. Rudolf Steiner, *Die Not nach dem Christus*, published by M. Steiner, 1942, p. 4 (not included in the GA).

85. H. Wiesberger, *Marie Steiner-von Sivers — ein Leben für die Anthroposophie*, p. 321.

86. Thomas Meyer, *Polzer*, p. 730.

87. Pfeiffer, op. cit., p. 99.

88. Pfeiffer, op. cit., p. 99. Author's emphasis.

89. GA 265, p. 452.

90. GA 265, pp. 455f.

91. GA 259, pp. 587ff.

92. GA 259, pp. 639ff.

93. Quoted in Emanuel Zeylmans van Emmichoven, *Who Was Ita Wegman?*, vol. I, p. 264 in the German edition.

94. Ernst Lehrs, *Gelebte Erwartung*, pp. 260f. We can regard the rhythm described by Lehrs as an amphimac (or also kreticus). Cf. also the slightly different account of these three blows in GA 260a, p. 90.

95. Published in GA 260; see also p. 209ff. in this volume.

96. According to a report by an unnamed person, Steiner 'entered with his head tipped backwards, and trembling all over'.

97. Archive of the Perseus Verlag.

98. Pfeiffer, op. cit., pp. 135ff.

99. Kirchner-Bockholt, p. 94. Author's emphasis.

100. P. Selg, *Ich bleibe bei Ihnen*, p. 77f.

101. Polzer-Hoditz, *Erinnerungen*, p. 199.

102. Rudolf Meyer to Johann Waeger, 7 October 1961. Archive of Perseus Verlag. Author's emphasis.

103. See *Der Meditationsweg der Michaelschule – Ergänzungsband*, pp. 241ff.

104. Polzer-Hoditz, *Schicksalsbilder*, pp. 28ff.

105. Both comments published in *Mitteilungen aus der anthroposophischen Vereinigung der Schweiz*, Easter 2003.

106. Thomas Meyer, Polzer, pp. 666ff.

107. Friedrich Rittelmeyer, *Meine Lebensbegegnung mit Rudolf Steiner*, p. 154.

108. The whole experience can be found in Thomas Meyer, *Polzer*, p. 418 (*Ludwig Polzer-Hoditz*, p. 323).

109. Miltitz does not include in her figures the members of the Dutch and British Societies, who were expelled en bloc.

110. Op. cit., p. 478. Author's emphasis.

111. Thomas Meyer, *Polzer*, op. cit., p. 592. See this also for a more detailed account of the matters outlined here.

112. According to an internal report by Henrik Knobel, February 1952. See also *Nachrichten der Rudolf Steiner-Nachlassverwaltung*, October 1952.

113. See Der *Europäer*, year 13, no. 11, September 2009, p. 10.

114. Around this time, in the West, literature of varying quality was published on related themes. Caroll Quigley's book *Tragedy and Hope* came out in 1966 and revealed the un- or even anti-democratic background to Anglo-American politics. In 1971 Gary Allens published *Now Dare Call it Conspiracy*, followed a little later by Antony Sutton's *Wall Street* books. Yet these volumes would have needed a deeper, spiritual-scientific foundation to give the protest movement more sustainable support and orientation.

115. Cf. *Der Meditationsweg der Michaelschule*, p. 452.

116. See *Der Europäer*, year 4, no. 5, March 2000, pp. 11ff, where this essay was reprinted with a commentary.

117. Published in *Der Europäer*, year 1, no. 9/10 1997, pp. 11f, and in *What is Happening in the Anthroposophical Society* (Newsletter), 26 February 1995.

118. This incident was described in a written statement to the author by a person who attended this conference.

119. Cf. *Der Meditationsweg der Michaelschule in neunzehn Stufen*, p. 452.

120. Carl Unger, *Schriften*, vol. II, p. 238.

121. Thomas Meyer, *Moltke*, vol. 2, p. 255.

122. Pfeiffer, op. cit., p. 22.

123. Printed in: *Mitteilungen aus der anthroposopischen Arbeit in Deutschland,* no. 46, 1958.

124. GA 344, 9 September 1922.

125. Published in GA 286.

126. Thomas Meyer, *Moltke,* vol. 2, p. 166. See also *Light for the New Millennium,* Rudolf Steiner Press, 2014.

127. Wolfgang Johannes Bekh, *Bayrische Hellseher,* Munich, 11th edition, 1998.

128. GA 343.

129. See Ekkehard Meffert, *Die Zisterzienser und Bernhard von Clairvaux,* Stuttgart 2010. Something similar must be sought in the anthroposophical movement of the future.

130. R. Steiner on 19 January 1915, GA 157.

131. *Wer ist der deutsche Volksgeist,* Perseus Verlag, Basel 1990.

132. GA 157, 19 January 1915.

133. It is an important task of spiritual-scientific research to discover which spiritual entity filled the vacuum left by the absent spirit of the nation.

134. Bruno Krueger, *Leben und Schicksal,* pp. 39f.

135. Goethe, *Gedenkausgabe,* vol. XII 1949, p. 527.

136. The whole poem was first published in *Der Europäer,* year 9, no. 5, March 2005, pp. 5ff.

137. George Adams, 'Rudolf Steiner in England', in: *Wir erlebten Rudolf Steiner* (ed. K. v. Poturzyn), Stuttgart 1957, p. 22.

138. GA 266b. Author's italics.

139. F. Rittelmeyer, unpublished notebooks, Perseus Verlag archive.

140. Cf. articles by G. Aschoff, G. Suwelack and A. Anderson in *Der Europäer,* year 16, February to June 2012.

141. In GA 260. Author's emphasis.

142. Thomas Meyer, *Moltke,* vol. 2, p. 291. This communication was received on the day when the Foundation Stone Meditation appeared in the members' newsletter.

Index